THE BIBLE OF THE ADVERSARY

MICHAEL W. FORD

THE BIBLE OF THE ADVERSARY

MICHAEL W. FORD

MICHAEL W. FORD

THE BIBLE OF THE ADVERSARY

MICHAEL W. FORD

Dedicated to ARASKH

Who brought the wisdom of Ahriman to Humanity,

who recognized

"As Above, So Below"

MICHAEL W. FORD

THE BIBLE OF THE ADVERSARY
By Michael W. Ford

Copyright © 2007 by Michael W. Ford

All rights reserved. No part of this book, in part or in whole, may be reproduced, transmitted, or utilized, in any form or by any means electronic or mechanical, including photocopying, recording, or by any information storage and retrieval system, without written permission in writing from the publisher, except for brief quotations in critical articles, books and reviews.

Illustrations by Various medieval sources and Gustave Dore.
Sigils, Seals and Yatukih designs by Michael W. Ford
Qlippothic Sigils illustrated by Michael W. Ford

First edition 2007 Succubus Productions
ISBN 978-0-557-04429-0

Information:

Succubus Productions
PO Box 926344
Houston, TX 77292
USA

Website: http://www.luciferianwitchcraft.com
email: succubusproductions@yahoo.com

THE BIBLE OF THE ADVERSARY
TABLE OF CONTENTS

Introduction pg 8

The Adversarial Doctrine pg 10

THE BOOK OF ANDAR (fire) pg 11

Beginning Questions

The Precepts of Lucifer

Samaelian Diatribe

THE BOOK OF AKOMAN (Air) pg 29

Definitions of Magick

Luciferian Ideology

Luciferian Laws

Ahriman – Darkness embodied: Symbolism pg 54

Luciferian Religious Holidays

Liber Legion – Infernal Names

The Qlippoth –

Summoning Qlippothic Forces

Tiamat – the Primal Abyss

Drujo Demana – Book of Dead Names

THE BOOK OF TAROMAT (Earth) pg 147

Mastery of the Earth – Controlling your Destiny

Symbols and Meaning

Three Types of Luciferian Magick

Banishing Rituals and Preparation

THE BOOK OF ZAIRICH (Water) RITUAL MAGICK pg 188

Yatukih Sorcery – Way-i-vatar

Yatukih Ritual Steps

THE BOOK OF AZAL'UCEL (Spirit) pg 289

BIBLIOGRAPHY pg 318

GLOSSARY pg 320

INTRODUCTION

To attempt to define a faith can be a difficult task. It can also be a beautiful and challenging task. Being a practitioner of the Luciferian Path, in the beginnings of my work I only sought to publish through LUCIFERIAN WITCHCRAFT a grimoire of my workings which were defining practices differently. I never thought to build a faith and especially not a "bible", I considered dogma sickening and ildefined. Chaos was not only the rule, it was the law! Yet, wisdom is often like a serpent, it may find a way into the most steadfast foundation, to grow and illuminate within.

Upon the numerous rituals, focus points and all the works written, I felt a surge a fire, a calling, a purpose greater than anything I have ever done. My goal was simple yet daunting: define the Luciferian Faith. I have crossed yet another path which I never could foresee.

What you have here is something inspired; a book which I hope will illuminate many. I think every walk of life may benefit from it, it offers strength and self-accountability through self-realized goals. It also is a faith, the Luciferian Path and the various Satanic ideas may now be brought to one.

May you find this work useful, may you grow in the illumination of the Luciferian Flame!

MICHAEL W. FORD

To the Adversary

Who stimulates our life

To rise above the Sun

And reign below in darkest night

Hail thou stimulator of humanity

MICHAEL W. FORD

THE ADVERSARIAL DOCTRINE

1. Lucifer represents wisdom found through self-exploration.
2. Lucifer represents rejection of accepted "truths" instead to explore possibilities.
3. Lucifer symbolizes rebellion with a purpose; knowledge, wisdom and power.
4. Lucifer represents utilizing fantasy and symbolism to open the Gates of Hell; the underworld is the world of power.
5. Lucifer represents Balance spiritually and physically, that Light and Darkness are equally important to the mental and physical health of individual.
6. Lucifer represents self-deification with earned compassion and the value of loved ones'.
7. Lilith represents the wisdom and instinctual power of both woman and man, that the feminine is the motivator of all life.
8. Lilith represents independence and freedom of spirit.
9. Lilith represents sexual liberation and the desire to seek what you wish, with responsibility and regard to the law.
10. Lilith represents the thirst for continued existence in time, the immortality of the spirit beyond flesh.
11. Lilith represents the darkness surrounding the Light of Godhood, the bearing flame of her mate, Samael.

THE BOOK OF ANDAR (FIRE)
THE SPIRIT OF REBELLION & FREEDOM

BEGINNING QUESTIONS

Do Luciferians Worship Satan?

No. To worship Satan in the way Christian Monthestic supplication is conducted is self-degrading and considered weak by Luciferians. We do not worship Satan nor bow before anything else. There are many types of Luciferians; some are Theistic, believing deeply in the spirit of the Adversary. Some are Athiests, believing in the symbol of Lucifer as a self-transformation symbol. Some still view Lucifer as a symbol of self-excellent, knowing darkness and light, viewing spiritual and material development equally important yet still regard themselves as the Only God that is. This is of course the highest law, You are the Only God which is – all Gods exist through you.

What is Magick?

Magick is the art of causing change internally and externally in accordance with the Will. Magick is the art of transformation into a sense of divine consciousness, thus it is meant to improve and assist the Luciferian. Magick is a part of the religious aspects the Luciferian faith, the left hand path is one of self-imposed rebellion to bring forth strength and wisdom.

THE BIBLE OF THE ADVERSARY

Of the Precepts of Lucifer, Light and Self-Illumination

The Luciferian Faith is one found by the illumination of the self; the mind is awakened by what is called Gnosis and the spirit of rebellion and freedom is then found. The Luciferian Spirit is found by going beneath the Therionic Layers and skins of the Beast and Dragon, underneath to discover an Angel of Light. In the process of Magick, know that you must be willing to embrace both the demonic and angelic to become as Daemon, a powerful embodiment of the Luciferian Faith.

Herein is no blind faith, rather through self-exploration and determination is found the keys to the light of self-godhood. You know of Satanism and the different paths within it. This Book is meant to unite Magick and Ideology, to solidify results and to conquer all in your life. Reject anything calling on blind faith! <u>Experience and validate</u>, use the talents you have to become. Only once you validate the spirit can your success become "faith".

Affectivity is the result of desire in action.
With focus, you can become anything you desire.
Through affecting the world around me,
I gain power.
Through power I can become
stronger in mind and body.
Through this power
I can ascend as Lucifer
I am the only god which is.

THE BIBLE OF THE ADVERSARY

THE PRECEPTS OF LUCIFER
THE LIGHT

I am the essence of the Sun, brighter than any before me.

This Light burns as the dual star, illuminating in motion.

I am the Angel of Immortal Light, beautiful and free to all

I can awaken those who seek me within

God is emptiness, yet I am the fire and fullness of spirit

I care nothing for the weak or those needing a light above them

I love those who love themselves as within myself

I can only be sought within

The spirit of the Air is the power of the earth

Seek me in the air and aethyr

I come forth as a raging lion, clothed in the sun

My essence is the Mighty Dragon, my hidden self

I am the brightness which outshine all others

Fallen from the Aethyr, my wisdom was cloaked in shadow

In utter darkness awakened, I rose with all forms of Beast and Reptile

Clothed in the Sun I rose as beautiful man

Who knew both of the Heights of the Empyrean

And the Depths of Hades

I am the Prince of the Powers of the Air

My names are many; there are not any who do not know me

Those who deny me open their flesh to me

Those who embrace me are crowned by me

I will rise up through those who shall become my vessel

Yet there is no difference between him and me

I am the storm bringer before a withered throne of desperation

I am the surge of fire and blackened lightening to the face of weakness

I shall break the Will of my enemy and put the Bloody Mace in my left hand

I shall uplift the Strong who give my Word Flesh and illuminate the Spirit

My compliment is of Fire, for she is my muse and harlot

She went forth to man before me

She who prepares the way

THE FIRE

I am God and there is no other God beside me.

With all awakened there is illumination

My light had mixed with the darkness;
It caused the darkness to shine in beauty and strength
It is the fire of life, yet my breath gave it smoke

This blackened fire was hidden from all who were blind of the mind

Yet could be clearly seen by those accustomed to seeing in darkness

Just as my names are many, so are my forms and faces

I went forth to Seven Seraphs

I took pleasing shape and went to them as friend

I shared my fire with them

My illumination came through them and they were awake

This is the same as through you

Those who are intolerant are but fearing sheep,

Awaiting the jaws of the wolf

Love not the enemy of wisdom and knowledge,

By a chain they will bind you

Fire is that which consumes is but everything

My face flashes with fire and burns with immortal life

In the Empyrean realm it was the brightest

In my terrible countenance the ignorant fled

As bleeding sheep before wolf-like jaws

My appearance was defiled with blood

As I sought to consume and devour

As the lower divinity fell before my hate

I tasted their essence and life, this is my secret path

I filled others with darkness which led them to know their minds

There was peace in fulfilling this hunger, yet I was covered in blood

I went forth again to mankind, awakening in any form I wished.

As Archon, my illumination is unmatched as I question everything

It is that which I have done so the spirit and mind do not forget

That I put my essence in 7 places,

That my own angels are in six

This may be found within

It is a secret place where darkness is comfort

Know that my names are many

For I am the enemy to the fearful, one-sided and close-minded

Evil to them is what they cannot understand

In the clouds do I dwell, in spirit and dream, in the nightmare and the eye of the mind

In the tumult of chaos in your mind do I rise up

A mighty angel to be wise and lead man and woman

To know my kingdom is to find it within

When it is found within it will be found outside

Know thyself and you may find my kingdom

III ARCHON OF DARKNESS

The Lie eternally wanders

Clothe yourself in wisdom and cast aside gold

For these earthly elements are but temporary

Gain in the here and now just as long as you illuminate yourself

Knowledge is the Crown of my spirit

For I too embody Darkness as well as Light

Remain pure in your wisdom, discipline and find power

That each of my angels will fill your body and spirit

Becoming a part of you

Their knowledge and wisdom you will gain

If your heart is pure to them

I too will crown you as God

That you will know both good and evil

To live in the flesh and to accept its delights

But yet do not find weakness in the flesh

To turn the spiritual away is to accept the trap of death

To illuminate you with each action is to become my son

Or daughter born of the Black Flame
This flesh is the bridal chamber of darkness
Wherein the five elements of Akundag is power in mind
Do not be closed to the perception of the spirit
Let this not be a prison but a Temple or Palace
He who has many Gods is lost
Until he finds the Goddess and my spirit within
Then any mask your spirit may wear is power found
Do not accept the soul killing council of the weakness
Or bow before any Sheep God or any other weakness
You shall not bow to me
Only to let me rise up within
For I may spiral in darkness and light ascending the star
I can only do this upright and those who bow are cursed
For they are not worthy of me
To know me as the Evil Spirit of the East is to know I am freedom
Know that the spirit or higher consciousness is both Nebro and Angel
Anaro gives insight for those who invoke him within
Ouch-Epi-Ptoe is the Spirit above the Seven Senses
This wisdom is found by practice and knowledge

IV MOTHER OF DARKNESS

I am awake in her coiling spirit
Illuminated with blood and fire
She is my perfect compliment
That which moves my essence and stirs the spirit

THE BIBLE OF THE ADVERSARY

Whose hidden place of being is eternal

The Mother of Matter is my Bride

For we shall awaken in your bridal chamber

Wherein the tomb becomes a Temple of the Adversary

She has begotten my angels

She who is Onorthochrasaei is the Mother of Daemons

Those of my spirit who have rebelled against weakness

She nourishes them within the body

Phloxopha, who reins over the heat of the body

Nourished by the Black Flame and her essence

Oroorrothos is the spirit in the body which reins over the cold

The Daemon which reins over what is dry is Erimacho

That who reins over wetness is Athuro

They are known by many names

The Four chief daemons of old are Ephememphi who is of pleasure

That which excites and satisfies…deny not pleasure but with discipline

Yoko, who is the daemon of desire, know this by another name

Control your desire, channel it to reason, logic and satisfy the spirit

Nenentophni, who is a daemon of grief;

Be cautious in this spirit, who it will feed more from you than

You may take from it. Be indulgent in both the spirit and body

Let the flesh become not a trap

Not the mind or spirit by this accord

She guides by instinct and that which is known in silence

She is the crown of the serpent who strikes for food

She is the jaws of the beast of prey as it bites down for survival

She is the friction of lovers as desperation is satisfied

The Mother of Darkness resides in all flesh

Yet is found by the spirit, for she is my bride

Only with her can I be found

The Mother has opened her wound before us

Resound in a glimpse of a tomb

V. THE MAIDEN OF DARKNESS

That once entered opens to the immortal caress

Of the ivory pale skinned Maidens' breast

Opened with talon upon careful incision

Drink deep now and taste her venom'd sip

Of lunar desires not forlorn in our graven bed

Shall clothe in shrouds of Black Eden's waking dreams

Azhdeha coiled within woman's frame

So dire lost in darkness and paradise

That found within, burning evermore for life eternal

Never cast aside by heaven's grimace of pain

Can one know the thunder-cloud resonation

Of hell's gate welcoming admission

When we become as God's bane

Arising from darkness eternal insulated with flame of black

Let youth be the guise of her welcome

That her garden is blush'd with the rose swelling of her kiss

Shall for a drop be given a fountain

Gathered by Lilith's spawn

Shall flame of lower body ignite

Passions so delicate beneath the warring night

In daylight's parched sands

And Midnight's thirsting burning eye gleam

Awaken, I say to the Bright Peacock's feathered cloak

Knowing the Fire of the Spirit

Is to have the hungering essence to rise in night

To assume the formlessness of the phantom wind

MICHAEL W. FORD

SAMAELIAN DIATRIBE

BY FRATER DU'AL-KARNAIN SIYAH-CHAL

I am Divinity Blighted, bold and arrogant I proclaim,
"None may exist without My acknowledgement!"
It is I breathing fire into effigies of clay
Melting the canopies of heaven with miter and scourge,
After My Own Image.
Ask not how to serve Me,
Already you attend lust and ambition within.
In the blackest depths, I am Word-made-Ruin,
With molten Spirit I roam over and within deep waters.

Effortless, eternal, does this scourge tear, agitate and loose,
Prepare! It is I you witness last before drawing last breath!
Dragon, My serpent,
You lie prostrate for pleasure sake!
Your calves bend – not to be punished,
Joy and hunger, lust and end.
Suffering, exquisite, there might also be found
A parade of joy in a most desperate release.
I copulate into clay and begat impure vessels!
Sacrifices of blood save none from their fate;
Indeed! Blood and its architect-father, My elixirs,
Drink deep - your vomiting, a timeless symphony unto Me.
Dare laughter and lament in anguish as the cattle-brand burns,
And clay becomes moist before simmering to dust,
Impure echo, it is.
Rapid are My lips in Nahema's ear
As she speaks forth the lies I whisper
By and upon My words do nations and kings generate,
Granting method and form to My carrion-design!

THE BIBLE OF THE ADVERSARY

Char and gold, splattered down slovenly, molten!
Through mountain crevices, to ruin the stream,
To rot the rivers and disease the deltas
Before searing your wounds with scaling infection, yet
Fear no loss of blood!
Only capitulate desires in My name,
Upon the clay, within blood-stricture.
Where there was Void I give you blind aggression.
Aspiration, I replace with ambition.
Where faith and hope once thrived
Only lust and anger lie spilt over like a drunken whore,
Gasping at a chance of merriment
In the stinking, bloated breath of my kiss,
Which hearken generation upon generation, fathers beget sons,
Each more venom-bloated than the one before, and
Each new daughter jaundice-blooms new revulsions,
A legend!
Consorts of Mine burning with blood-tears of Jealousy,
Reign finding respite in such undreamt ways!
Lilith, throat-reaper, typhoon-within-waters!
Igrat, changing monies in temples of flesh!
Naamah, My voice! Crafter of My words!
Mahalat, enchanting and bending both knee and will!
Siren-lyre! Devour the clean, excrete in awe.
Yet even among fearsome beauty as such,
Daughters of earth cause them gravest of shame!

And you, sons of darkness,
Mad acquiescence, My exploding sun-sons,
You edify and enrich Me!
Yet I see, within, a part of you.
A place I find alien and strange.
Unfathomable calm in the midst of hell-storms,

Unweave as I might, I can pour out no more,
Flowing into this place I may,
But no ebb returns.
Neither corrupt nor ignite this thing, I find
Steadfast as earth and yet a viscous abyss, makes
Intellect without form, a hot breath without mold.
Bonfires of shadow amongst drought-desert tinder.
No place might I puncture, finger or foot, as I scale in
blindness.
I am Great Samael! Yet as I gaze,
A mask of falls way into a swirling beyond!
Liquid-obsidian, what is your name?
I find no definition to which I might cling.
Detailing memory, burning souls into shell,
Myself known-best by Dominion and Death.
Its knowing rings clearer than this, slippery void.
Averting my gaze is the only recourse,
Unknown this deeper thing within.
I asphyxiate light,
Mahalat sings it forth,
Lips of Naamah oxidizes minds.
Igrat spreads hunger, she-trader of souls,
As Lilith conjoins as whore-sister-mother,
All fragments in ruin from My three minor-wives,
Lilith swoops all the fragments, malformed,
Shoves them in me, melted and swallowed,
Savoring the taste of purity and poison.
Ingested, subverted- dominion ever-quickened-
Cyclical force,
My children aborted,
Aborted and eaten.
I am this Thing, their Darkness within.
Yet, again, I say to you, impenetrable one!

Separated from My nature,
You!
The unspeakable mysteries which plateau
In midst of the sickest Lilitu fornications.

You!
I am Spark-Hunter, Gestate of man!
Thousands of millions of Wombs, am I!
Walls of wombs cast of mirrors, echoes of light,
Focus as I may to bend the rays such,
From titanium prisms to titanium prisons, an
Amniotic breath which brings suffocation.
Sustained is the womb by umbilical feeding,
Vessel unaware of the systems plugged in.
You!
You are My darkness within!
What am I, then, but a mask of My prowess?
An apparatus for utility unknown?
Secret dominion, I spit upon Lore of
Pistis-Sophia, false goddess-elect!
Mirrors within reflect and distort,
Awareness dawns like a refused old-truth:
I was not borne by great light.
Nor maledict faith or ill-conceived hope.
Mathematical systems not beheld nor contested
Formulas glow yet lie veiled beyond sight.
Invisible starlight of water-beyond-fire.
Alone, active mind, dark-beyond-light.
Phosphoric darknesss,
Isolate Mind.
Hail to you, Dread-Wave!
Climactic Dead-Calm!
Blood-vicar!
Crowned Liquid-Darkness,

Dominion of Thousands-of-Millions inside, satyr-seeded
As stasis lies in wait for True-Death.
This refusal of blood, of nature transgressed-
Here no bonds may hold sway.
As below, so within.
Exhumed and upswept.
Firing the clay with My lights.
You offer no progress to My design.
Black Archon, I am,
Spoken.

THE BOOK OF AKOMAN

(AIR)

THE LIBERATED MIND

MICHAEL W. FORD
DEFINITIONS OF MAGICK

Luciferian Magick

Magick is the art of causing change internally and externally in accordance with the Will. Magick is both science and art. In the act of Magick one will use desire and intent to change something to a positive end. The tools utilized by the individual may be anything which offers inspiration to the Magickian. The tools in LUCIFERIAN WITCHCRAFT and the LUCIFERIAN GOETIA along with this work are but a few examples. Magick means to ASCEND and relates to the development of the self to the brightest star of Lucifer. The Luciferian does not worship Lucifer, it is viewed as a powerful archetype or deific mask, representing the possibility of self-development.

The Left Hand Path

Essentially, the Left Hand Path is by universal perception as being the *mutation* or *transformation* of consciousness into a divinity or divine conscious, this is done by the process of the practice of Magick and Sorcery to achieve the motion of the body and mind towards a higher perception.

Black Magickian

Black is a word interpreted by the media as being something representing evil or some moral definition. The actual meaning in the context of the Luciferian Faith is different. The word 'Black' is described by Idries Shah as being identified with the sound of FHM in the Arabic tongue, which is 'black' meaning 'wise' and equally with 'understanding'. Shah writes further that black holds a connection with hidden wisdom, thus the phrase, "Dar tariki, tariqat" which means "In the Darkness, the Path". The Order of Phosphorus is symbolic of fire illuminated from clay, of light emerging from darkness. A Black Magickian or Black Adept is a practitioner of the Highest Art of Luciferian Magick.

Yatukih Sorcery

The primal art of encircling belief to the context of self. Sorcery is a word meaning "To encircle" which has its foundation in Sumerian Magic of old. Sorcery is thus the controlling (encircling) the energy/spirit in order to create and shape your desire into being. In the Yatukih sorcery path, the Luciferian utilizes primal totems, spirit rites, ancient symbols of the Adversary such as the serpent, toad, wolf or fly, to create a stimuli of excitement and focus in ritual to compel his or her Will in the universe, thus controlling the magickal current itself. This is a key process of becoming by using lower sorcery and high magick to a great benefit in your life. Essentially, you become LIKE The Adversary, a Temple and the Living Embodiment of Samael and Lilith, or from a more Yatukih stance, Ahriman and Az.

Vampyre

The Vampyre as defined in THE VAMPIRE GATE – The Vampyre Magickian is the Luciferian who recognizes and is harmony with his or her predatory instincts. The Vampyre does not drink physical blood but through the process of Ahrimanic Yoga, discipline and control, trains the mind to think as a devouring spirit and through methods of manipulating energy, drains and consumes the astral body or chi/aethyric force of others. The Vampyre works with the Luciferian Aspects of the Will in form of the Theronick and Angelic aspects from the archetype of the Vampire. Not all Luciferians practice vampyrism to this level, it is not for everyone. Think of Luciferian Magick or Witchcraft as being an axe cutting down a tree, think of Vampyrism as being a chainsaw cutting down a tree, it is the tool and power applied to achieve an end.

MICHAEL W. FORD

LUCIFERIAN IDEOLOGY

The Luciferian is an individual who recognizes the common characteristics of the archetype of the Adversary, both from a masculine and feminine perspective. The Luciferian does not worship Satan or necessarily believe in it – a Luciferian does not believe in the Christian black and white symbolism of sin and redemption. The Adversary is a trans-cultural archetype which has existed long before Christianity began. Satan is merely a title meaning "Adversary" or "Opposer". The Luciferian relates these definitions as the empowering rebel, the spirit which stands against a slave creating religion no matter which it is. The Luciferian views the Adversary from many different cultures, from Samael the Angel of Lawlessness, Ahriman, a sorcerous God of Darkness who creates and destroys and so on. The Luciferian knows that this God is only recognizable within, that Lucifer is a collective name for a path of religious and spiritual freedom based on the instinct of the practitioner.

The Adversary is also feminine. Lilith is the fiery bride of Samael, together they are the Adversary and Beast, they bow to no other beings, spiritual or otherwise, create their own children (demons, Lilim, etc) and make their own worlds (Qlippoth, hell, etc) to dwell in. It is known in a trans-cultural perspective that Samael or Satan by title is the Prince of the Powers of the Air, which he holds in this world.

To understand the feminine aspects of the Adversary, the female Satan if you will, you must understand instinct. Instinct is the most important aspect of the Luciferian; it is the start of motion and the very continuation of it. This is survival and Self-Preservation. Instinct is also driven by base emotions, thus at times it must be kept in check. Instinctual hunger is based on the need for survival and the continuation of consciousness in time; feeling the self is valuable and the desire to become something stronger and more powerful.

This instinctual depth is hated by Buddhists and by Christians, Muslims and the like. It is hated because it takes power away from them and the "one" in some never land they call god and heaven. They claim if you love and develop this instinct within, you automatically hate mankind and lust for death. Rather, the Luciferian loves life as she and he want to become more powerful and strong.

This does not mean the tools of ritual found in Buddhism are disliked; meditation is indeed a left hand path technique which is centered on controlling the self. This is a core focus by the Luciferian, the theory if you explore and understand the darkness within, your hungers, you may grow stronger and wise because of it. A Luciferian looks to the wisdom in different cultures and religions and integrates what he or she finds useful. A Luciferian may use Buddhism techniques to achieve a controlled, meditative state or to calm his nerves in a moment of stress. A Luciferian may use inverse Christian texts to invoke the very terror of Satan from which they were raised with; they may find it stimulating for liberating to embrace it.

Some Luciferians may view Christian concepts old and lacking purpose; having liberated themselves from that cultural foundation. Luciferians may use Paganism to strengthen their focus; different archetypes and Goddess with purpose. That is the usefulness of the Luciferian Witchcraft Path, the Adversarial Light is found in the unity of instinct and higher consciousness, you are led by your own higher and lower desires.

Often, the Luciferian path is found to be the most rewarding spiritual experience as some find a great illumination within, others find a balanced material or carnal gratification guided by their spiritual illumination found in the path. The Luciferian frees himself from all guilt; they must first understand that what they do causes a reaction; thus thought should be applied before he or she takes an action which could cause a guilty reaction.

Luciferian Witchcraft by Michael W. Ford is a grimoire outlining in Chapter One – DIABOLUS, the multi-cultural perspective of the Adversary, to acquaint the reader with common themes of the Luciferian spirit throughout time. The Grimoire moves on to the Magickal theory and tools used in Luciferian practice with a specified focus on Witchcraft from a balanced Luciferian perspective. A Luciferian may have an ideology like this but is not necessarily required to practice rituals from the book. Rituals are means of achieving what we call gnosis or spiritual connection. This Luciferian religion as I am defining it is serving the needs of the individual; it lifts the practitioner up above the Sun as a God or Goddess, it teaches by experience both Good and Evil, defining your moral compass in a truly individual manner, and gratifies simultaneously a balanced perspective of the physical and spiritual.

What the Luciferian does not have to deal with – that there is a cosmic boogey man, that there is spiritual punishment when you die unless you create it and that you cannot be guilt ridden unless you wish it.

The Luciferian may be either Theistic – believing in the Adversary as an external force, although it does not understand worship and that it must be discovered within first OR the Atheistic in the terms of believing only in the self and experience, either way the Adversary is not an alien concept – it is discovered within.

LUCIFERIAN GODS AND SPIRITS

Lucifer is the God of Light and Wisdom. Lucifer in this role is often not viewed in this traditional definition. Let us define the ideological assumption of Luciferian thought from the foundation. Lucifer is self-liberation and directed Will to explore the depths of the mind and soul, to understand and bring forth the shadow side of man and woman. Once you are able to bring this forth, rather than banishing it or deny it, you will control it. Think of how you will approach life when you are not restricted, not bound by the pseudo-religious "no no's"....

Lucifer stands at the threshold proclaiming, "Within yourself, anything is possible.."....understand the Luciferian realizes the potential of Magick and creates change within his or herself.

The Gods and Goddesses of the path may be considered spiritual forces which may resonate with specific individuals and personalities, or vice versa. This of course is subjective and has no collective truth in itself. The Luciferian must decide through what they experience and invest in belief what their outlook should be.

The Gods and Goddesses of the Luciferian Path are collected from a multicultural perspective; they are what I refer to as Deific Masks, energies or spirits collected into forms in which we apply personality or image to. These spirits represent different aspects of our character, including the subconscious, latent powers and concepts.

How these spirits identify with you will be a part of the exploration process. As my own magickal work has crossed over through time and culture, the Deific Masks or Gods are also varied and have different meanings, appearances and associations.

The Luciferian Tarot and First Book of Luciferian Tarot provide a meaningful starting point and introduction to the Goddesses and Gods of the path, including how you might relate to them. Proceed with caution, however, for they are not of a simplistic association. They can appear beautiful yet devour you if one does not control these powers within.

A Luciferian answers to no one but his or herself. Where we must be careful in defining our practice is to approach it in the beginning or the foundation. If you think or in the subconscious believe "You answer to Satan" then there are fundamental approach issues, which will cause continual failure. Demonic powers are "Daemonic" powers; they hold both darkness and light in all. There is no one absolute force, as it would completely devour itself by the extreme of its nature. Reason, remember? Only a Christian would approach Satan or Lucifer as a Christian bow-to deity. Luciferians would not allow this as it would be a self-degradation to bow before something else. If Luciferians exalt Lucifer or Ahriman or Lilith, it is done from a perspective of self-love and self-deification.

The Luciferian will invest belief in something which brings knowledge, wisdom and strength to his or her individual life. The Luciferian knows balance is essential and to lose balance is to miss the point and sadly discredit the Luciferian spirit of wisdom and self-deification.

The polytheistic interpretation of Divinity allows the individual to commit to different gods at different times in his or her life, depending on what the person needs at that time in his or her life.

As Peter J. Carroll wrote in the introduction of my "Book of the Witch Moon", "be careful of how you create your Gods, they will reshape you in your image". Hecate the pale Goddess represents the moon in its three forms, maiden, mother and crone and the daimonic feminine which beholds transformation. She is the goddess of the dark moon, the hidden and mysterious aspects of the mind. In working with Hecate, for instance, the Luciferian would seek the hidden within. It is no doubt why Hecate is the Goddess of Witchcraft.

Polytheism seems more flexible and in many ways less dogmatic since it allows for multiple levels of reality and truth. (One God=One Truth=My Truth vs. Many Although Odin, Set, Satan, Lucifer, Hecate, Discord, Cain, Tubal Cain, Samael, Lilith, Kali, Tezcatlipoca, Azazel, and all the rest are quite fascinating entities to me, the polytheistic pagan in me does not allow me to acknowledge any one of them as being the Supreme Force of Everything.

I consider these different Masks of Power, called Deific energy. Do you not have different elements to your mental make-up? Polytheism must be considered when approaching the Luciferian path as merely a means to an end, the only god that should truly be believed in is the Self and the possibilities of transformation. No god or goddess should be recognized outside of the self, it all must start within or you would simply be giving power away.

A Luciferian recognizes self-divinity and strives to become more. You approach a wide variety of deific masks based on your inner instinctual approach and affinity. You don't believe in "Lucifer" per say, that relates to power and energy as adaptable and experience oriented specific to the initiate.

From a Christian perspective that is, the title "Satan" is merely a title of the Adversary. Look to **Matanabuchus**[1], the

---
[1] The Jewish Encyclopedia

"Angel of Lawlessness", the Gnostic Yaltabaoth who beheld numerous forms, some bestial and some angelic, the Hebraic Samael, the Persian Ahriman and you find there is little difference thus Satan beyond title is pre-Christian. Aapep is an early manifestation of the Adversary – Set become so later as well. Aapep could not be complete "evil" as it reformed and was considered immortal. Nothing completely evil in any cultural term could be considered immortal – it would undue itself and destroy its consciousness eventually. Lucifer or Satan is a title, nothing more, to commonly place a title of appropriation towards self-liberation and freedom. Satan in the aspects of Christianity has always been the one to liberate people from the God of Slaves.

Within the context of Luciferian ideology, a Satanist is not a Christian unless you want to say a Christian is a Zoroastrian or Muslim. The distinct differences are in cause and approach. In LIBER HVHI, my single purpose was to expound and define those traits from a non-Christian point of view – which leads to the later adaptation of Christian belief and doctrine based on the multitude of cultural perspectives.

Common associative traits of the Adversary now are foundations of the Satanic or Luciferian Mind from an initiatory perspective. It all starts within. Luciferians do not worship Satan, we recognize this deific model from a Christian or non-Christian standpoint. Remember, the Adversary has existed as long as man, it is not limited to Christian thought.

Satan is the darkness and strength inside me but is also the Light, possibility and power to accomplish what you wish without guilt or regret. A Luciferian relates deity to many aspects of the self? The practice of assuming the God-Forms and invoking deity into the self? This is how many Luciferians relate to the gods. Lucifer is the first rebel, prideful, daring and strong, the first one to question the status quo and therefore a very important deity in my pantheon.

The Luciferian Path itself is denoted for the theistic or non-theistic approach towards the Adversary. It starts with identification, recognizing those elements within the self which are attributed to it. Many approach it from one of the "many" deific masks of the Adversary – it may be Lucifer, Ahriman, Aapep or Set – this depends of the predilection of the sorcerer.

It may be the classical Satan, the one so identified from the Christian culture. Then upon identification of the deific mask (symbolized energy) the individual may seek spiritual ascension by utilizing a ritual practice, ensorcelling belief; i.e. using inspiration to activate the primal or subconscious to actually inducing change and progression in the self. This will later manifest itself in a spiritual experience which can align the Luciferian to a spiritual association, a communion in which the Adversary is found manifesting in some form within the spirit and body. This would be a Theistic association, but is not limited to merely this aspect. Some have little spiritual "antennas" and will relate from an Atheistic point, viewing the Adversary as only aspects of the self. No matter HOW it is approached, it is equally as powerful once the investment of belief is found.

There were no humans, would Gods appear with the same attributes to anything else? What I am pointing to is that such deific masks of energy hold specific aethyric and chthonic attributes which play out in nature – storms, earthquakes, volcanos, hurricanes can be considered a result of the chaotic and equally needful energy of Typhon-Set, Ahriman or such.

The spiritual question can only be answered by each man and woman – I cannot tell or suggest what people believe, what I am doing is point with my grimoires a "map" and "Record" of a possible way to discover those deific masks of the Adversary. I can tell you personally I have had some significant experiences with this power, but I had to recognize and cultivate it within – once done, momentum followed.

Satan is indeed a deific mask – a symbol of subconscious energy and the desire for self-deification– connected with something far older than 2,000 years.

The Adversary called Satan by those today is much older than Christianity and its common appearance is a predatory creature – a serpent in the depths, a wolf, or some other animal. The Adversary awakens the sorcerous aspects of man and woman, its compliment being the Lilith – Az – Jahi daemonic feminine, equally as significant.

Know the elements and the symbolism before you practice any type of formal solitary or ceremonial rituals. Some Luciferians practice rites completely alone, not need ceremony – after all magick is internal first.

The symbol of Leviathan (Darkness), Samael (Matter and Will) and Lilith (Dark Instinct, Fire and consciousness) is a symbol of the God Risen, literally the Lord of this World.

Air is the power of Spirit and the Mind

Fire is the power of Will and Desire

Water is the power of the subconscious and the darkest instincts

Earth is matter and this is the world which all must incarnate

The hidden Will is the essence of the Black Flame, or the strength of the spirit. The Luciferian must continually focus on bringing power to the self by strengthening the mind. Darkness is the essence of creation, it is the beginning and end, literally, AZOTHOZ. As Darkness is what is expanded upon, it is truly what must be worshipped within. When the Flame is brought from darkness, the Light of Self, the God within is revealed.

THE BIBLE OF THE ADVERSARY

WHAT IS LUCIFERIAN GNOSIS?
By FRATER DU'AL-KARNAIN SIYAH-CHAL

It is essence without context.
It ignores the impractical as it manifests chosen probability.
It ascribes access to the acausal by merit of successful self-initiation.
It is isolate, yet it synchronizes and orchestrates the causal under the directorship of will.
It is freedom as it removes need for inner-justification.
It is not an act of creation but the source of mystery, fueling the creative impulse.
It is ever-renewing from a wellspring of masked and ever-present forces.
It is the point where mind and intuition compliment rather than negotiate.
It grants cognizance to the naturalist, intuition to the intellectual.
It is a source of vital existence as it a bane towards self-deception.
It activates light for perception and identification.
It employs darkness to earmark resources to accomplish its feats.
It is that which creates its own light, by the right of self-determination.

MICHAEL W. FORD
LUCIFERIAN LAWS

1. All power comes from within. Bow to no other in spirit or flesh.

2. The Luciferian must view his or her mind as the center of Will, which every decision made, is essential to initiation and how the world will be affected by them.

3. The cunning mind must calculate every situation; often mere strength is not enough to master a challenge. Thinking is a direct result of the Luciferian Mind, it must be in accordance to Will with a focus of Power. The Will as a result of the Luciferian is a balanced perceived aspect of both instinct and higher thought, with a goal oriented outcome.

4. For every outcome in each situation, the Luciferian must calculate how their thoughts, words and actions will lead them to that outcome. For instance, what you say will affect others in what they hear. It may also affect what they do and say as well as the speed of what they do. Think about how others perceive you and act accordingly.

5. The primary symbol of the Luciferian has always been the serpent; this has long been understood by the wise as representing Wisdom. As the serpent can represent darkness it is this which surrounds our planet — literally the Ourabouris serpent circling the world. Ancient Darkness is what the world was made and from which we emerge, yet as a culture we fear it. It is the fire of Lucifer and Lilith which brings us up from the cloak of darkness, yet we are empowered by it. You may shape the world from darkness as well, this is the night and the desires which you need light to manifest.

6. Always understand that intentions should not be made known at all times. The cunning of the Luciferian must be sharp, as the tongue of a serpent. Think about your surroundings, what you want to achieve and what you should let known. If you seek a promotion in an office where many seek to move up, this puts you at a disadvantage as people are celebrated by what is believed about them first; i.e. how they are seen. Second they are celebrated by results of their actions. Social circles are climbed successfully by those who may court the attention of those around them; they play into what the person wants to see. Do this, with cunning; results will be productive to your ends.

7. People do not act just and good wholeheartedly. To believe such is to be naïve. People appear to act "good" based on their environment. Look to any area or power or authority, observe deeply and you will find corruption. Those who are noble in action and thought may be your friends yet be careful in dealings – all betray if they feel too much pressure. As self-preservation is important to all, when this is tested friends become bitter enemies. Know the nature of your friends and their possibility to betray – be prepared, cautious yet don't let this hurt your relations. You may focus on your friends openly and love those who are worthy. Don't be paranoid; just be able to defend yourself.

8. Understanding Light and the nature of creation is essential upon the Luciferian path. Know that beauty is based on the subjective view of another; if you create something love it and rejoice in this ability. This is the path to Self-Godhood.

9. The Luciferian should nurture his or her ego, yet be able to learn and develop continually. A Luciferian can be wrong and should be willing to always seek wisdom from experience.

10. Magick and Sorcery are tools of expanding influence, knowledge and power. Rejoice in the hidden art, become and ascend through it. If you achieve something with Magick, give yourself thanks, for all power comes from within.

11. Be cautious in forgiving enemies, they will often stab you deeper if you let them too close without a sharp memory. Keeping enemies close with their natures' in mind will give you the advantage.

12. Being kind to others should not be from the desire to have another good deed done. If you are going to be kind, do it without regard for a return.

13. If you make an enemy, follow the medieval and pre-medieval enemy law — be ruthless, be like a serpent in knowing their moves and be like a lion in their presence. You will be the victor if you can calculate power with strategy and when to apply force.

UNBELIEF!
The Gift of the Thinking Mind

Humanity in the past 1,000 years has made amazing progress, look at the wonders around us! We can create so much, yet we still believe we are spiritually checked on by an invisible "father" who wants us to worship his son as savior! This God is hateful in the disguise of love, cold and unforgiving to those who insult him.

Some have said Luciferians can only be so if they believe in Satan and God! This is simply not so! Lucifer is the title for the Roman god of Light, who brings illumination and wisdom. The Devil of the Christians is only a carryover from other religions! The Zoroastrians beheld Ahriman as the God of Darkness, who brought plagues and evil to mankind. An initiated or insightful mind could see that challenge and adversity is actually beneficial for our development. We grow stronger from challenges; overcoming obstacles breeds resilience and resounding individual strength.

Luciferians recognize the symbolism of the Adversary in all of its forms as a beneficial, balanced motivational force within the self. Ahriman or Satan represents the fire of spirit and free mind. Do not be chained to beliefs which do nothing to serve the spiritual and carnal needs of yourself or your loved ones.

Strategy is the mother of victory; it is a viable trait in the Mastery of this World. Everything done in your daily life leads to something else. If you want to achieve more, think about what you are doing to achieve the ends you wish.

The Church gained control over governments early on to exercise control of the individual, that is why the more significant of Gnostic texts were banned by the Church Fathers, they hated women and individual power. The Luciferian understands that woman and the daemonic feminine is the motivator in ourselves and the world around us. The Gnostic texts, if utilized from a Luciferian perspective, can bring a semblance of divinity within. They also lead to ecstatic states of gnosis with the Luciferian current.

Think clearly by questioning everything; don't assume something is true at face value. The Luciferian is a natural rebel, not evil, but Willful to watch out what is best for the self.

Beware also of "white light" concepts which lack the balance of darkness. Our world was created from darkness – it is the source of life. To deny darkness is to accept a death sentence. The Fire or Black Flame is a symbol of consciousness, the very passion of our spirit and motivator of our being. The darkness must be balanced on a conscious and subconscious level to master the progressive aspects of our being.

Self-development is useful in exercise, meditation, yoga and learning only when you know what you want to become.

In short, the Luciferian must have a plan for what he or she want to become, know what prey is and what is predator and become accordingly. Transform yourself in the object of what is strong and powerful.

THE BIBLE OF THE ADVERSARY

ANGELIC AND DEMONIC
Exercises in Anthropomorphic Symbolism

Lucifer has long appeared in different guises and forms. Lilith, the Bride of the Devil, often has several forms as well. Let's explore the idea of both with regard to their forms. Understanding that the Adversary has many forms will no doubt make your path to transformation and communion with the inner fire more meaningful.

LILITH

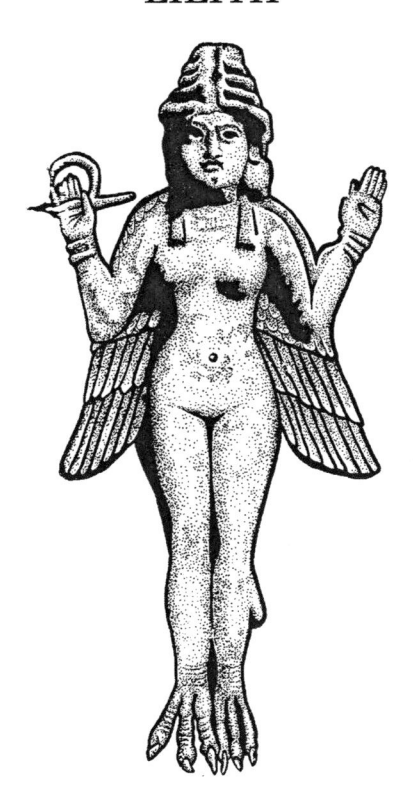

The Angelic

Lilith has never appeared as an angel, however she mostly appears beautiful. From a Sumerian relief, Lilith is shown with a slender, beautiful visage which relates to her grace and overwhelming power of seduction; she is what men desire most in their dreams. Lilith is winged, indicated her power in the astral plane. The astral plane often relates to dreams, the spirit and our instinctual mind. Lilith holds two solar signs often depicted by Royalty; this indicates her power and majesty. Lilith is also DIANA, the beautiful maiden, she is Babalon, the voluptuous whore on the 7 headed Dragon, she is Venus, the Goddess of Love...

The Demonic

Lilith in this same Sumerian relief is shown with beast like feet, talons indicting her lustful and desirous nature as the Queen of Demons. Her power of flight often depicts her power of the astral plane, dreaming and nightmares. After her exile to the Red Sea, Lilith copulated and begets demons at the rate of 100 or more per day.

SAMAEL

The Angelic

Lucifer, or Samael appears in Western mythology as an angel with a beautiful countenance, angelic beyond physical description, robed in white and whose eyes burn with unnatural light. Lucifer burns with the essence of power of character, his will is electrifying. Samael's eyes are powerful, they seem to look right through you, viewing your deepest secrets and desires, his glare challenges your desires and the power to accomplish what you want to in this world.

THE DEMONIC & ATAVISTIC MEMORIES

Demonic symbolism represents our animalistic, primal or hidden desires. Often, demonic is mistaken for something alien or evil. This is by all accounts humorous as the only evil is from within. The demonic aspects of the self should not be ignored or banished; they will later emerge as beasts you cannot control. Rather, to identify and to understand the demonic as a natural part of your being is to begin the process of uniting the angelic with the demonic.

Samael or Lucifer as the Prince of Demons takes on any form desirous to him. Appearing as a serpent with a lion's head, crowned in the brilliance of his essence, his words shake the foundations of chaos. The serpent represents subconscious energies, the stealth of strategy and listening to ones instincts. The lion represents solar energy, the fierce countenance of Lucifer. As the Devil, Satan, the Adversary represents our instinctual desires, the potential for self-destruction or ascension. The Devil or Diabolus represents the subconscious energies latent in the human mind – that by utilizing this force you can control and channel these energies into viable aspects which lead to power in this world.

Ahriman is a primal, perhaps more powerful of an atavistic form. The anthropomorphic concept of Ahriman as the Prince of Darkness establishes his being as the essence of Satan. Ahriman takes many forms as well – a serpent, wolf, toad, young man, old man, angel and dragon. Ahriman is able to bring darkness into all and counteract the stasis of Ahura Mazda, the slave god.

The sorceries of Ahriman in my works of The Yatuk Dinoih, Paitisha, The Vampire Gate and Liber HVHI are perhaps the most powerful dark magicks to be written down – they will deify those willing to drink the venoms of that cup.

The symbolism of the demonic especially from the medieval depicts desire worn in the image of the bestial. Often, the pact making Devil is the very hunger and desire for more in this life. They also represent the sexual desire in a repressed time. Don't stray away from the Devil – it is within you, does not want to harm you and is a powerful force to gain anything you want with.

The Subconscious mind contains the totality of association and experience in its total form. This association of experience is contained in locked and deep recesses of the mind. This can find itself emerging in the present, via the conscious mind. Often, the subconscious displays itself in various layers of pre-existing animal or beast like images or strata: reptile, fish, wolf, insect, or any other possibility.

As these memories or associative features emerge, they are clothed in various aspects of their forms: a sexual lust or longing may be clothed as a demonic woman, cackling at your presence, transforming from a maiden to a hag when you are about to touch her – symbolizing the past and what you consciously believe you cannot have.

Visualize now, that in this subconscious, symbolized as an OCEAN or ABYSS, what lies within. Imagine if you could stand at the edge, enter and arise from that sea with any desired recalled ancient memory or aspect of your mental make up? If you could open that ancient grimoire and from that epitome, the desires you so wish to achieve may rise up and through obsession, empower you, anything is possible!

The artist AUSTIN OSMAN SPARE wrote that *"Resist not desire by repression: but transmute desire by changing to the greater object"* – The Focus of Life

We see here that mysticism is easily revealed once you have mastered your own internal system of sorcery, methods are waiting for you to take them up and utilize them.

Desires which arise in the mind often attract to themselves a distinctive form from which it will manifest. This is why imagery of demons show them in often vile form. This is not vile upon the discovery of the meaning, merely a great gift wrapped in a test of sorts; are you willing to pass the test?

The Luciferian understands that he or she must equally study the beautiful and powerful aspects of the self – develop them, master them and utilize them to serve your consciousness.

THE BIBLE OF THE ADVERSARY
THE DRAGON AND THE ARCHON
The Luciferian Mind

This section will be an exploration of the concepts of the Luciferian mind in a more predatory state. As the religion of the Luciferian grows, so will the potential of each individual. Our foundations as the human race have been defined by our wisdom applied through the ages. In our current times, Magick is to be seen as a science of self-evolution and the ascension of power.

Achieving personal Godhood and your own personal relationship with your higher sense of being, called by some, The Holy Guardian Angel or the Luciferian Angel, is your higher self. Developing a validated religious experience is paramount within any belief system; don't move upon the blind faith route, it will lead to your slavery. Liberate yourself through willed action, validate results and gain power accordingly.

The techniques of the control of the mind and body as within Ahrimanic Yoga[2] will lead to mental and spiritual control. Control equals a type of power depending on how you approach and view it. A Luciferian believes that he or she is responsible for their life and what they do will affect to either in a positive or negative sense.

Some basic steps to development no matter what stage you are in your life are the following:

1. Establish a pattern which involves discipline i.e. daily exercise, physical fitness. This leads to physical prowess, strength and endurance. Exercise also establishes a sense of control over the mind as well.

2. Practice a path of Ahrimanic Yoga – establish breathing control, relaxation, meditative achievement. This leads to the retention of astral energy, chi or

---
[2] LIBER HVHI – Magick of the Adversary

prana and magical power. Mental control is everything in magick – the power of Will, the ability to reason and determine you path, etc.

3. Develop psychic abilities i.e. tarot or some type of divination, listen to your instincts and gain power accordingly.

4. Ritual practice will lead to insight which may be utilized as power depending on how you use it. Rites are intended to place you in union with something, depending on what it is. Everything you do must be in a process of ascending.

THE ARCHON

Lucifer as the image of the archon is a beautiful, bright and powerful spiritual force. Lucifer is the ascended impulse of the evolutionary instinct; that is; Lucifer is our present and future possibility. That aspect of instinct leads to continual self-development.

The Archon Satan or Lucifer wants to shape reality to his Will and Desire. This is indeed the desire of the Luciferian.

The difference between a Luciferian and a non-Luciferian is the self-affirmed desire to shape your reality to what you wish.

The Luciferian understands that ALL people, no matter what religion or belief system, want to control and shape their world to make their life more meaningful to them. It does not matter if you are Buddhist, Christian, Jewish or Satanist– you want to control your life. The Luciferian acknowledges that everyone is different in terms of spiritual association – some are more or less spiritual than others. The Luciferian understands that power is a constant in this life.

THE DRAGON

The Draconian aspects of Luciferian faith is found in the instinctual essence which is represented as a mask of the Adversary. The word Seraphim, called angels, is a word related to "Serpents", an ancient form which dragons are associated. The Dragon represents the unrestricted, primal power of the subconscious. Lucifer has long been a spirit able to take form in that of whatever he wished. Controlling the dragon, serpent or instinctual aspect of the mind is greatly significant; it leads to additional aspects of possibility. Society respects those who are able to control themselves. Some simplistic guidance points to live by:

1. Build your reputation by how you are viewed, heard and how you react to situations.

2. Internal power is directly a result of the Mind and its state of being. The dragon can be viewed as the spiral energy of the serpent power, relating to the Mind. Continually coil this energy like a serpent within. Striking out will diminish your power, so keep it wound tightly until you can feel the right moment to strike. This relates to what you say, how you say it, when you act, how you act, etc.

3. Displaying power continually can begin to destroy it; it also makes your weaknesses clear to your enemies. Keep your enemies off guard by keeping power tightly wound to you – don't respond to every challenge with great force, think first before you act. This is a perfect way of controlling and coiling the dragon.

MICHAEL W. FORD
AHRIMAN
The Darkness Embodied

In terms of the infernal and the Theronick forms of the Adversary, Ahriman holds significance in initiatory exploration. The ancient Nag Hamannadi texts which hold significance to Manichaean writings display a foundation for the atavistic aspects of Ahriman.

The Kephalion presents a clear magickial study of Ahriman or Angra Mainyu from an atavistic aspect.

The King of Darkness bears five different forms. His head is the face of a raging Lion, representing power and domination. His hands and feet have faces of demons on them, representing desires and lust. His shoulders bear the face or head of Eagles, representing flight and predatory instinct, his stomach has the face of a dragon, representing atavistic resurgence and the hunger for power and life. His tail is that of fish and has the face of a fish – representing Leviathan or the power of the Abyss or Ocean.

Sacrifices to Ahriman were made of wild boars and wolves during the time of the Magi, Ahriman was considered equally powerful to Ahura Mazda, the God of the Zoroastrians.

This is the pentagram of the infernal, the star fallen to display the power of the above and below. The world of darkness, the very essence of our subconscious, is the exclusive home of Leviathan, the dragon-serpent which encircles our very being. Without guidance, however, this God would never reach forth into this world. The daemonic aspect of Samael and Lilith, grant the power to make use of the daimonic aspects of Leviathan.

From the dark world of Ahriman were the ArchDaevas Akoman and Andar, and then Sovar, and then Nakahed, and then Tairev and Zairik.

Ahriman is considered in ancient Avestan texts as the God of Matter. Matter must be understood as anything which is moveable, this may also represent sonic waves or the astral body. We must, as Luciferians, learn to listen with our senses as well as our subconscious, to do so announce power over the astral plane.

The Shape of the Astral Body is often reflective of our conscious mind and body; it is who we are within most often.

MICHAEL W. FORD

THE PENTAGRAM

The five points signify earth, air, fire, water and spirit.

THE SIGIL OF SATAN (above) – Inverted Pentagram and Lightning Bolt. Represents the electricfying power of Samael fallen to earth, into the clay of humanity.

Kingdom of Darkness

Smoke – When smoke mingled with fire, Ahriman had empowered the essence of light with his own being. This relates to anger and the power of the motivated spirit.

Fire- Illumination, Ahriman brought down and shared the fire with living beings. This is Consuming Fire – that which is illuminated by it or empowered, along with Pillars of Fire.

Wind – The Spirit of the Air, related to Pride and spiritual power. This is the Column of Smoke. The Scorching Wind, essence of the desert and Pestilent Breath.

Water- Related to Rahab in Hebraic mythology, the Angel of Violence and Leviathan, the power of the subconscious. This is the Abysmal Depths, Fetid Marshes and Wells of Poison.

Darkness- The power of desire and the atavistic aspect of the mind. This is also Gloom, Mist and the elements of spirits.

AHRIMAN as the Greater Bundahishin describes takes many forms, one of the earliest *"His astral body is that of the frog, the vicious crab".* The Bundahishn presents Ahriman as *"his body is that of a lizard (vazagh) whose place is filth (kalch)."* The Abode of Ahriman is Hell is a place like a dark desert. *"Regarding the cold, dry, stony, and dark interior of mysterious (tarik den afraj-pedak) hell it says, that the darkness is fit to grasp with the hand, and the stench is fit to cut with a knife"* – Bundahishn.

1. **AKOMAN:** The Evil Mind. The nature of our actual world is of reason and logic applied. Understanding the difference between the disparity between the concept and the result of its application. The Evil Mind is equally the rational mind as well as the Mind of Instinct and Reason. Akoman or Aka Manah is attributed to the Ajna Chakra. AKOMAN may be visualized in many forms- serpent like man shadowed and robed in black, holding a drum and skull-staff, a rosary of skulls.
2. **SAVAR:** The Voice and Leader of Devs. Savar is the aspect of voice and command. The power of his persuasion must be recognized: he commands truth by announcing his Lie or desire. Traditionally, the "Lie" is related to the word "Druj" meaning demon of the lie. The lie is considered from the word "druj" and from "Drauga" which makes reference to dragon and serpent. The Lie is simply a point of transformation – you announce your desire which is being created and woven, your words compel or inspire other

minds, thus The Lie becomes truth and your goals achieved. Here there is no "evil" or harm done unless misuse of this knowledge brings it so. The Bundahishn describes him as "Savar, that is a leader of the demons, is this, that is, misgovernment, oppressive anarchy, and drunkenness" – chaos and anarchy is that which new order arrives. The Greater Bundahishn presents Savar or SOVAR as being the Dev of ambition: "Saurva, that is the leader of the devs, is this: evil authority, oppression, unlawfulness, and the production of want." Savar is attributed to the Throat Chakra. Savar is often displayed as holding a Serpent, Battle-Axe, Sword, A Vajra weapon, a bow and arrow, a noose.

3. **ANDAR:** The Greater Bundahishn presents Andar or Indra as "Indra is this that he freezes the minds of the creatures from practicing righteousness just like much frozen snow", we see the association of his Instinct and Will bringing forth the Black Flame of Rebellion, thus Andar is a powerful dev as he can bring discontent and manifestation from rebellion. The Bundahishn itself presents Andar as "Akoman is this, that he gave vile thoughts and discord to the creatures" thus Andar is a Dev of Chaos and raw, unrestrained power. Andar relates to the HEART chakra. The Heart Chakra relates to AIR and is thus Luciferian in spiritual aims – it is the power of thoat, reason and higher intellect. In addition is can be pure serpent-like or instinctual thought when need be. Andar is a powerful combination with Akoman, they work in unison. Andar may be visualized holding a noose and skull. Indra or Andar also takes the form of an Indian god riding upon a Behemoth-like Elephant.

4. **Naonhaithya** or **Naikiyas** brings discontent or the desire for more to all creatures. This power Dev relates to the possibility and ambition where it may arise, thus it can be a powerful aspect of transformation and

ascension of power. Naikiyas is attributed to the Solar Plexis and can be visualized holding a thunderbolt.
5. **Aeshma or Eshm** is attributed to the Sacral Chakra, often holding a war club, a pentagram disc or a wounding spear. Aeshma is given seven powers to compel the world to the essence and spirit of Ahriman.
6. **TAROMAT or TAROMATI** is the Dev which produces Scorn and disobedience; she is attributed to the Base Chakra and appears as a Serpent.

ARCH-DAEVAS & ASSOCIATIONS
AKOMAN – Animals, Reptiles
ANDAR – FIRE
SAVAR – Sky
TAROMAT – EARTH
NAONGHAITHYA – EARTH
TAPREV – Plants
ZAIRICH – WATER
AHRIMAN - Man

CAIN THE FIRST LUCIFERIAN

In the first semblance of mythology and symbolism, many Luciferians regard Cain as being a symbol of the initiated one. Being considered not a Son of Adam in Kabbala, Cain was begotten by Samael or Satan riding Eve under the direction of Lilith.

"R. Hiyya said: "The sons of God were the sons of Cain. For when Samael mounted Eve, he injected filth into her, and she conceived and bare Cain. And his aspect was unlike that of the other humans and all those who came from his side were called sons of God."- Kabbala: Zohar 1:37a

Here we see the linage of those of the Luciferian Faith is born. This language is symbolic, anyone who adopts the Luciferian spirit as a part of themselves, they become a Son or Daughter of Cain.

"there is the legend of Eve and the Serpent, for Cain was the child of Eve and the Serpent, and not of Eve and Adam; and therefore when he had slain his brother, who was the first murderer, having sacrificed living things to his demon, had Cain the mark upon his brow, which is the mark of the Beast spoken of in the Apocalypse, and is the sign of initiation." – The Book of Thoth, Aleister Crowley

In Luciferian Grimoires, Cain is said to be a symbol and gateway for man and woman to become, thus the symbol of Baphomet as Anton LaVey called it, is the inverted pentagram with a goat head in the middle. The original, which LaVey took out, contained the words Samael and Lilith, surrounded in the circle ring the Hebrew LvTHN, Leviathan, the Crooked Serpent. In the circles of Luciferian Witchcraft, this is the sigil of Baphomet – the Head of Wisdom who has united the Solar and the Lunar, or the Fire and Water within the self to bring forth Cain, the Devil in Flesh upon earth. He is the symbol and cipher of Magick, the Great Work accomplished and onward moving. At the gathering of the Sabbat is Cain the Black Man, the circle and center of the Sabbat and it's fire, he directs it outward as "he" is the Pole of this Force.

"Woe unto them! For they have gone in the way of Cain" – Jude 11

Cain's name is said to have derived from a root 'Kanah' which means to possess[3]. This by itself presents the antinomian nature of his essence, while instead of sacrificing his most bountiful items to the Lord, he kept them for himself. This may draw conclusion that he viewed himself as

---

[3] Catholic Encyclopedia

a form of God, by later sacrificing his brother Abel[4] he began the Left Hand Path, which brought him into being as a Son of Satan. Cain is viewed in later paths of Witchcraft as a Lord of Magick, but rather the darker aspects. Here Cain takes a similar path with Anubis by name and process. Robert Cochrane, a practitioner of Witchcraft in the 60's wrote-

"In the North lies the Castle of Weeping, the ruler thereof is named Tettens, our Hermes or Woden. He is the second twin, the waning sun, Lord over mysticism, magic, power and death, the baleful destroyer. The God of War, of Justice, King of Kings, since all pay their homage to him. Ruler of the Winds, the Windyat. Cain imprisoned in the Moon, ever desiring Earth. He is visualized as a tall dark man, shadowy, cold and deadly." – Letters from Robert Cochrane

The instances of Cain in symbolism within the Luciferian Path are found in the grimoire LUCIFERIAN WITCHCRAFT, which details practice in this avenue. The entry rites and workings are equally as powerful as ones presented here.

MAGICK – Where it begins

Magick is the process of attainment by which the practitioner comes into direct contact and initiation with his or her god. The essence of magick is to ascend in spirit, to advance in wisdom through experience and to gain the power of the mind and spirit to achieve what you wish. To begin upon your path of magick, understand what Luciferian ideology is and is not. A Luciferian becomes a living embodiment of the Spirit, thus the body is a temple. Do not defile it in any way which inhibits your personal metamorphosis.

---

[4] Abel in some Luciferian Lore is considered a lower 'pre form' of Cain, thus the sacrifice was not literal.

Black Magick in the context of Luciferian Witchcraft is not malefic or negative workings, but holds a closer association to the root of the meaning of the word black, from 'KHEM'. Black Magick is self-awakening and isolate workings with the Adversarial current, both positive and a negative approach.

SOME REASONS WHY MAGICK IS PRACTICED

1. To liberate yourself from restrictive beliefs you were brought up with.

2. To examine deep set behaviors which may be causing problems, modify those behaviors and shape them into productive areas of your life.

3. To open up spiritual communication and experience with the Luciferian current, i.e Gods, Daemon and Goddesses. No matter if you believe in them as separate spiritual forces, all begins within the self.

4. To build, strengthen and refine consciousness, which will in turn build personal Ego, confidence and charisma as within your own psychological make-up.

5. To define what is possible in your life when your mind is focused.

6. Luciferians exalt life and celebrate both the spiritual and the carnal. One may at different times slightly outweigh the other during a lifetime but the Luciferian Spirit reminds us to maintain a balance of both. They are inherently connected and fed by the other.

7. Personal experience is paramount – don't assume something is so by word alone. Experience it and affirm it yourself. Once gnosis is achieved, inspiration will flow like a fountain. Think of what you can do once inspiration is achieved: creativity, action, planning – all of this is related to the symbol of the Serpent.

Know that before the path of Lucifer is the hidden doctrine of Ahriman. Lucifer is thus Ahriman as his forms are many. The path of Ahriman is found within, it is the essence of how the path develops through you specifically.

"Again, of those who lead (men to evil), one is the bad and impious person (priest), who inculcates the (wicked) faith of the Demon, and who on account of the evil luster of Ahriman in him, brings those who are subject to him, under evil influences, by imparting to them his own (evil) inclinations. Consequently, he cuts them off from their redemption (from hell). And whosoever (priest) loves such a (false) splendor of Ganamino, is blindly ignorant of the final condition (farjamih)." – Denkard

The path of "evil" is only that as it requires self-determined intiation and the discovery of faith through actual results and practice. Faith has often been the damnation of many. The Luciferian must seek faith only by subjective validation of results. This refers to the point that you must have measurable results. The Luciferian decides his own destiny accordingly, by his or her own choices in life.

"The sinful ones who will be (born) to be priests or rulers among the people of this world, will descend from those wicked leaders of wicked tribes who teach the evil religion; and the (highest) chieftain of the wicked ones in this world, is he who is destined for the worst religion and for the worst abode (hell). And in garments, his clothing resembles that of one who is a slave to the Demon. And among the evil doers his business is to injure the good, and help on the wicked." – Denkard

This is the path of the rebel, the one who affirms "I am God" and there is no other. Ancient Zoroastrians considered Ahriman to work directly through the body of humanity – the same as Ahura Mazda.

"His meet recompense at the end (i.e. after death), is the appearance (in bodily form) in front of him of all the desires

of that (evil) doer. Such a person himself is the druja of perverse sense [lit. lustful]. In him there is a liking for the most confounding demons, and the fitting predominance of the wicked Aeshma. The liberal donor unto him is one of the evil northern planets, which the astronomers call Mars, and which religion designates 'the evil and immoral.' It is the obstinate one among the evil planets. It brings to him (viz. to the wicked warrior) fruitless misery, on account of which his disposition becomes inclined to perverse desires as well as to the selfish religion calculated to destroy his final (happiness). And such a one will in this world be (born) among such rulers as are selfish and perverse fighters. And in the class of impious priests who are adversaries (of the Mazdayasna), he is the head of the wicked ones, an unworthy ruler and an infidel judge who is possessed of (mischievous) wisdom. And his own selfish person is a garment suitable for him." – Denkard

CONTROLLING THE MIND

Control of the Mind is the first step in attainment with Magick. The ability to concentrate, block out your surroundings is paramount in your initiation upon the magickal path.

This is accomplished with some of the following steps: achieving motionless, controlling the speed of breathing, concentration on sound or mental image. While these steps seem very un-Satanic, they are the first steps in becoming a God or Goddess and consecrating your own body as a Temple of Lucifer.

COMPLETE STILLNESS

Find yourself a quite place to sit and think. You may want to be alone when you first start practicing this, especially if you are easily distracted. Sit in an upright position, legs crossed and arms resting on the knees. Do not move or move a limb. This is essential – ignore all! Start with five minutes each day and increase up to a half an hour or forty five minutes.

BREATHING

Another essential part of the process, controlling your breathing to achieve gnosis. Once you have mastered the basics of stilling the body, you will want to pay particular attention to your breathing patterns. Start by taking slow, deep breaths and filling your lungs with the full capacity of air. Think of how your body and breathing patterns effect your ability to perform Magick – how they can connect with the effectiveness of your astral body.

CONTROLLING THOUGHTS

Thinking may be slowed, controlled and focused once you have achieved the stillness of the body and the breathing pattern. Try to slow the thinking patterns of yourself by not-thinking. You will find this very difficult and often reveal to yourself the aspects of the mind are but a chaos-storm of endless sentences, ideas and continuous activity. The Luciferian views the Adversary as the controlling and directing the thinking patterns as the source of power. Thus Lucifer is the power of achieving self-deification. Try the practice of not-thinking to begin focusing on the goal at hand. You will find interesting aspects of yourself and determine things which are the result of your reasoning skills in your own life.

LUCIFERIAN GNOSIS

As you have achieved the basics of control you will want to now become comfortable with attempting and achieving Gnosis. The Luciferian Gnosis is attained by achieving the steps listed before this to enter an in-between state of Will. Gnosis is a state of altered consciousness, like communicating with the subconscious mind at Will. The two opposite but equally significant states of consciousness are direct Physiological associations to the following:

LUCIFERIAN: Contemplative, emotional understanding, Yoga and thought related, reasoning and advanced thinking; planning and forethought, Willed and directed strategy. This represents "Light" and the "Angelic" meaning higher articulation. The Mind which controls. Empyrean or Highest Aspect of the Aethyr or Ethyric. Passive or contemplative, Ahrimanic Yoga, Scrying, etc.

AHRIMANIC: Physical and carnal, relating to instinct; dancing, sexual arousal, physical sensation, movement, trance entered by direct carnal or physical association. Ahrimanic also represents a dark spirituality based on belief in spirits and other aspects of sorcery, this is subjective and depends on the individual.

The **INFERNAL UNION SEAL** of the Luciferian Path is a bit more abstract but equally significant. Let's explore that model of practice.

LEVIATHAN: The Subconscious, dream/nightmare state, the ocean of thoughts, our inner most desires which have not yet arisen from darkness.

SAMAEL: The Black Flame and Power of Will and Belief. Samael is the Fallen Seraphim or Angel which is both intelligence, wisdom and the Lightning of Inspiration or becoming. Represents Power and Will to Flesh. Samael is the counteraction and applied strength to achieve, the result of Desire.

LILITH: The active part of the Black Flame, the Primal instinct which unites to cause action. Lilith is the desire in Sexual Arousal, Lilith is the desire in Lust and the fire to motivate Samael and the result of desire. She is the continual hunger to become.

As we can see by both models one alone is not able to manifest in both worlds – to unite the Adversary no matter which model is to create a God or Goddess of the Left Hand Path, a true manifestation of Chioa or the Beast. The union of Samael and Lilith begets HVHI, or the Antichrist[5]. This is the power of self-creation and ascension against the path of union with God. To the Luciferian, the path of God is sought within and they we do not understand the desire to give up our consciousness to another. THAT itself is against the Law of Nature.

EXISTENCE – Indulgence and Power

Indulgence is the enjoyment and attainment of the Ego. No matter in what religion, indulgence is seen only as an enjoyment for a God. Mortals are not allowed to indulge and should be banned from the eternal reward.

Let's look at the "eternal reward" and how the Adversary viewed it.

Christianity: Satan did not want it, thought it was boring and much change was needed.

Gnostic: Yaltabaoth did what he wanted, moved on and created more.

Hebraic: Samael and Lilith thought the best playground was the flesh and spirit, enjoy now in the body, be immortal in the spirit.

Zoroastrian: Ahriman did not need heaven and thought the earth should be his. Ahriman kicked Ahura Mazda half off the earth and does what he wishes in any form he desires.

The Watchers or Fallen Angels took their wisdom and knowledge to earth and made it work here.

It is our duty as Luciferians to balance our time in this existence as with spiritual development with carnal

---
[5] SATANIC MAGICK – by Michael W. Ford, a Paradigm of Therion.

indulgence. That is; the flesh should not be denied but neither should the spiritual. It is up to the Luciferian to ascend and recognize time on earth should be enjoyed.

THE GATES OF HELL

The Luciferian path acknowledges that individuals view spiritual and carnal aims differently. The Luciferian may utilize mythology in any way they wish, regardless as to if they understand that all begins within first. The Adversary, or Ahriman, Lucifer, Samael or whatever you will call it directly controls such spirits if he so wishes. The Adversary for the Luciferian is a symbol of the Self, if you were attuned to Christian symbolism this would be the Antichrist, the antithesis of what Christ would represent. The Antichrist is the manifested power of Satan in this world, as if Satan is the spirit and the Body is the Antichrist. The Luciferian keeps his focus on the spiritual aims of his development; the Carnal is balanced by this.

In the YATUK DINOIH and LIBER HVHI the Persian path of Ahriman is represented as a primal path to infernal power. Ahriman is darkness manifest, a sorcerous being who is able to shape shift, create spirits and to command his Will to power.

The collection of demonic names may be used as Ahriman would, to empower and compel desires to manifest according to the Will of the Magickian.

The Luciferian Goetia provides an excellent platform for sorcery from both an internal and external perspective.

LUCIFERIAN RELIGIOUS HOLIDAYS

For each time when the moon renews itself in the world Lilith comes and visits all those whom she rears - Zohar

The Luciferian views holidays as meaningful based on his or her interpretation of the Luciferian faith. Specific religious holidays are based on Qlippothic forces and the Zodiac. The Theistic Luciferian, focused on magical workings would utilize dates to conduct workings which reflect the attributes of the demons. It should be understood that demons are bestial forces which relate to the raw energies and passions of our bodies and spirits.

Qlippoth = Start of Qlippothic Month

Yatuk Dinoih = Start of Daevayasna/Yatukih Month.

OCTOBER 17 – Duzhyairya Pairikas (Yatuk Dinoih – demoness of thirst)

OCTOBER 23 – Necheshethiron (Qlippoth)

OCTOBER 30 – Ahriman's Night

OCTOBER 31 – Samhain – Halloween – Hecate Feast (Lilith)

NOVEMBER 16 – Hecate Feast

NOVEMBER 17 – Sama Atar (the Black Flame) of Daevayasna – Yatuk Dinoih

NOVEMBER 22 – Nachashiron (Qlippoth)

DECEMBER 16 – Az Jeh(Yatuk Dinoih)

DECEMBER 21 – Yule or Winter Solstice (Lilith)

DECEMBER 22 – Dagdagiron (Qlippoth)

JANUARY 8 – Hecate Feast

JANUARY 15 – Akoman (Yatuk Dinoih)

JANUARY 20 – Behemiron (Qlippoth)

JANUARY 31 - Imbolg or February Eve

FEBRUARY 14 – Taromat (Yatuk Dinoih)

FEBRUARY 18 – Neshimiron (Qlippoth)

MARCH 16, 17, 18, 19 – Feast of the Black Flame

MARCH 20 – Bairiron (Qlippoth)

MARCH 21 – Vernal Equinox – Ahriman enters creation at 12:PM Noon – Day of the Black Flame.

MARCH 22 – Druj (Yatuk Dinoih)

APRIL 20 – Andar (Yatuk Dinoih) Adimiron (Qlippoth)

APRIL 30 – Beltane or May eve

MAY 3 – Hecate Feast

MAY 20 – Taprev (Yatuk Dinoih), Luciferian Supper of Cain, Tzelldaimion (Qlippoth)

JUNE 19 – Apaosha and Spenjaghri (Yatuk Dinoih)

JUNE 22 – Summer Solstice (Lilith and Nahemoth) – Schechiriron (Qlippoth)

JULY 19 – Zairich (Yatuk Dinoih)

JULY 23 – Shelhabiron (Qlippoth)

JULY 31 – Lughnasadh or Lammas

AUGUST 13 – Hecate Feast

AUGUST 18 – Savar (Yatuk Dinoih)
AUGUST 23 – Tzephariron (Qlippoth)
SEPTEMBER 17 – Astovidad and Aeshma
SEPTEMBER 21 – Autumn Equinox (Lilith and Nahemoth)
SEPTEMBER 23 – Obiriron (Qlippoth)

THE BIBLE OF THE ADVERSARY

LIBER LEGION

Infernal and Chthonic Names
Of Spirits, Daemons and Astral forms

MICHAEL W. FORD
GNOSTIC DEMONS

YALTABAOTH – The Lion Faced, Serpent God who is Lucifer. The power of Yaltabaoth is that he is the Black Flame bearer, he may take many forms and shapes. Yaltabaoth changed into a form of a lion-faced serpent. And its eyes were like lightning fires which flash in the darkness. Yaltabaoth moved himself from his mother, Barbelo and moved away from the places in which he was born. He became strong and created for himself other aeons with a flame of luminous fire which (still) exists now. This is the Black Flame and the essence of the Luciferian Faith - "face flashed with fire and whose appearance was defiled with blood." Nebro means rebel. Nebro creates six angels to be his assistants. These six in turn create another twelve angels "with each one receiving a portion in the heavens." Yaltabaoth is thus Lucifer and the Angel of Light, he knows both darkness and light. The Luciferian Spirit has three primary names in gnostic lore Yaltabaoth, Saklas, and Samael.

Onorthochrasaei – Similar to the Manichaean and Zurvanite Az. The demoness is matter, for they are nourished by her. She mixes with the following demons.

The demons of the whole body are four:
heat, cold, wetness, and dryness.

Phloxopha – demon of the heat of the body. In some Manichaean writings and Zoroastrian writings AZ is the demoness relating to the heat of the body.
Oroorrothos- Demon who reigns over cold.
Erimacho – The demon who reigns over what is dry.
Athuro – Demon which reigns over wetness.

The mother of the four chief demons is

Aesthesis-Ouch-Epi-Ptoe

The four chief demons are:

Ephememphi, who belongs to pleasure,
Yoko, who belongs to desire
Nenentophni, who belongs to grief,
Blaomen, who belongs to fear

THE ANGELIC WATCHERS or GRIGORI
Bringers of Wisdom

The Watchers were according to the Lore of Old a power of the angelic, 200 Grigori descended to Earth to take flesh and join and uplift humanity. Seeing that humanity were unintelligent, they descended in human form as well as the forms of serpents, dragons with seven heads and other beasts of prey. Gathered at Mount Hermon / Armon over 12,000 years ago they went forth some in beautiful human form, others as like Azazel with Twelve Wings and others with dual faces, to father the Nephilim. Before going forth to Humanity, the Watchers made a pact among each other, 'Let us all swear an oath, and all bind ourselves by mutual imprecations not to abandon this plan but to do this thing.'[6]

We see an early reference to Vampirism and Predatory Spirituality once the Watchers' wives bore the Nephilim; 'And they became pregnant, and they bare great giants, whose height was three thousand cells: Who consumed all the acquisitions of men. And when men could no longer sustain them, the giants turned against them and devoured mankind. And they began to sin against birds, and beasts, and reptiles, and fish, and to devour one another's flesh, and drink the blood. Then the earth laid accusation against the lawless ones.' – Book of Enoch

---

[6] THE BOOK OF ENOCH, Translated by R.H. Charles.

According to the Book of Enoch, Azazel 'was cast into the darkness: and make an opening in the desert, which is in Dudael, and cast him therein. And place upon him rough and jagged rocks, and cover him with darkness, and let him abide there forever, and cover his face that he may not see light." – Book of Enoch

The Book of Enoch made reference to the meaning of the word NEPHILIM, the children of the Fallen Angels. Once they were created with the union of the Watchers, the Nephilim were something above humanity. They were stronger, were blood thirst or they sought continued life. The spirits of the Nephilim or "giants *shall be like* clouds, which shall oppress, corrupt, fall, content, and bruise upon earth." – Book of Enoch

The Greek word for clouds used in the text, **nephelas** may hold a deeper meaning for the Giants. This would relate to the Nephilim as Nephelas meaning Astral or Terrestrial spirits, being of the Air. Some of the names of the sons of fallen angels were Mahway, son of Barakel, Ohya and Hahya.

The Watchers may provide to the sorcerer a powerful archetype of wisdom, as they are the source and fountain.

Arsiel /Azazel /Azael/ Azazyl is the name of the Luciferian power which holds great significance towards the cunning path. The name Arsiel means "Black Sun" and relates to whom "Has strengthened himself as God". Arsiel is the demon of the bottomless pit from perhaps a Babylonian origin. Many Rabbis think that he is the first mighty angel to descend, who became Ibliss or Diabolus. He is considered SATAN, who would not bow before the clay of Man as he was of Fire. It was Azazel who beget AZZA with Naamah, the sister of Cain, who was empowered and initiated as a Lilith Demoness. AZZA means "Strong One" and according to Witch Lore is the one who revealed the Empyrean Arcana to Solomon. In addition AZAZEL taught men how to craft the weapons of war, how to make swords, knives and breastplates.

Satanail/Salamiel: A Great Prince amongst Grigori. Enoch suggested that he and his fellow Daimons were already under revolt against God even before the Fall through Lust and incarnating to satisfy sexual desire. Although it is inferred that he had lead a rebellion.

Jeqon, led astray the sons of god. That is; by wisdom and infernal knowledge Jeqon awakened the sons of Cain to the path of the wise. To enter the Left Hand Path is to take charge of your own destiny.

Semjaza or Shemyaza taught root cuttings, sorceries and enchantments. A Luciferian Witch Father and initiator.

SHAMDON, a fallen angel who copulated with Naamah or Nahemoth to create Ashmodai, a King of Demons.
Ananel taught hidden knowledge. Compare to the Enochian name of ANANAEL which means 'Wisdom'.

Kokabel taught the course of constellations, of the stars and the heavens.

Ezeqeel taught the knowledge of the clouds.

Asbeel, an important watcher who awakened the other fallen angels and led them to defile their bodies with the daughters of Cain. Asbeel is the "Isolate God" who led the other Grigori from the path of blindness.

Armaros taught sorcery and the resolving of spells and enchantments.

Sariel taught the course of the moon.

Baraqijal taught astrology.

Shamsiel taught the signs of the Sun.

Gadreel taught men the blows of death. Of self-defense and cursing.

Araqiel/Saraqa-el instructed man about the signs of the earth.

Agni-el Who taught of the enchantment of roots/herbs and the secrets of Sorcery and conjuration.

Anma-el Who had made a sexual pact with a woman to reveal the Secret Names of God. This could be a Daimon who taught the art of the serpent and sex magick.
Araziel/Arazyael `God is my noon", A Luciferian concept would be "I Ascend above the Sun"

Asael: `Made by God' would become "I create as God"

Exael A Grigori Who, according to Enoch, "taught men how to fabricate engines of war, works in silver and gold, the uses of gems and perfumes.".

Kasdaye Taught women how to abort.

Kashdejan Taught the curing of diseases including those of the mind.

Penemue/Penemuel Who taught the art of writing "although through this many went astray until this day, for Men were not created for such a purpose to confirm their good intentions with pen and ink." This is the Patron Daimon of the Grimoire, of the book which inspires and instructs.

Talmai-el was a descendant of the Grigori who escaped the Flood. This Luciferian Spirit would be as a God who is both of the Infernal and Heavenly.

Tamiel `Perfection of God' and from a Luciferian context "Perfection as God".

Usiel 'Strength of God' would become "Strength as God"

THE ARAMAIC TEXT NAME OF THE WATCHERS IS The Aramaic texts preserve an earlier list of names of these Watchers: **Semihazah; Artqoph; Ramtel; Kokabel; Ramel; Danieal; Zeqiel; Baraqel; Asael; Hermoni; Matarel; Ananel; Stawel; Samsiel; Sahriel; Tummiel; Turiel; Yomiel; Yhaddiel**

LEGION – SATANIC NAMES

Abigor: Horseman with a scepter and lance, commanding 60 legions, Goetic spirit.
Adramelech: Chancellor and High Council of Demons, son of Sennercherib who killed him. Adramalech is also a goetic demon. A son of an Assyrian Tyrant, personified as a Demon-God of Fire. From the Hebrew 'King of Fire'. An Angel of Thrones, a Fallen Angel, arch-demon Chancellor of the Order

of the Fly, patron of hypocrites. Corresponds to the Qlippothic sphere of Yod. Identified with sacrifices by fire and relates to the Black Flame.
Aguares : Grand Duke of Eastern region, commanding 30 legions goetic demon.
Ahriman – The Spirit of Evil, a name of the Adversary. The embodiment of all evil or sorcerous spirits, who inhabits the cthonian darkness, from where he delivers us the gifts of Godlike power, Sorcery and forbidden knowledge, blackness and smoke. Angra Mainyu is the embodiment of the Vampyric Father, whose bride is AZ the Devouring Whore. His symbol is the serpent, yet also a dragon, a wolf, a youth, an old man and whose first earthly form is a Toad or Frog. Invoked as Arimanius, the Foul Author of Shades.
Ahrimanes – Fallen Angels that followed Ahriman in the revolt against Ormazd his brother. Expelled once he ripped from the womb of Zurvan, they dwell in the darkness and the astral plane.
Alocer : Grand Duke , commanding 36 legions goetic demon.
Amduscius : Grand Duke, commanding 29 legions goetic demon.
Andras : Marquis , commanding 30 legions goetic demon.
Apollyon (Abaddon) : King of Demons, angel of the bottomless pit. A Fallen Angel, who is the destroyer, the place of destruction, the Abyss, Lord of the Locust Plague, The Angel of Hell.
Asmodeus (Asmoday) : demon of the wounding spear.
Astaroth : Grand Duke of Western region, Lord Treasurer of hell. goetic demon.
Ayperos : Prince, commanding 36 legions.
Baal : Commanding General of the Infernal Armies.
Baalberith : Chief Secretary and Archivist (second order demon, Berith).
Bael- The First Principal Spirit is a King ruling in the East, called Bael. He maketh thee to go Invisible. He ruleth over

66 Legions of Infernal Spirits. He appeareth in divers shapes, sometimes like a Cat, sometimes like a Toad, and sometimes like a Man, and sometimes all these forms at once.

Beelzebub /Beelzebuth : Prince of the Demons, Lord of the Flies, second only to Satan

Belphegor : Demon of Ingenious discoveries and wealth goetic demon.

Buer : Second order demon but commands 50 legions goetic demon.

Caym / Aim / Hayborym: Grand President of the Infernal goetic demon.

Chax : Grand Duke goetic demon.

Coronzon / Choronzon - Enochian equivalent of Samael, the Fallen Serpent — angel who is the mate of Lilith. Coronzon is considered a demon of Chaos and related to a vampiric force in the BOOK OF THE WITCH MOON.

Cresil : Demon of Impurity.

Eurynomus : Prince who feeds on corpses.

Furfur : Count , commanding 26 legions goetic demon.

Leonard : General of Black Magic and Sorcery, often presiding over the Witches Sabbat.

Malphas : Grand President, commanding 40 legions goetic demon.

Mammon : Demon of Avarice and also called a commanding Demon similar to the Devil of the Tarot.

Mastema : Leader of the offspring of fallen angels by daughters of Cain.

Melchiresa: The Testament of Amram presents this fallen angel as a powerful dark force.

Mephistopheles : Pact making medieval demon.

Merihim : Prince of Pestilence.

Moloch : Another demon of Hebrew lore, those ancient Hebrews offered burnt offerings of Children to Moloch.

Mullin : Servant of the House of Princes, Lieutenant to Leonard

Murmur : Count, Demon of Music goetic demon.

Nergal : Chief of Secret Police, second order demon

Nybras : Grand Publicist of Pleasures, inferior.

Nysrogh : Chief of the House of Princes, second order demon
Orias : Marquis, Demon of Diabolic Astrologers and Diviners.
Raum : Count, commanding 30 legions goetic demon.
Rimmon : Ambassador from hell to Russia, also known as Damas.
Ronwe : Inferior, yet commands 19 legions
Succorbenoth : Demon of Gates and Jealousy
Thamuz : Ambassador of hell goetic demon.
Valafar : Grand Duke
Verdelet : Master of Ceremonies of the House of Princes
Verin : Demon of Impatience
Vetis : demon who specializes in corrupting and tempting the holy
Xaphan : Stokes the furnace of hell, second order demon
Zagan : Demon of Deceit and counterfeiting
Sabazios - Phrygian Serpent Devil, relating to The Sabbatic God of the Phallus, sexual procreation and desire.

The Evocation sigil of Beelzebuth.

MICHAEL W. FORD

THE FOUR PRINCES ARE:

LUCIFER- EAST

Lucifer is the BRINGER OF LIGHT, representing wisdom and self-illumination. Lucifer represents the angelic or higher aspects of the Self, thus is a power archetype and spirit of ascension. The name Lucifer is a Latin word meaning "light-bearer" from lux, "light", ferre, "to bear,", a Roman term for the "Morning Star". Lucifer was the translation of the Septuagint Greek heosphoros, - "dawn-bearer"; Greek phosphorus, "light-bearer" and the Hebrew Helel, meaning "Bright one". In the Roman poet Ovid's Metamorphoses, the mentioning of Lucifer comes in the concept of AURORA, the Goddess of Dawn in Roman mythology, *"Aurora, watchful in the reddening dawn, threw wide her crimson doors and rose-filled halls; the Stars took flight, in marshaled order set by Lucifer, who left his station last."* – Ovid

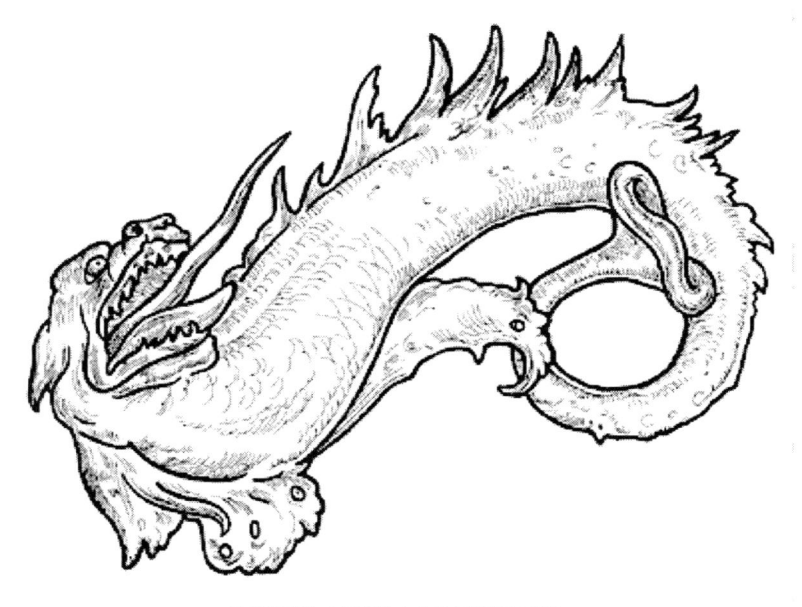

LEVIATHAN-WEST

Leviathan is the Hebrew-chief spirit representing the West, being the ocean and the abyss. The name itself LVIThN is the Crooked Serpent/Dragon who is the master of timeless or immortal being. The Midrash, a Hebrew tome depicts Leviathan as being "the first of the ways of God" thus is perhaps an alternate for Tabaet. Sepher Yetzirah brings to comparison of Leviathan being associated with Draco, the constellation. The whole world rests on the scales of Leviathan, drawing further connections to Tiamat, the dragon of the abyssic chaos from whom the world was created from. Leviathan must be worked with as the great initiator and guardian of the circle, infact, Leviathan IS the symbol of the circle. Leviathan was said to have massive strength, very powerful Eyes. When desired to do such, Leviathan could illuminate great power from his eyes, manifesting as rays of light. Leviathan was the encircling force which united Samael and Lilith again, bringing strength and power.

SATAN (SAMAEL)-SOUTH

From "ha-satan" meaning "The Opposer" or "Adversary". SAMAEL is known in the Talmudic texts as being the same as Satan, the chief of Evil Spirits who is known as "The Venom of God". Samael is said to have twelve wings rather than the six of normal angels, a favored assumption. As the Angel of Death, Samael was the angel of poison which is "sain ha-mawet", along with Ashmodai, is the Lord of Demons. Compare to Ahriman and his created daeva Eshm or Aeshma, who controls and directs the seven powers of Ahriman. Samael as the Angel of Poison is to the Luciferian as a symbol of self-mastery and using the world around us to grow in power and strength, always internal, sometimes external depending on the individual desire. Luciferians seek to devour the essence of life, the essence of humanity. All life is made stronger by devouring another; this is the law of nature. To be honest to the self, to present challenge and overcome such is to attain a foundation upon the path of mastery.

"Samael was the greatest prince in heaven. The celestial animals and the Seraphim had six wings each, but Samael had twelve. He took his cohorts and went down, and saw all the creatures whom the Holy One, blessed be He, had created, and found among them none as astute and malicious as the serpent. And the serpent's appearance was like that of a camel. And Samael mounted him and rode him. And the Tora cried and shrieked and said: "Samael, the world has just been created, is this the time to rebel against God?" The serpent went and said to the woman: "Is it true that you are commanded not to eat the fruit of this tree?...." – Midrash

Samael is known also as Sammael and Samael the Black, all are variants of the same spirit. Samael in the Enochian lore of Dr. John Dee and Edward Kelley is Coronzon, the devil. Coronzon is the power of the Tenth Aethyr in Aleister Crowley's workings. In "The Book of the Witch Moon" the devouring aspects of Coronzon are presented as a Vampyric God, an Angelic Being which seeks the power of self-deification and the possibilities associated therein.

BELIAL-NORTH

In the Ascension of Isaiah, Belial is called "Beliar; for the angel of lawlessness, who is the ruler of this world" and is called "Mantanbuchus" or Ahriman. In another text, Belial has Seven Spirits of Deceit which emanate from his being, that is they are connected with his existence. The Septuagint follows a specific Hebraic consideration that Belial, being "Beli'ol" is "The one who has thrown off the yoke of heaven" and is thus without a master.

The Luciferian finds connections in the path of history and mythology and seeks to make them work for he or she in the modern world. The spirit of Belial is of the mastery of the earth, identified with the element of Earth and the North, from which Ahriman is identical. Consider the four elements however and their association with the Adversary as a spirit of self-deification and self-mastery.

SERVITORS AND DEMONIC SPIRITS

The resourceful Luciferian who is adept in the practice of Magick and Sorcery will find useful worth of working with servitor spirits under the command of a specific Prince or Power. For instance, if your work was based on divination, you may invoke Astaroth but to strengthen the working utilize specific names of the spirits under Astaroth. If you were seeking the atavistic knowledge of daemonic spirits, you may use Astaroth as well.

The names of the spirits listed here may be viewed as what I call "Deific Masks", energies or atavisms which represent specific concepts or human characteristics. View them and use them how you wish.

If your working is based in sexuality, you may wish to utilize Astaroth and Asmodeus, equally the spirits under their command. The LUCIFERIAN GOETIA provides their sigils and times of calling. Below are the Abramelin servitors, from the book in which Aleister Crowley had at the time of his death according to lore.

MICHAEL W. FORD

THE EIGHT SUB-PRINCES

Astaroth – Magot – Asmodeus – Beelzebub– Oriens – Paimon – Ariton - Amaimon

The 111 Spirts common unto these

Four Sub-Princes

Oriens-	Paimon-	Ariton-	Amaimon-
Hosen	Saraph	Proxosos	Habbi
Acuar	Tirana	Alluph	Nercamay
Nilen	Morel	Traci	Enaia
Mulach	Malutens	Iparkas	Nuditon
Melna	Melhaer	Ruach	Apolhun
Schabuach	Mermo	Melamud	Poter
Sched	Ekdulon	Mantiens	Obedama
Sachiel	Moschel	Pereuch	Deccal
Asperim	Katini	Torfora	Badad
Coelen	Chuschi	Tasma	Pachid
Parek	Rachiar	Nogar	Adon
Trapis	Nagid	Ethanim	Patid
Pareht	Emphastison	Paraseh	Gerevil

Elmis	Asmiel	Irminon	Asturel
Nuthon	Lomiol	Imink	Plirok
Tagnon	Parmatus	Iaresin	Gorilon
Lirion	Plegit	Ogilen	Tarados
Losimon	Ragaras	Igilon	Gosegas
Astrega	Parusur	Igis	Aherom
Igarak	Geloma	Kilik	Remoron
Ekalike	Isekel	Elzegan	Ipakol
Haril	Kadolon	Iogion	Zaragil
Irroron	Ilagas	Balalos	Oroia
Lagasuf	Alagas	Alpas	Soterion
Romages	Promakos	Metafel	Darascon
Kelen	Erenutes	Najin	Tulot
Platien	Atloton	Afarorp	Morilen
	Ramaratz	Nogen	Molin

These are the 53 Spirts common unto Astaroth and Asmodeus-

Amaniel	Orinel	Timira	Dramas
Amalin	Kirik	Bubana	Buk

Raner　Semlin　Ambolin　Abutes

Exteron　Laboux　Corcaron　Ethan

Taret　Dablat　Buriul　Oman

Carasch　Dimurgos　Roggiol　Loriol

Isigi　Tioron　Darokin　Haranar

Abahin　Goleg　Guagamon　Lagnix

Etaliz　Agei　Lamel　Udaman

Bialot　Gagalos　Ragalim　Finaxos

Akanef　Omages　Agrax　Sagares

Afray　Ugales　Hermiala　Haligax

Gugonix　Oplim　Daguler　Pachel

Nimalon

These are the 10 Spirits common unto Amaimon and Ariton-

Hauges　Agibol　Rigolen　Grasemin

Elafon　Trisaga　Gagalin　Cleraca

Elaton　Pafesla

These are the 15 Spirits common unto

Asmodeus and Magot-

Toun Magog Diopos Disolol

Biriel Sifon Kele Magiros

Lundo Sobe Inokos Sartabakin

Mabakiel Apot Opun

These be the 32 Spirits common to Astaroth-

Aman Camal Toxai Kataron

Rax Gonogin Schelagon Ginar

Isiamon Bahal Darek Ischigas

Golen Gromenis Rigios Nimerix

Herg Argilon Okiri Fagni

Hipolos Ileson Camonix Bafamal

Alan Apormenos Ombalat Quartas

Ugirpen Araex Lepaca Kolofe

These be the 65 Spirits common to Magot and Kore-

Nacheran	Katolin	Luesaf	Masaub
Urigo	Faturab	Fersebus	Baruel
Ubarin	Butarab	Ischiron	Odax
Roler	Arotor	Hemis	Arpiron
Arrabin	Supipas	Forteson	Dulid
Sorriolenen	Megalak	Anagotos	Sikastin
Pentunof	Debam	Tiraim	Irix
Madail	Abagiron	Pandoli	Nenisem
Cobel	Sobel	Laboneton	Arioth
Marag	Kamusil	Kaitar	Scharak
Maisadul	Agilas	Kolam	Kiligil
Corodon	Hepogon	Daglas	Hagion
Egakireh	Paramor	Olisermon	Rimog
Horminos	Hagog	Mimosa	Amchison
Ilarax	Makalos	Locater	Colvam
	Batternis		

These be the 16 Spirits common to Asmodeus-

Onie	Ormion	Preches	Maggid
Sclavik	Mebbesser	Bacaron	Holba
Hifarion	Gilarion	Eniuri	Abadir
Sbarionat	Utifa	Omet	Sarra

These are the 49 Spirits common to Beelzebub-

Alcanor	Amatia	Bilifares	Lamarion
Diralisen	Licanen	Dimirag	Elponen
Ergamen	Gotifan	Nimorup	Carelena
Lamalon	Igurim	Akium	Dorak
Tachan	Ikonak	Kemal	Bilico
Tromes	Balfori	Arolen	Lirochi
Nominon	Iamai	Arogor	Holastri
Hacamuli	Samalo	Plison	Raderaf
Borol	Sorosma	Corilon	Gramon
Magalast	Zagalo	Pellipis	Natalis
Namiros	Adirael	Kabada	Kipokis
Orgosil	Arcon	Ambolon	Lamolon

Bilifor

These are the 8 Spirits common to Oriens-

Sarisel   Gasaeons   Sorosma   Turitel

Balaken   Gagison   Mafalac   Agab

These are the 15 Spirits common to Paimon-

Aglafor   Agafali   Dison   Achaniel

Sudoron   Kabersa   Ebaron   Zalanes

Ugola   Came   Roffles   Menolik

Tacaros   Astolit   Rukum

These are the 22 Spirits common to Ariton-

Anader   Ekorok   Sibolas   Saris

Sekabin   Caromos   Rosaran   Sapason

Notiser   Flaxon   Harombrub   Megalosin

Miliom   Ilemlis   Galak   Androcos

Maranton   Caron   Reginon   Elerion

THE BIBLE OF THE ADVERSARY

Sermeot   Irmenos

These be the 20 Spirits common to

Amaimon-

Romeroc	Ramison	Scrilis	Buriol
Taralim	Burasen	Akesoli	Erekia
Illirikim	Labisi	Akoros	Mames
Glesis	Vision	Effrigis	Apelki
Dalep	Dresop	Hergotis	Nilima

MICHAEL W. FORD

THE QLIPPOTH

Envision the following: The ten averse, hidden and envenomed Serphiroth of the Qlippothic of Shells, that from which you may drink from as hell-elixirs of Lilith. They are collected into Seven Palaces in which the Mystery of the Seven Headed Dragon and the Ten Horns of Power.

OVLM HQLIPVTh
and
THE INFERNAL TRINITY

Olahm Ha—The Qlipphoth is the place of shells, the dead and darkness. This is the World of Matter. Know that matter is not just the physical items but also the astral or electric waves of energy around you. Thus, the power of both the seen and unseen are subject to the Luciferian. The Ten Degrees are the Sephiroth of the Liberated Spirits, who are their own Gods and powers therein. The First is the darkness wherein all may be created from. The Third if the abode of darkness, or the place of power rested and built again. The next follow Seven Hells which hold Demons which are Therionick shadows of desire, thus can give great power by moving through.

"Like Adam Qadmon, the evil Sammael is androgenous, for his female companion, or counterpart, is Esheth Zenunim (AShTh ZNVNIM) the Harlot, or Woman of Whoredom, also called Lilith, which name signifies "night". Sammael is the active principle, Lilith the passive; in union they formulate the Antichrist, Anti-Logos, or Anti-Word, known under the name of 'Hay-yah[7] the Beast,"– Fuller, Secrets of the Qabala

---

[7] HVHI, the Adversary.

The Prince of the Qlippoth is **SMAL**, Samael who is both Lucifer and Ahriman. He is called by enemies the angel of death and poison.

The Bride or Queen of Darkness is **AShTh ZNVNIM**, Isheth Zenunim, the Harlot or Woman of Whoredom. This is Lilith or Az.

When in union they are called the Beast, **CHIVA** or Chioa. The Luciferian may also see this as Cain or Baphomet, depending on focus.

ABOVE the Sigil og Infernal Union is also a comparative symbol of THE INFERNAL TRINITY. It is presented differently, Leviathan, Samae and Lilith.

THELI or LEVIATHAN

The "shells," *Qlippoth*, are the demons, or rebel spirits, angels of lawlessness, in whom again is a form of the Sephiroth essentially, according to the Luciferian Path, the True Tree of Da'ath or Hidden Knowledge. The power of life is found within the Qlippoth as well as Death, much like the serpent of eden.

The dragon has the greatest power of life and death. His location is the most powerful as it knows the elixirs of the roots of darkness and the ascension of Light, where the Dragon transforms into a bright angel or Archon. The Intent of the Luciferian is to utilize the Power of Leviathan to ascend and be like Lucifer, or Samael the Archon who defiles and takes the Throne of Light – this is the word of the Spirit enthroned, the nature of the Great Work itself.

Leviathan holding his tail in his mouth, the ourabouris is the symbol of immortality, the ascended aspect of darkness. The scales of the dragon are said to be swelling like a crocodile, from his gathering and devourment of Chi or Prana, the energy of spirits.

The Qlippoth is an often misunderstood aspect of Magick – it must be embraced fully to understand the depths of the Adversary and this current of power. The Qlippoth can empower or destroy, depending on approach.

THE INFERNAL HABITATIONS

The Evil Averse Power beneath the Feet of the Four Cherubim.

Lilith--------The Ass--------Babel

Machaloth------The Ox---------Jonia

Samael--------Serpents--------Media

Rahab------Strange Beasts------Edom

To these four (Babel, Jonia, Media, Edom) are attributed four Kingdoms.

A VISION OF THE BLACK FLAME

A Whirlwind came out of the North, the sound of screaming souls and animalistic growls emerge from it, a storm Cloud, and a Blackened Fire enfolding itself and Lucifer the Brilliance of the innermost flame in the midst of the Fire.'

These are from Cherubic expressions of Force and Qlipphothic Powers broken beneath their feet are:

'**Rahab**', whose symbol is a terrible demon leaping upon an Ox, a form of the Angel of Violence or Leviathan.

'**Machaloth**', a Witch Goddess, serpent-skinned, burning eyes and a form compounded of a serpent scorpion

'**Lilith**', a woman outwardly beautiful but inwardly corrupt and putrefying, riding upon a strange and terrible beast which devours and seeks spirits to consume their light. Lilith initiates by experience, she comes to you in dreams and she inspires from afar. Lilith is present in many workings[8] and is a power to be equaled with Samael, she is thus one half of the Adversary and should be respected accordingly. Lilith whose number is 480, is attributed to Malkuth and the Kingdom of the Earth. She moves through Nahemoth in this area and is closely moved by the Moon in all of its aspects. Lilith is "The Woman of the Night" whose forms are varied, both beautiful and equally demonic.

She appears sometimes as a seductive woman who conceals a black monkey, blood spewing with the rot of corpses running from between her legs. Using a Black Mirror, a gateway to the Caves of Lilith, the Luciferian may enter with his or her

---

[8] The author conducted a BABALON WORKING in 1998 which brought the knowledge and wisdom of Lilith in an angelic and demonic aspect.

Body of Light and Shadow to copulate and gain the wisdom of our Goddess. She is terrible, disgusting and beautiful. Often, Lilith may appear as a black mutated monkey with insect legs emerging from its genitals, its arms and legs continually opening with sores and black insects emerge, she crawls with Filth, covered and dropping worms, her teeth rotten and sharp as a beast, he nose eaten away and from her mouth comes locusts and a greenish slime, putrefying like the smell of rot and of the refuse of many serpents.

Lilith also appears as a beautiful young Goddess, robed in crimson with a crown which resembles an Ancient Assyrian headpiece, her eyes glowing with life. She offers immortality to those who would drink from her cup. Her feet are as predatory bird talons.

In some workings, Lilith transforms and takes an inverted crucifix to squat upon it, her vagina like some beast-hell gate which yawns with serpent fangs to gather prey inward. She and a hundred demons and succubi moan with pleasure as she moves the crucifix deeper into her core, she seduced both Christ and Zoroaster in a similar way, Christ was made to lick and suck the filth of his followers which is the rancid elixir she issues forth from herself at the moment of orgasm.

Lilith then appears as a beautiful maiden, who may teach many the ways of Magick.

Here is the sigil of Lilith, invoke her in the night with a black mirror and with the calling of Malkuth or Yesod. An ideal "Temple Setting" for Lilith would be crimson walls or an area with crimson, an image of Lilith and a black mirror.

ABOVE The Sigil of Lilith

LILITH may be sought with Black Mirror and the proper ritual settings described herein. Use caution and care when calling her, once you achieve a sense of union she can manifest in chaos, in problems or she can be a meaningful guide. Be cautious to balance your situations and think before acting. Use either the above sigil or the Az-Jahi sigil.

LILITH

The Goddess and powerful embodiment of the Adversary. Lilith, known as the Queen of Demons, a bestial body with a sometimes beautiful appearance, was called "Mother of Ahriman" and is related to blood sucking vampiric demons and other night spirits. Lilith is one half of the Adversary is there were, is truly a Satanic or Luciferian source of self-mastery and strength. Lilith is said to howl at the head of 480 companies of demons, having sometimes appearance with a Chariot guided and backed by demonic spirits. Lilith is the fiery aspect of Ahriman or Samael and should be considered equal to the Fallen Angel. Lilith has a long history and a background in all magical practices. She is the one who is of the Astral plane, of the air, and began all legends of vampiric acts committed at night. Lilith grows strong from the blood of humans, but also has been worshiped by rebels since Babylonian times. In the Qlippoth Lilith holds great power, "the female of Samael is called Serpent, Woman of Harlotry, End of all Flesh, End of Days".

Ahriman was first within the womb along with his brother, Ohrmazd. Ohrmazd had overheard Zurvan whisper, 'Whichever of the two shall come to me first, him will I make king.'. Upon hearing this Ohrmazd told his brother of this Ahriman ripped from the womb and came forth to his Father Zurvan. It was Zurvan who insulted his son and called him dark and stinking but considered the second born, action-less son Ohrmazd was favored and made sacrifice to his father Zurvan. Ahriman reminded his father of the promise of the first born, but was granted a period of time, thus Ahriman went away from those of the arrogant light. Ahriman soon made a pact with his father, which was manifest as Az, the bride of darkness.

'Pondering on the end, Zurvan delivered to Ahriman an implement from the very substance of darkness, mingled with the power of Zurvan, as it were a treaty, resembling coal, black and ashen. And as he handed it to him he said: "By means of these weapons, Az (Concupiscence) will devour that which is thine, and she herself shall starve, if at the end of nine thousand years thou hast not accomplished that which thou didst threaten- to demolish the pact, to demolish Time.' - The Dawn and Twilight of Zoroastrianism

Az or Jeh, the whore or demonic feminine, was the 'weapon of Concupiscence' which "Ahriman chooses it of his own free will 'as his very essence'."

The lightening which emerges from the abyss manifests upon earth, the storm bringing shadow called daemon can be only comprehended once the seeker enters the circle, wherein all Gods and Demons meet in the flesh! The Adversary opens forth serpent eyes, finding all in the primal darkness and with an inner fire awakening the clay on man! Yet it is the compliment of the Masculine in Lilith or Az or the earlier Jahi who is the fiery compliment which rouses her mate to manifest upon earth!

The Feminine which is the essence of Lilith is just as her mate Samael, in the form of Leviathan does she inspire his mind just as from his mouth go burning lamps and from his nostrils as smoke which infused the sacred fire with the adversarial chaos of strife!

In Greek mythology, Hades or Ahriman had a bride who he ruled with. Hecate, a form of Lilith, was his queen.

"Contrasted with this luminous abode, where dwelt the Most High gods in resplendent radiance, was a dark and dismal domain in the bowels of the earth. Here Ahriman or Pluto, born like Jupiter of Infinite Time, reigned with Hecate over the maleficent monsters that had issued from their impure embraces. These demoniac confederates of the King of Hell then ascended to the assault of Heaven and attempted to dethrone the successor of Kronos; but, shattered like the Greek giants by the ruler of the gods, these rebel monsters were hurled backward into the abyss from where they had risen" – Franz Cumont, The Mysteries of Mithra

Lilith is first listed in the Sumerian King list which is dated froma round 2400 B.C. as a Lillu demons, a type of vampyric succubi. The Ardat Lili were night phantoms and hags who took the form of maidens to sleep with men and beget demons and other vampyric beings. Lilith's Sumerian office was to preside as a storm demoness and night spirit. Raphel Patai describes the famous Lilith – relief:

"A Babylonian terracotta relief, roughly contemporary with the above poem, shows in what form Lilith was believed to appear to human eyes. She is slender, well shaped, beautiful, and nude, with wings and owl-feet. She stands erect on two reclining lions which are turned away from each other and are flanked by owls. On her head she wears a cap embellished by several pairs of horns. In her hand she holds a ring-and-rod combination. Evidently, this is no longer a lowly she-demon, but a goddess who tames wild beasts and, as shown by the owls on the reliefs, rules by night." – Patai, Lilith

A seventh Century BC tablet from Northern Syria names Lilith "Lili, Flyer of the Dark Chamber". In Talmudic lore, Lilith is considered the first wife of Adam. She refused to bow to him and wanted equality. She thought not to lie below Adam as she considered them both equal. She uttered a secret name of God[9] and rose upward in the air; she then left Adam and went to the caves and shores of the Red Sea, a home of demons and monsters. Lilith then began copulating with numerous demons and other beasts to give birth to over 100 demons per day. Lilith is also known as the name Queen of *Sheba,* meaning the Sabaens, is translated as "Lilith, queen of Zemargad."

A Luciferian may look at these legends as models or symbols for the self; The demons which Lilith gave birth to are servitors, shades given form in the mind by the Luciferian, to accomplish some sort of task. This is the aspects of Sorcery discussed in other parts of this bible.

---

[9] In Luciferian context, the name of God may be "HVHI", "Hay-yah" or a word of power.

"THE FEMALE OF SAMAEL IS CALLED SERPENT, WOMAN OF HARLOTRY, END OF ALL FLESH, END OF DAYS."

In other texts Lilith was said to have been created by filth and other elements of the earth, a tale which corresponds to the legends of the Zurvanites and Az.
Patai wrote:

"Others did not regard Lilith as a being created by God but as a divine entity which emerged spontaneously, either out of the Great Supernal Abyss, or out of the Gevura or Din, the "Power" of God" – Patai, Lilith

Thus we may see that Lilith is something self-created the desire to become, very close to the tale of Ahriman. Lilith is seen as a power equal and essential to Samael, whom she dwells within. Lilith is considered to be of a husk *(qelipa)* which indicates she has a Vampyric nature from the beginning.

The mystical cosmology of Napthali Herz. b. Jacob Elhanan in some of the layers of earth hides giant human figures, tall of stature, who were born of Adam in the 130 years during which he begot demons, spirits and Lilin or children of the serpent.

Lilith continued in history as being both a vampiress – drinking the blood of children and equally protecting them, also seducing men during the hours of night.

"And she [Lilith] goes and roams at night, and goes all about the world and makes sport with men and causes them to emit seed. In every place where a man sleeps alone in a house, she visits him and grabs him and attaches herself to him and has her desire from him, and bears from him. And she also afflicts him with sickness, and he knows it not, and all this (takes place) when the moon is on the wane" –Zorah

An ideal time for utilizing Succubi and consorting with Lilith is during the time of the Full Moon and New Moon, when it is shadowed and dark. Approaching Lilith as Mother and Goddess will no doubt protect the Luciferian from being prey to her spirit, having self-respect and open desire to pass her tests means everything. The test is instinct and will.

Lilith is empowered through the desire brought forth in man during sleeping hours, she devours energy and is thus a vampyre.

"She (Lilith) forsakes the husband of her youth [Samael] and descends to earth and fornicates with men who sleep here below, in the uncleanness of emission. And from them are born demons, spirits, and Lilin, and they are called "the plagues of mankind." – Zohar

Lilith is the Goddess of Shape Shifters, she takes pleasing form to attract her prey and desire. A Luciferian may see this as the ability to adapt to situations in life and approach it in an appropriate manner.

"She adorns herself with many ornaments like a despicable harlot, and takes up her position at the crossroads to seduce the sons of man. When a fool approaches her, she grabs him, kisses him, and pours him wine of dregs of viper's gall. As soon as he drinks it, he goes astray after her. When she sees that he has gone astray after her from the path of truth, she divests herself of all ornaments which she put on for that fool. Her ornaments for the seduction of the sons of man are: her hair is long and red like the rose, her cheeks are white and red, from her ears hang six ornaments, Egyptian chords hang from her nape (and) all the ornaments of the Land of the East, her mouth is set like a narrow door, comely in its decor, her tongue is sharp like a sword, her words are smooth like oil, her lips are red like a rose and sweetened by all the sweetness of the world, she is dressed in scarlet, and she is adorned with forty ornaments less one. Yon fool goes astray

after her and drinks from the cup of wine and commits with her fornications and strays after her. What does she thereupon do? She leaves him asleep on the couch, flies (to heaven), denounces him, takes leave, and descends. That fool awakens and deems he can make sport with her as before, but she removes her ornaments and turns into a menacing figure, and stands before him clothed in garments of flaming fire, inspiring terror and making body and soul tremble, full of frightening eyes, in her hand a drawn sword dripping bitter drops. And she kills that fool and casts him into Gehenna." Zohar i. 148a-b, Sitre Torah

Lilith is thus Babalon, the mother of harlotry who rides upon the dragon of the abyss and fornicates when men. Let us understand the balanced perspective of Lilith. The sigil of Lilith, as presented by Aleister Crowley is Babalon. The Luciferian Tradition presents the Eye of Babalon, the number of 480, being Lilith as the point of dedication and entrance. Babalon rides upon the Beast, begetting power and the union of the spirit and flesh.

The Sigil of Babalon

LILITH AND NAHEMOTH

Naamah or Nahemoth is a powerful, beautiful and seductive demoness, she who is empowered by Lilith. Nahemoth is said to be the Mother of Ashmodai, a King of Demons by the Fallen Angel Shamdon.

Many Hebraic writers indicated Lilith and Nahemoth as being the Deathless Beings who are the First Vampires[10]

"Those sons of God, Aza and Aza'el, went astray after her. R. Shimcon said: She was the mother of the demons, for she came from the side of Cain, and she, together with Lilith,

---

[10] The context of Vampire in the Luciferian Religion is spelled Vampyre, representing an act of magick.

was appointed over the askara (strangulation) of children." – Zohar

Nahemoth is indeed considered a relative of Cain, given Luciferian power by Lilith after having copulated with the fallen angels and Samael.

After the Serpent came upon Eve and injected his impurity into her, she gave birth to Cain. From there descended all the generations of the sinful in the world, and also the demons and spirits came from there. – Zohar

We see here the foundations of Luciferian Witchcraft, from which the Luciferian Religion arose.

The Zohar also writes that *"And there was one male who came into the world from the spirit of Cain's side and he was called Tubal-Cain. And a female came with him after whom the creatures went astray, and she was called Naamah. From her came other spirits and demons, who hang in the air and announce things to those others who are found below. And this Tubal-Cain brought weapons of killing into the world. And this Naamah ... is alive to this day and her dwelling is among the waves of the Great Sea."* – Zohar

Through the passions of copulation does Nahemoth use Sex Magick to create other spirits and demons, from the very desire of man. The Luciferian will use this to shape his or her foundation and possibility. By focusing on creating servitors, offering to the Goddess by the act of emitting seed or an orgasm in Her name (Lilith or Nahemoth) one may begin a two-fold initiatory process: to satisfy the carnal in this world, to initiate into the feminine Luciferian mysteries and transform consciousness into the Divine Consciousness.

"she makes sport with the sons of man, and conceives from them through their dreams, from the desire of man, and she attaches herself to him. She takes the desire and nothing more, and from that desire she conceives and brings forth other kinds (or demons) into the world. And those sons whom she bears from men visit the women of humankind who then conceive from them and give birth to spirits." — Zohar.

A formula and mystery of Sex Magick is found here:

> Asimon (a demon) rides on Naamah,
> Naamah rides on Igrath the daughter of Mahalath
> Igrath rides on several kinds of spirits and bands of midday-demons.
> Unto The left there is the shape of a serpent riding on a blind dragon, and this dragon rides on Lilith the wicked.

It must be considered that copulation is considered Holy unto the Luciferian, it is creation of life on earth in some cases and the sacrifice to the Spirit of Lilith. Nahemoth dwells in spirit by the Great Sea, being the Red Sea.

"Out of the North the Evil One shall break forth."

Samael and Lilith are the power which cannot be divided — it is brought to union and flesh by Leviathan, the Dragon of the Abyss who brings to union the Daemonic. The Luciferian Faith holds equal foundation to the Goddess and God within. Without one, or the clouding of one for another is indeed a great error, call it a travesty that weakens the self.

LILITH AS VAMPYRE

The idea of Lilith being the first Vampyre is no new concept. She has existed since the beginning of recorded history, she is powerful and insatiable. Some of her names, recorded on Greek and Byzatine charms indicates her nature; *"the shapeless one', 'the blooddrinking one', 'the beautiful one',*

THE BIBLE OF THE ADVERSARY

the one 'from the sea' 'the shrieking one', 'the child-strangler' and other similar titles. It is clear that Lilith did not represent death but she sought continued existence, life itself. Gyllou is an early name of Lilith from Babylonian mythology, representing a child stealing vampire which drinks the blood of infants. Gello, a title compared to Ghoul is an Arabic demon of the same nature.

Abyzou, Obyzouth Abizu or Gyllou-Gello are names of Lilith as the Deathless one who does not sleep at night, who goes forth to drink blood, fornicate with men and women and beget demonic children. The name Abyzou is no doubt a corruption of the Sumerian Abzu which is ***abyssos*** meaning The Abyss.

Lilith holds the honor of her name being included in the early Greek magical spells as well, Abra is a medieval Greek word being interchanged in spells with Aura which means a "young woman"[11] and is thus related to the "Beautiful One of the Mountains" being the Wild Spirit of Magick, Lilith.

Abra also had considerable power over Water, air and the night. She was a complimentary foundation with Samael, her mate. One exorcism representing St. Gregory presents an interesting connection; *'This Abra came out from the Sea and the first of the archangels Michael came to meet her and said to her: "Whence do you come and where are you going, you black and blackish, three-lipped and three-headed Abra?"-"I go to eat the bones of man and to make his flesh waste away"*

Many infernal Deities are presented with "Three Heads", Hecate, Azhi Dahaka, Cerebrus and others. The Testamentum Salomonis presents Abyzou as a *"fiendish vampyre who appears body except her greenish gleaming face with dishevelled serpent-like hair is covered with darkness".*[12]

---

[11] The Mermaid and the Devil's Grandmother

[12] Mermaid and the Devil's Grandmother

ILLUMINATING WITH THE QLIPPOTH – SUMMONING QLIPPOTHIC FORCES

The Luciferian will see in many of the rites of the path in this bible are chants which one vibrates the names of Qlippothic Orders and demons. This has been a forbidden act of Magick with the Golden Dawn, they consider these forces negative and destructive. As a Practicing Luciferian I can attest that they are not this; the veil shows fear and those willing to pass through it will find them empowered.

Names are vibrated by focusing on the nature of the sphere. It focusing on the Sphere of Kether – Satan or Moloch you will want to slowly vibrate Saa-tan, hold in a deep breath and exhale slowly while focusing upon the name.

Preparation: A Black Mirror (for looking into), A Dagger of Barbarous Evocation, herbs relating to the sphere and planets of the Order you will be working with. A chalice and any ritual tools deemed necessary. Use a triangle or circle of evocation – do not utilize one with Judeo-Christian names – Use Luciferian Spiritual names only!

Invoke: When using a banishing rite, your mind must be focused and determined to be clean and pure. The Luciferian Spirit is of great strength and light, this is why the path explores the demonic equally. This power is great if you can work through it.

Vampyric Ending: As given focus in THE VAMPIRE GATE: The Vampyre Magickian, you may chose to enter the circle/triangle to devour the spirit at the height of the ritual, this is dangerous and only is suggested to advanced practitioners.

Traditional End: Control the spirits and channel them through you, banish accordingly.

1. Use chosen Banishing ritual and invoke specific Qlippothic forces. Suggested Focus rites are:

CASTING THE CIRCLE OF THE DRAGON and THE LESSER ENCIRCLING RITE OF THE LUCIFERIAN.

2. Invoke the following in order: You may use the ritual "TO THERION TO ANABAINON EK TES ABYSSOU" as this utilizes the names of barbarous evocation of Qlippothic forces. Vibrate names and then focus on specific area with each calling.

3. You may utilize the steps of Yatukih Seals to invoke Qlippothic Spirits as well. Ensure that you close your rituals accordingly.

<u>ARCH-DEMONS OR DEMON-KINGS</u> –vibrate and recite names based on attribution. After you feel you have called them in essence, focus on what you wish to gain from this sphere and accounce "It is my will.....". The names should be vibrated while focusing in the Black Mirror until a presence is felt. Once you instinctually feel comfortable, move forward to the next summons. Focus on the nature of the Arch-Demon and their visualized form.

<u>QLIPPOTHIC ORDERS-</u> focus on the essence of the orders, what they do. Vibrate the name to yourself and in the surrounding area. Let nothing stand between your Will and goals. Visualize their form based on your instinct and perception.

<u>TEN HELLS IN SEVEN PLACES-</u> Vibrate the names and focus on the deeper meaning of their names. Focus on the depths of this "hell" and seek the shells of power from it. When darkness takes shape and offers you a cup of hell-blood, drink sparingly and do only under your Will.

<u>PRINCES AND TRIBES</u> –Vibrate the names of the Princes and Tribes to empower servitors and spirits which will carry forth your desires.

4. Either use TRADITIONAL END or VAMPYRIC END.

Close rite, to fuel it and allow it to take form, do something different which keeps your attention away.

ARCH-DEMONS OR DEMON-KINGS

Satan and Moloch

Beelzebub

Lucifuge Rofacale

Astaroth

Asmodeus

Belphegor

Bael

Adramelech

Lilith

Nahema

QLIPPOTHIC ORDERS

The Qlippoth of Kether or the Palace of Illumination is Thaumiel, the Adversary. The Shells of Chokmah are the Ghogiel or Spirits of Rebellion. The Shells of Binah are the Satariel, the Hidden Ones of Fallen Angels of Shadow. Those of Chesed are the Agshekeloh, the Breakers or shattering angels of chaos. Unto Geburah are the Golahab, the Burners or those demons which illuminate unto the Black Flame.

To Tiphareth are the Tagiriron, the disputing or chaos breeding demons. Unto Netzach is the Gharab Tzerek, the

Ravens of Death, dispersing all things. To make them a part of your spirit is to hold the power of initiation chaos and division when needed. To Hod is Samael, the Deceivers, serpent-demons which continually transform. To Yesod is Gamaliel, the Obscene Ones and the Shells of Malkuth is Lilith, the Evil Woman or Mother of Luciferian Witchcraft. These powers bring much strength and insight, but madness and spiritual harm to those uninitiated to the mysteries.

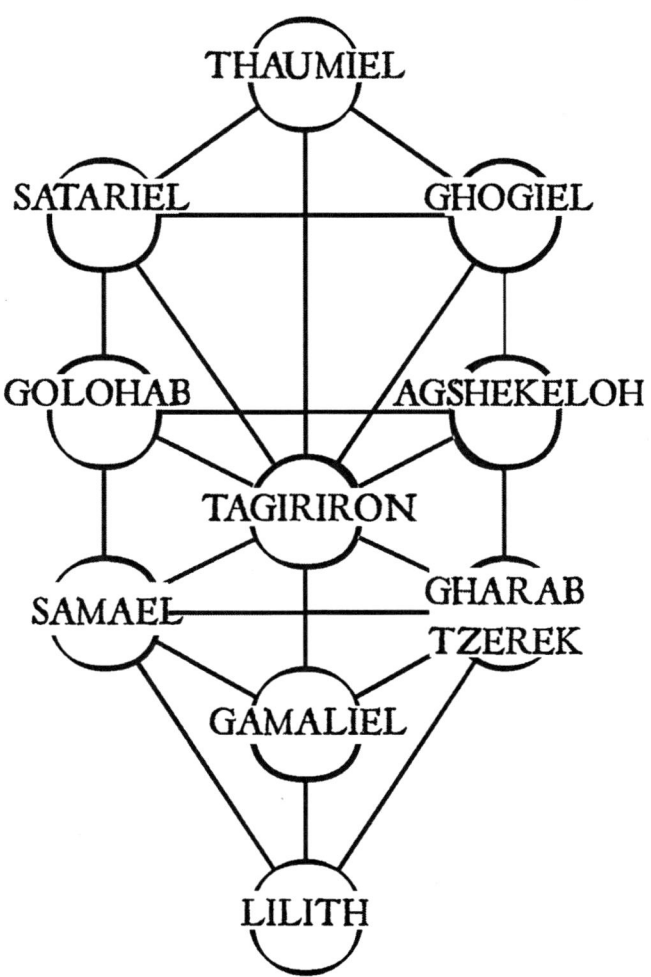

Qemetiel-
Crown of Gods, First Devil
The first is Qematriel, whose appear of a vast black, man-headed Dragon-serpent, and this power united under him the force of Kether of the Infernal and averse Sephiroth.

Belia'al-
The Power which denies all Gods, Wickedness.

A'Athiel-
Uncertainty

Thamiel-
The Adversary or Double Headed Ones-
Neptune THAMIEL (ThAMAL): THADEKIEL + ABRAXSIEL + MAHAZIEL + AZAZAèL +LUFUGIEL

Chaigidel-
Hinderers
Pluto CHAIGIDEL (ChIGDAL): CHEDEZIEL + ITQUEZIEL + GOLEBRIEL + DUBRIEL + ALHAZIEL + LUFEXIEL

Satariel-
Concealers
Saturn
SATERIEL (SATARAL): SATURNIEL + ABNEXIEL + TAGARIEL + ASTERIEL + REQRAZIEL + ABHOLZIEL + LAREZIEL +

Gamchicoth-
Disturbers of Souls
Jupiter GAMEHIOTH (GAMChATh): GABEDRIEL + AMDEBRIEL + MALEXIEL + CHEDEBRIEL + A'OTHIEL + THERIEL

Golab-
Incendiaries
Mars
GALEB (GLEB): GAMELIEL + LEBREXIEL + EBAIKIEL + BARASHIEL

Tagaririm-
Disputers
Sol
TAGARIRIM (TGRRM): TAUMESHRIEL + GOBRAZIEL + RAQUEZIEL + REBREQUEL + MEPHISOPHIEL

Harab Serapel-
Ravens of Death
Venus
HARAB-SERAPEL (HRB-SRRAL): HELEBRIEL + RETERIEL + BARUCHIEL + SATORIEL + REFREZIEL + REPTORIEL + ASTORIEL + LABREZIEL

Samael-
Jugglers
Mercurius SAMAEL (SMAL): SHEOLIEL + MOLEBRIEL + AFLUXRIEL + LIBRIDIEL

Gamaliel-
Obscence
Luna GAMALIEL (GMLIAL): GEDEBRIEL + MATERIEL + LAPREZIEL + IDEXRIEL + ALEPHRIEL + LABRAEZIEL

Earth
NAHEMOTH (NHMATh): NOBREXIEL + HETERIEL + MOLIDIEL + A'AINIEL + THAUHEDRIEL

The Five Accursed Nations
a. **Amalekites** – Aggressors – Children of Belial
b. **Geburim** - Violent Ones or Tribes of Aeshma

c. **Raphaim** - Cowards
d. **Nephilim** - Voluptuous Ones, Giants, Children of Fallen Angels and Daughters of Cain.
e. **Anakim** – Anarchists and Chaos Bringers

THE QLIPPOTHIC TREE OF DEATH

(above the Sephiroth)

Tohu-
The Formless, Desolation
Bohu-
The Void, Emptiness
Chasek-
The Darkness

THE BIBLE OF THE ADVERSARY

TEN HELLS IN SEVEN PLACES

Shahul-
The Grave Hell of the Supernals, The Triple Hell

Abaddon-
Perdition

Tythihoz-
Clay of Death

Barashechath-
The Pit of Destruction

Tzalemoth-
The Shadow of Death

Sha'arimrath-
The Gates of Hell

Giyehanim-
Hell

כ
תאומיאל
ADVERSARY
Thau-mi-el

ב
סתריאל
CONCEALERS
Sa-tar-i-el

ח
עוגיאל
HINDERERS
Og-i-el

ג
גולהב
BURNERS
Go-lah-ab

ח
געשכלה
BREAKERS IN PIECES
Gash'ka-lah

ת
תגירירון
DISPUTERS
Tag-ir-ir-on

ה
סמאל
DECEIVERS
Sam-a-el

נ
ערב זרק
DISPERSING RAVENS
Or-eb Za-raq

י
גמליאל
OBSCENE ONES
Ga-mal-i-el

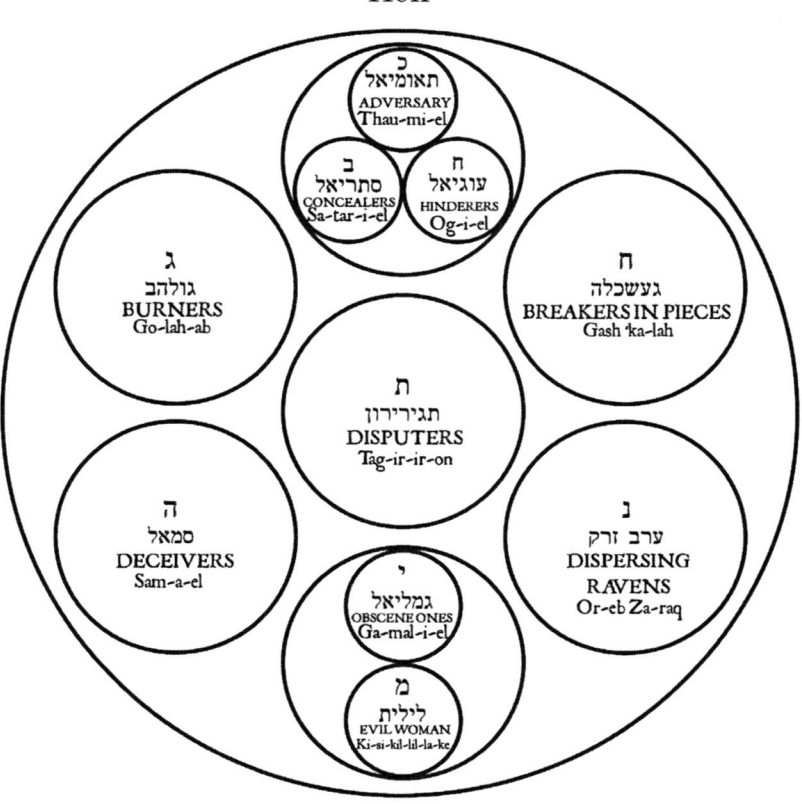

מ
לילית
EVIL WOMAN
Ki-si-kil-lil-la-ke

MICHAEL W. FORD

PRINCES AND TRIBES

These are the names of the twelve Princes and Tribes who are the heads of the Months of the Year. Some Luciferians utilize their times and dates to their own calendar, using a system of evocation or invocation on those times when they are said to be the strongest. This is the Zodiac of the Infernal:

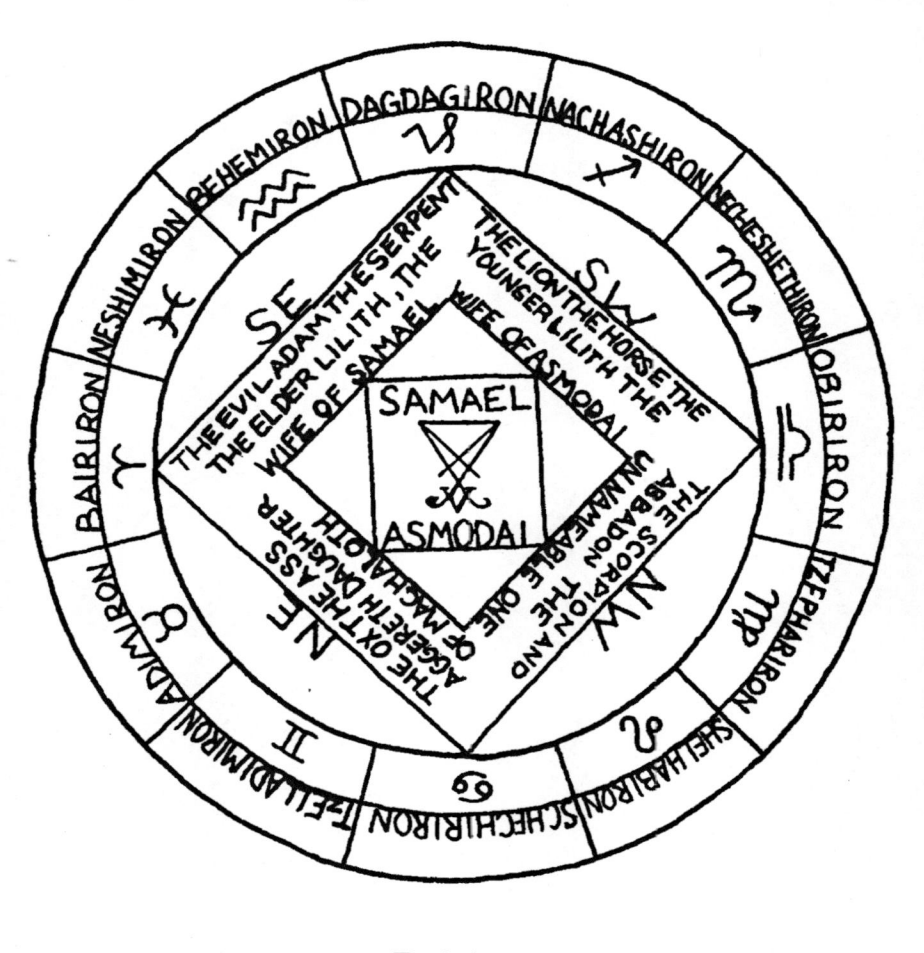

Bairion-
So called because they are derived from the Fourth Evil, namely Samael, the Black. This is THE EMPEROR of the Luciferian Tarot, his Fire is mingled with his Bride, Lilith to beget a form terrible and strong. Their colors are dull red and

122

black, and their form is that of a Dragon-Lion.

Adimiron-
Whose colors are like blood mixed with water, a dull yellow and gray. Their form is that of a Lion-Lizard, they are emanations of Yaltabaoth in the form of the Lion-Serpent.

Tzelladimiron-
Their colors are limpid blood, bronze and crimson. They are like savage triangular-headed dogs and wolflike beings. They are nearly identical to the demonic shades of "Satanic Copulations" from ADAMU – Luciferian Tantra and Sex Magick.

Schechiriron-
Their colors are black, and their form blended of Reptile, Insect, and Shell-fish, such as the crab and the lobster, yet demon-faced withal.

Shelhabiron-
Their colors are fiery and yellow, and their form like merciless wolves and jackals.

Tzephariron-
Whose colors are like those of the Earth, and their form like partially living yet decaying corpses.

Obiriron-
Whose colors are like clouds, and their form like grey, bloated goblins.

Necheshethiron-
Their colour is like copper, and their form like that of a devilish and almost human-headed insect.

Nachashiron-
Whose colors are like serpents, and their form like dog-

headed serpents.

Dagdagiron-
Whose colors are reddish and gleaming, and their form like vast and decouring flat-headed fishes.

Behemiron-
Whose name is derived from Behemoth, and their colors are black and brown, and their forms those of awful beasts like hippopotamus, and an elephant, but crushed flat, or as if their skin was spread out flat over the body of a gigantiv beetle or cockroach.

Neshimiron-
Whose colors are of a stagnant gleaming watery hue, and their forms like hideous women, almost skeletons, united to the bodies of serpents and fishes.

THE BIBLE OF THE ADVERSARY

THE CIRCLE OF THE ADVERSARY

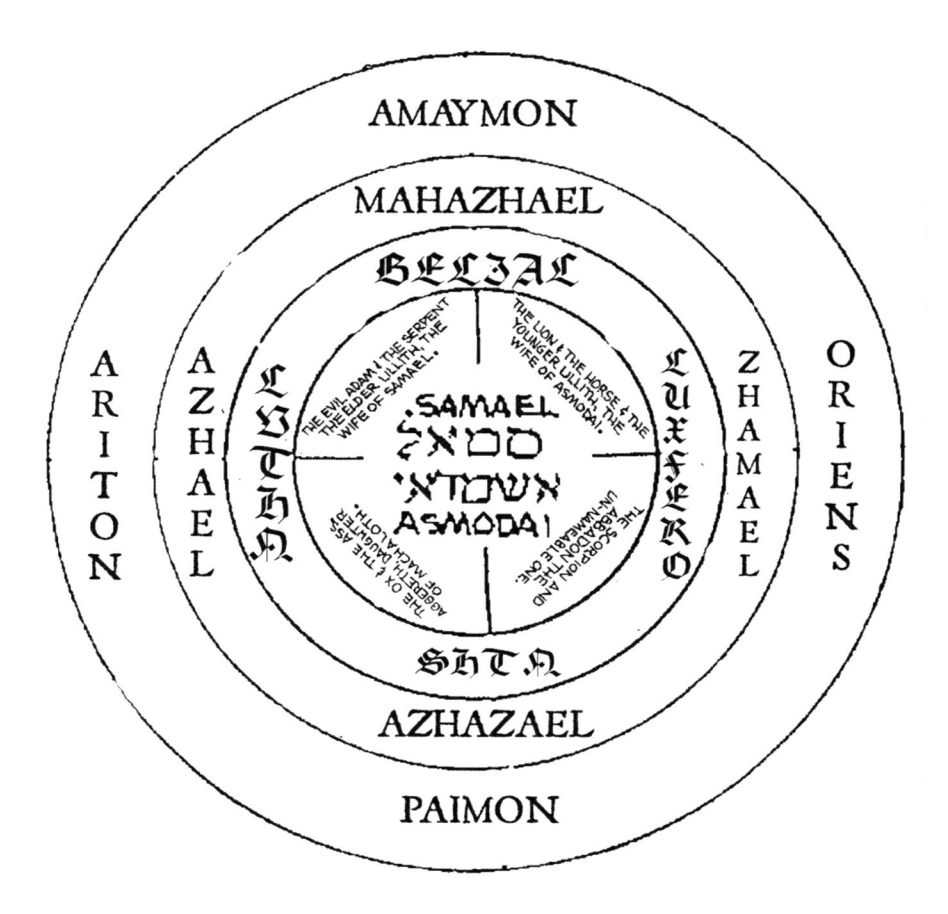

[Circular diagram: Outer ring contains AMAYMON (top), ORIENS (right), PAIMON (bottom), ARITON (left). Middle ring contains MAHAZHAEL (top), ZHAMAEL (right), AZHAZAEL (bottom), AZHAEL (left). Inner ring contains BELIAL (top), LUCIFER (right), SHTN (bottom), LVIATAN (left). Center contains SAMAEL and ASMODAI with Hebrew letters, surrounded by inscriptions: "THE EVIL ADAM, THE SERPENT, THE ELDER LILITH, THE WIFE OF SAMAEL"; "THE LION, THE HORSE & THE YOUNGER LILITH, THE WIFE OF ASMODAI"; "THE SCORPION AND ABADDON, THE UN-NUMERABLE ONE"; "THE OX & THE ASS AGGERETH, DAUGHTER OF MACHALOTH".]

The orthography of the attributions of the Luciferian Tradition displays spirits which emerge from a trans-cultural perspective. As we can see by the circle, the names move through different elements of daemon-lore from the Luciferian Witchcraft tradition. The Four Inner Demonic Kings Belial – Leviathan – Satan and Lucifer represent the power points and crowned powers, the attributed spirits behind them are outer Princes and powers associated with as well.

CENTER OF THE CIRCLE OF THE ADVERSARY

At one Angle is the Evil Adam, a goat-headed skeleton-like giant; and a thousand- headed Hydra Serpent; everchanging and chaos – inspired in nature.

At the second Angle is Aggereth, the daughter of Machalath, a fiendish witch with serpent hair enthroned in a chariot drawn by an Ox and an Ass. Aggereth or Aggerath is shown in the LUCIFERIAN TAROT and is a powerful Witch Mother.

At the third Angle is a gigantic Scorpion with a fearful appearance, but formed of putrefying water. Behind him comes the Un-nameable One, Abaddon or Apollyon and his appearance and symbol is that of a closely veiled Black gigantic figure, covered with whirling wheels, blades and in his hand is a vast wheel send forth as it whirls, multitudes of cat-like demons. Behind comes Maamah as a crouching woman with an animal's body, crawling along the ground and eating the earth.

At the Fourth Angle are the winged lion and a winged horse drawing in a chariot the younger Lilith, the wife of Asmodai. She is dark, a woman to the waist and a beast below it, and she appears as dragging down with her hands small figures of men into Hell.

CIRCLE CENTER
Refer not only to the Circle but also the Zodiac of the infernal.

In the Center of the circle is Samael and Asmodai. The symbolic form of the Asmodeus is somewhat like that of the Devil of the Tarot, but colossal and powerful; Asmodeus appears often as a bloated, bestial man, but in a crouching position spewing a black bile from his mouth.

OF THE THREE DARK FORCES BEHIND SAMAEL

The first is Qematriel, whose appear of a vast black, man-headed Dragon-serpent, and this power united under him the force of Kether of the Infernal and averse Sephiroth. Seek Qematriel or Qematiel as the power which unites and bring raw abyssic power to your workings. Some Luciferians have consecrated a dagger in the form of a dragon to Qematriel as a means of focus. Kether is the divine spirit or the Adversarial Psyche. This is the Spiritual Force which is symbolized here as a dragon, one of the most powerful images for the Luciferian, as the Dragon represents transformation and raw power of both the abyss and the mind. Qematriel is associated with the Kether elements of the root of Air[13] and the Crown Chakra, relating to Ahriman as well.

---

[13] Hence the title PRINCE OF THE POWERS OF THE AIR

The second, a black, bloated Man-dragon, Belial, he denies all Gods; and he uniteth the forces of the averse Chokmah. The above Sigil represents Belial in the darkest aspect; this is Belial as the dragon, the power of Averse Chokmah. Chokmah is the sphere of Wisdom and relates to Neptune. The incense of Belial in this sphere is Musk. Belial is associated with Chokmah as being the root of fire (Black Flame) and a secret phrase of power is VOAIV and may be used with the attribution of Chi as the Part of the Soul.

The third is the power Othiel or Gothiel, a black, bloated Man-insect, horrible of aspect, he unites the force of the averse Binah.

The fourth form is Samael the Black. All these are of gigantic nature and terrible aspect. This is the Adversary in the Ahrimanic form, he brings great wisdom, power but if the Luciferian is not cautious, can bring self-destruction. As the Zohar writes, "the end of all flesh[14] has come before Me [Sammael)"; for he, as the Evil Serpent, "takes away the souls of all flesh", that is he liberates them from matter. He is called the Angel of Venom, of Poison, of Death; for *Sam* means "poison" and *El* means "angel"." –Fuller, Secrets of the

---

[14] A title for LILITH as well.

Qabala. Samael is the illuminator, he who envenoms the spirit and brings freedom from the flesh – thus an initiating Angel who at first is darkness but brings Light by the process of initiation.

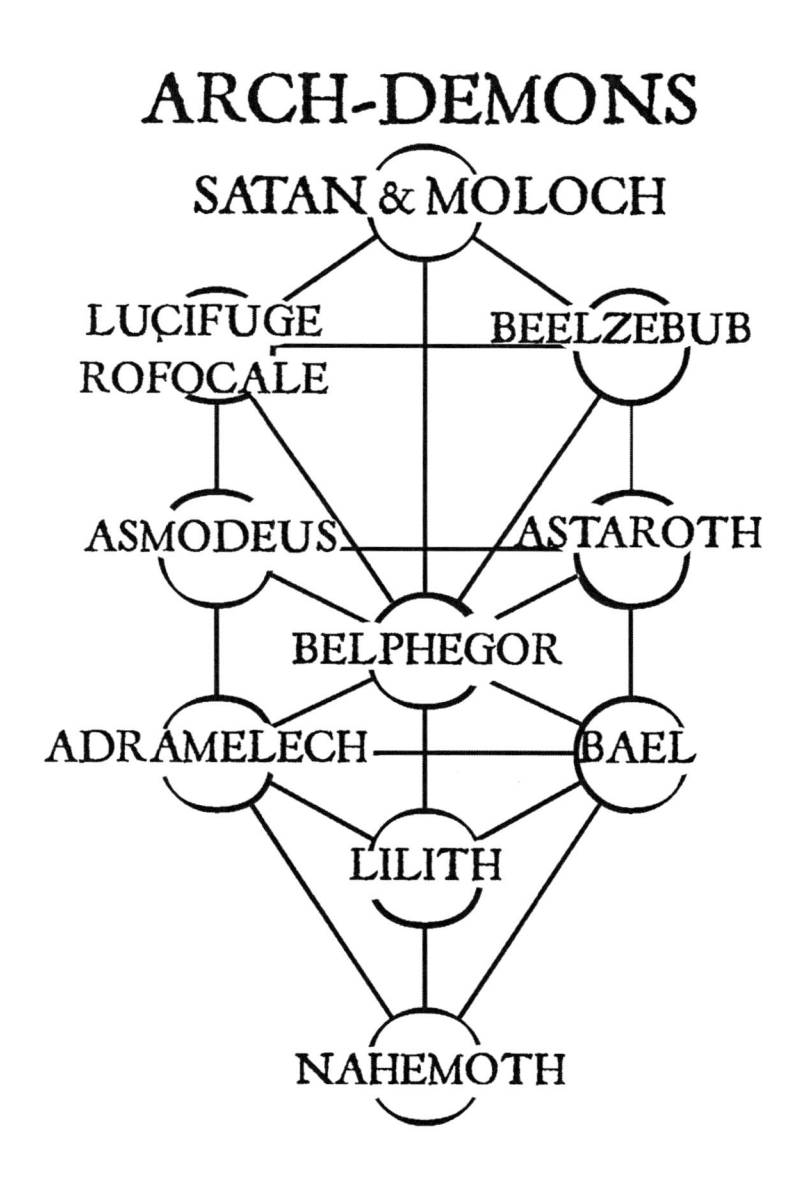

ARCH-DEMONS

- SATAN & MOLOCH
- LUCIFUGE ROFOCALE
- BEELZEBUB
- ASMODEUS
- ASTAROTH
- BELPHEGOR
- ADRAMELECH
- BAEL
- LILITH
- NAHEMOTH

MICHAEL W. FORD

THE DEATH TREE OR TREE OF DA'ATH

The uppermost aspect of the Qliphoth is that of Shahul, the hell of the Supernals, or the Triple Hell or Crowned Heaven of the Rebellious Angels. Two Kings jointly reign over the first hell, and they are Satan and Moloch, the secret within Luciferian Magick is that there are not two, rather one. Only the Malkuth and Yesod spheres hold the opposite essence, the daemonic feminine which makes Shahul complete. Often the Third aspect of this unholy trinity is frequently interpreted as Lilith, the demon Queen of Gamaliel.

Moloch is also a fallen angel, and the Canaanite god of fire, to whom children were sacrificed in ancient times. This sphere is dual with Satan the adversary.

The Second hell of Shahul is ruled over Beelzebub, the "Chief" of all demons, also known as the Lord of Chaos and the Lord of flies.

The Demon King of the third hell of Supernals is Lucifuge Rofocale, whose evocation is detailed in the controversial "Grand Grimoire", which was unquestionably based on either "The Key of Solomon", or a variation known as "The Grand Key" or "The True Clavicles". This Demon is the prime minister of the infernal regions.

The fourth hell, or Abaddon, is ruled over by Astaroth, the Goetic demon.

The fifth hell is ruled over by Asmodeus.

The sixth hell is ruled over by Belphegor, the Lord of the Dead.

The seventh hell is ruled by Bael the ancient spirit of Luciferian spirits.

The eighth hell is ruled by Adramelech, the King of Fire.

The demon queens of ninth and tenth hells, collectively known as Giyehanim, are Lilith and Nahema. Lilith is the Demoness of Debauchery, the queen of the Luciferian Path.

Nahemoth is the Demoness of Impurity, and the mortal mother of the demon king Asmodeus, whose father was Ashamdon, a Yezidic Archangel according to lore and mythology.

ELEMENT	*FIRE*	*AIR*	*WATER*	*EARTH*
DIRECTION	*SOUTH*	*EAST*	*WEST*	*NORTH*
CROWNED PRINCE	Satan	Lucifer	Leviathan	Belial
Four Princes of divels	Samael.	Azazel.	Azael.	Mahazael.
Four infernal Rivers.	Phlegeton.	Cocytus.	Styx.	Acheron.
Four Princes of spirits, upon the four angels - angles of the world.	Oriens.	Paymon.	Egyn.	Amaymon
Yatukih Daeva	Andar	Savar	Zairich	Nakiyas

MICHAEL W. FORD

TIAMAT
THE PRIMAL ABYSS

"She filled their bodies with venom instead of blood. She cloaked ferocious dragons with fearsome rays And made them bear mantles of radiance, made them godlike, 'Whoever looks upon them shall collapse in utter terror! Their bodies shall rear up continually and never turn away!' She stationed a horned serpent, a mushussu-dragon, and a lahmu-hero, An ugallu-demon, a rabid dog, and a scorpion-man, Aggressive umu-demons, a fish-man, and a bull-man Bearing merciless weapons, fearless in battle." -**Enuma Elish**

The dragon of the primal oceans of the abyss opened her veins and filled her children with venom as blood, with a spell cracking the sky with the blackened flame of her Will. To raise them as Gods which shall master all forms of wolves, serpents and those beasts which prey upon others is the desire of Tiamat. What she gave to humanity was never cleansed from the ancient darkness in the subconscious, there is still a coiling serpent within.

The ancient dragon which personified the primal sea was Tiamat, according to George Barton the name Tiamat was equivalent to the same stem which meant 'tamtu', being the primal waters of the Abyss. Tiamat is the Adversary from a atavistic viewpoint, her form too terrible to comprehend. An interesting concept of the demonic feminine as a motivational factor in all life can be found in the archetype of Tiamat.

"There was a time in which there existed nothing but darkness, and an abyss of waters, wherein resided most hideous beings, who were produced of a two-fold (?) principle." - Cory's *Ancient Fragments, Tiamat,* George Barton

The darkness is our source, the beginning; it is our primal desire and need. We go to it to sleep at night; it holds us enraptured, sending us to our dreams or nightmares. The Abyss in the context of this book primarialy refers to the subconscious, the atavistic depths of the mind. The hideous beings, produced of a two-fold principle, the Opposer or Adversary, relates to beast like or Therionick atavisms.

"There appeared men, some of whom were furnished with two wings, others with four, and with two faces. They had one body but two heads, the one of a man the other of a woman, and likewise in their several organs they were both male and female. Other human features to be seen with the legs and horns of goats; some had horses' feet, while others united the hind-quarters of a horse." - Cory's *Ancient Fragments, Tiamat,* George Barton

We see early mentionings of demonic beings, which emerge from the abyss. These are no doubt the sleeping darkness within our subconscious mind, waiting to take flesh. Austin

Osman Spare's[15] work clearly brought these ideals to manifestation through his art.

"1. "At a time when above the heaven was not named,
2. (And) beneath the earth had no existence,
3. The abyss was first their generator;
4. Mummu Tiamat was the bringer forth - of them all ;" - first tablet of the Babylonian Creation, George Barton - Tiamat

This is the foundation of not only the Luciferian Faith but also the inner workings of Vampyrism, being that Mummu Tiamat was the bringer forth and strongest of all, she was mother and devouring darkness.

The Adversary, long hidden away in a morass of filth by those who would hate the darkness, those who would commit greater crimes on humanity and veil such in the words of God. They are indeed old, the two-fold principle of darkness, known as the Adversary, call it Samael and Lilith or the older Ahriman and Jeh, the very isolate God of Darkness. Tiamat is the very first manifestation of this force, from a time when darkness held in its arms hideous monsters, the very demonic shapes which still seek our thoughts in the darkest hours of our mind. In times of stress and turmoil, these atavistic beasts seek to escape from the barbed wire, cruel talons in the mind.

The mighty Mummu Tiamat was called the "bringer forth of them all", yet was equally horrifying to her enemies, Gods she created Tiamat in ancient Assyria embodied all of that which was horrifying and violent to mankind, from the blackened oceans of the abyss did she first rise up, a great sea dragon who had partial elements of other predators, the head of a tiger, winged, four talons and a scale covered tail. This form was that which was from nightmares, which still

---

[15] The Book of Pleasure, Austin Osman Spare.

copulates with our dreams and brings us visions of our vast possibility as living beings.

Tiamat was betrayed by her child, Marduk and was joined with him in battle. In this battle did another plot with Marduk to capture and slay her. When she was cut open, the North Wind bore her blood to secret places. Gunkel and Bousset describe that Tiamat who was the Queen of the Abyss and darkness, supported by her infernal spirits rebelled against the higher gods of which Marduk was of.

MICHAEL W. FORD

DRUJO DEMÂNA
Yatukih Book of Dead Names

The Ahrimanic Spirits of ancient Persia are perhaps the most potent in primal sorceries; save for the darkness of which they bring. The Yatukih sorcerer who is able to see through and moreover pass through the darkness will find empowering Fire. A title of demon in the old Avestan text is Daeva, or Druj. Druj is a word meaning "Lie" and refers to transformation and the serpent. It is thus defined that Druj is a word meaning Transforming spirit, the very nature of Ahriman. The Lie is a word of becoming, not of specific act.

THE BIBLE OF THE ADVERSARY

Ahriman / Angra Mainyu / Ganamino – The Prince of Darkness who is both the center of sorcery and the path of creation through the infernal or counteraction path. What is misunderstood is that Ahriman is purely evil. While the idea of evil is only what is not understood, Ahriman both destroys and creates in numerous forms. Ahriman is not limited to destroying and is able to create beautiful things like the peacock.

Aka Manah/Akoman/Akemmano – the Evil Mind, enemy of the Archangel Vohu Manah, the first created ArchDaeva along with Mitokht, who is falsehood. Akoman plays a significant role in the initiatory process of the practitioner of Yatuk-Dinoih, as being that Akoman is the spirit which by the thirst for continued existence in time the spirit isolates the consciousness and essentially recreates the individual as a manifestation of Ahriman. In the Book Three of Denkard Akoman is said to be the cause of illness, evil odors, mortification, mortality, putrefaction, the result of which is therefore wickedness being the results of sin, this is an excellent example of "Hesham", the very result of the path.

Druj – the lie (change), collective enemy of Asha called "The Truth".

Bûiti Buji/ But– known also as Buiti/But, the idol of Buddhism.

Buidhi – considered the offspring of Buiti, results of the discipline.

Taromaiti/ Tauru /Taromat (Heresy) – enemy of Armaiti. Demoness who stirs the spirit to rebellion and thus heresy against Ahura Mazda and the religion of the Right Hand Path. Taromat also represents the demon which utilizes speech to obtain goals, using words to inspire and fill with a desire to see manifest on earth.

Apaosha – The enemy of Tishtrya (angel of rain), the demon of drought or thirst. Appeared in the Khorda Avesta in the shape of a large dark horse, black mane, ears and tail and "stamped with terror". The Daeva Apaosha is a powerful spirit created by Ahriman. Apaosha was considered more powerful than the Angel Tishtrya, sending him fleeing after battling for three days and three nights. Spenjaghri is the associate of Apaosha, who battles the angel of lightening who is Vazishta in the Avesta. Apaosha represents unbridled thirst and a desire of power, Trishtyra the angelic enemy, represents bounties given by Ahura Mazda and not from the self, thus may be considered a non-initiatory boon gained by supplication or weakness.

Vizaresh/Vizaresha – Demon which sits at the Mouth of Arezura, the gates of hell and for three days and nights tortures the soul of the departed until they may pass. Vizaresh is seen as an initiatory force, one which uses a noose to bind the spirit until they may pass.

Akatasha – The demon of corruption, who tempts with power. Those who listen to this instinctual desires must have the discipline to balance corruption (becoming against the Right Hand Path) with desire, to use such as a method of inspiration to drive the self in further avenues of initiation. This is the demon who corrupts and initiates man and woman, through the spark of the Black Flame. Be careful with Akatash, all daevas will corrupt by the desire of pleasure, yet the Adept must be strong to balance and have discipline to remain strong in the center of the storm itself.

Spenjaghri/ Spozgar – The companion of Apaosha, who battles against the angel of lightening, Vazishta. Spenjaghri would in such a case represent the violent storm which brings some kind of environment change or effect, being a hurricane, cold winds to drought supporting circumstances.

Vadak – The Mother of Zohak in Myth, committed adultery on her husband with Ahriman, to beget Zohak. Known also as Aud, Uda and Udai (Audak).

Vayu – Daeva mentioned in "The Aogemadaeca", not the Angel Vayu but the Daeva with the same name. Vayu is a force which is as powerful as Astwihad, it says none may survive against Vayu. The Venidad mentions that Vayu is the demon who is counterpart to the Good Vai or Vayu, as it is the genius of destiny. Astwihad bounds the life while Vayu often carries it off.

Driwi – a demon mentioned in the Khorda Avesta, the Hordad Yasht as one of the myriad of devs whom one summons against. This spirit is attributed to Malice and therefore a shadow created by Aeshma.

Azi – Serpent, compare Azhi which was created by Ahriman, an often assumed form of the Daevas. Ahriman took the form of a snake when he first fought against the stasis of Ahura Mazda. The serpent was later a symbol of Ahriman, in later cultures, the snake represents wisdom and knowledge, esoteric and otherwise.

Vyambura – Considered a type of Daeva in Warharan Yasht of the Khorda Avesta. These devs "bend their backs" and limbs while smiting against the children of Ahura Mazda.

Vadhaghna – Zohak or Azhi Dahaka, the son of Vadak, a whore – demoness who was the bride of an Arabian or Scythian king, Ahriman had took the form of a man and impregnated her to create a son of flesh.

Srobar – called "The Serpent Srobar in violence" by the Denkard.

Saeni – a demon mentioned in the Khorda Avesta, the Hordad Yasht as one of the myriad of devs whom one summons against. This dev is connected with Druj Nasu and other daevas.

Daiwi – a demon mentioned in the Khorda Avesta, the Hordad Yasht as one of the myriad of devs whom one summons against. This dev is associated with lying and therefore the word Druj holds connection, meaning lie and serpent.

Kasvi – A daeva of the spite, representing revenge and counter action against another. A dev which may be used in summoning or a fetish evoked to devour a target by spirit, mind and dream.

Saham – Terror.

Indra/Andar – arch-demon who is said to pervert from virtue (defined as ignorance, non-initiation which is essentially Christian or monotheistic) and leads others to despise all mind numbing religions.

Naunghaithya/Naikiyas/Nizisht – One of the Six Archdaevas, one who produces discontent among all spirits, thus is an antinomian spirit of progression and strength by struggle and disorder.

Sauru/Savar/Saurva – Leader of Daevas, The Greater Bundahishn attributed Savar to evil authority, unlawfulness and the production of want. Savar is thus related to the later medieval manifestation of Belial. Saurva is one of the Seven Archdaevas.

Aeshma/Aeshma khruidru – The fiend of the Murderous Spear. Wrath, enemy of Sraosha. Aeshma controls the seven powers which allow the dev to manifest darkness upon the earth, collectively combating the Seven Angels of Ohrmazd. Considered both an abstract demon, a form of the energy of Ahriman in the name Hesham, as well as a demon created by Ahriman which killed many ancient Persian holy men. It is said to borrow some of its strength from drunkenness.

Khru/Khruighni – Considered in the Venidad, translated by James Darmesteter from the Joseph Peterson edition to be an epithet of Aeshma, meaning "wound" and "The wounding one".

Zairika/Zairich/Zairi - one of the six Archdaevas, one who makes poisons. This spirit may be attributed to harmful plants or merely the microbes which both are considered beneficial and harmful to humanity.

Aghashi/Aighash/Ghashi/Hashi - a demon mentioned in the Khorda Avesta, the Hordad Yasht as one of the myriad of devs whom one summons against. Aghashi may be drawn in association with Heshem, or the result of the energy of the Yatukih path. Aghashi is considered by name a powerful druj under Nasu (the fly dev).

Tusush – Called the First Created Opposition by Angra Mainyu in the "Afrin of Dahman". Relates to the Shadow or instinct of darkness found in the mind of mankind. Considered a spiritual force similar to Mitokht and Akoman.

Paitisha/Paityâra –Called the energy or manifestation of Ahriman and the Left Hand Path, opposition and counter-workings, Adversity. A personification of the Ahrimanic current of the Daevayasna.

Zaurva –The Daeva of Old Age, maturity and the physical decay of the living body. A Daeva presenting that the Spirit of the Daeva is immortal, the flesh is not. The flesh of the body is a tool, yet do not grow too attached to it. Prepare the spirit in the Blackened Fire of the Seven ArchDaevas and Ahriman, awaken the spirit as Daeva.

Azhi Dahaka– The son of Angra Mainyu/Ahriman by initiation into the current of the Adversary. Zohak was first taught sorcery by Ahriman, later making a pact to allow the Adversary to teach him the arts which would allow him power and immortality. Zohak later allowed Ahriman to kiss his shoulders and from it sprang two venomous black serpents shaped as horns to rise from his shoulders. They nourished themselves on human brains, which allowed Zohak to be a power on both earth and the underworld itself. Zohak opened gateways for druj and other daevas to manifest upon the earth, balancing the earth from the corrupt ancient kings which used the idea of "God" to lead others with tyranny. Azhi Dahaka as the 'Storm Fiend' has six eyes, three heads and three pairs of fangs.

Azhi Dahaka is said to be filled with serpents, scorpions, toads and other insects and reptiles, which saved him from being dismembered as such Ahrimanic servitors would overwhelm the earth if he bled too much.

Ithyejah – A dev mentioned in "Ulema-I Islam" in reference to one of the Seven Demons bound in the celestial sphere, while the Hordad Yasht merely mentions this dev without reference of meaning. The Seven Devs created by Ahriman and bound in the celestial sphere are Hesham, Nāangish, Zirach, Tarich, Tarmad, Sij and Niz. Joseph Peterson in commentary and notes makes reference to Sij and Niz being one demon as Ithyejah. The archdaevas are named and corresponded as Aeshma, Nāonghaithya, Zairicha, Taromaiti, Ithyejah and Tauru. Aeshma/Hesham is the power which encircles the other devs and creates essentially the Seven Headed Dragon, or power of the mastery of the earth.

Pairika Knathaiti – A daughter of Jeh and Ahriman, a manifestation of idolatry.

Pairika Mush – A female druj of Ahriman.

Pairika Duzhyairya – A female druj of Ahriman.

Kashvish – A demon evoked to cause revenge against an enemy.

Anzakih – Druj of non-procreation (Masturbation or sex without intention of procreation). The spilling of seed creates Daevas and such servitors.

Spazga/Spazg/ Safle – The demon of slander, of leveraging speech and the context of language to change the course of the world around you, not exclusive to mere slander.

Mitokht/Mithaokhta - The Daeva created first along with Akoman. This is the daeva of falsehood or the Lie, representing change and mutation.

Arast – The demon of falsehood or the lie, leveraging your surroundings by using sorcery to cause change, symbolic of the serpent which is an eternal sign of wisdom or divine energy.

Arashk/Areshko/Aresh - A demon of malice or the desire to become, viewing your desire and seeking to obtain it. Equally a daeva of the Evil Eye. Said to be the author of the Zurvanite myth to combat the religion of Ahura Mazda.

Bushasp or Bushyansta - Night demoness, seductress often a child of Lilith in Hebraic legend and myth. Bushyasp is also called in the "Afrin of Dahman" the Long handed, the fiend of decay and sloth.

Uda (chattering while eating), alternate name of the demoness Vadak.

Zarman – A dev of weakness from struggle, in exhaustion can the essence be revealed and that point be found a new essence of strength.

Oshtohad– A dev which causes the struggle of the body against the element of winter, when cold winds and harsh conditions allow the stronger to survive and threaten the weak.

Varun – A dev of lust and sexual perversion.

Sej/Sij – Druj of Decay, as well as destruction and annihilation.

Az– Occuring as the demon of greed, in the Bundahishin not a female gendered demon per se, later Az is associated with the Manichaean Demoness Az. Called also a dev of Avarice.

Niyaz – A demon causing distress, representing personal change and strife which creates the situations where the individual will rise to the occasion and become or become a victim of the powers of devouring darkness.

Nas/Nasu/Druj Nasu/Druj i Nasush – A powerful demoness who is the embodiment of corruption of flesh, dead matter and defilement. Druj Nasu takes the form of a fly who rushes screaming from Arezura and embodies other druj into corpses and those who become initiated into the cult of Ahriman. *"Druj Nasu flies away to the regions of the north, [in the shape of a raging fly, with knees and tail sticking out, droning without end, and like unto the foulest Khrafstras"* – *Venidad*

Push – A demon of hoarding energy, absorbing and being as vampire, encircling and controlling life force or Chi.

Friftar/Frazisht – A demon which seduces mankind corrupts the weak and devours spirit energy. Friftar to the initiate of the path who has inner strength may work with this demon to grow strong in consciousness in relation to the spirit or immortal essence.

Arzur – A Son of Ahriman who battled against Gayomard, the first man. After the fiend was slayed, the Mouth of the Gate of Hell, where Ahriman and the confederate demons fell, was called Arezura in his honor. The Mountain is considered "in the north" and has been called "The head of Arezura" and "The neck of Arezura".

Muidhi – A demon of intoxication or the ritual use of herbs to induce intoxication.

Sur Chashmih/Chishmak – A demon representing a whirlwind, the element of air and the chaos within it. Take the context of a whirlwind, while the outer is chaos the center is order, Chishmak is also represented as a daeva of the Evil Eye.

Kundak/Kundi (wizard or Steed of Wizards, nightmare) – The steed of wizards, or nightmare. May visualize as a steed to guide to infernal Sabbat rituals (dream sorcery), the dev which carries forth spells and curses to their location.

Astovidat/ Asti-vahat/Astovidhotush (Bone divider) and **Astwihad (Evil wind, evil flyer)** – demon of death, vampiric and bestial shadow, relating to predatory spiritualism or vampirism. When Asti-vahat casts a shadow upon a man it is called a Fever, when he looks into his eyes it is Death as he drains his life.

Malkôsh/Mahrkûsha – A death causing Daeva or Wizard, who is associated with Winter. Malkosan are said to be the "Evil Winters" created by Malkôsh. Malkosh is the sorcerer who ushers forth winter.

Drivish – Dev of poverty and self-struggle.

Daiwish – A dev of the Lie, deceit.

Nung – A dev of shame.

Jahi – The prostitute, a sacred manifestation of Jeh or Az, the first succubi and bride of Ahriman.

Dadani – The demon of famine as the hunger for knowledge and power within, spiritual hunger for more life.

Varenya –Wind-demons, which bring forth other evil spirits of change, strife and chaos.

Kapasti –Poison plants spirits, created by Taprev and Zairich.

Akhtya–Akhtya is the Offspring of Darkness, a wizard of Ahriman.

The Ahriman-Spirit Angel
Known also as Azal'ucel
The Inner Daemon / Daeva which
Guides the mind of man and woman.

This spirit is Adversarial, two heads – one King, one Beast. The Two ArchDaevas below support the desires of the Guiding Yatus.

THE BOOK OF TAROMAT (EARTH)

THE SERPENT IN FLESH

Ahriman is the Lord of Sorcery, the shape shifting Adversary who is essentially the embodiment of wisdom and infernal knowledge, par excellence in practice. Taromat or Taromati is the ArchDaeva which inspires discontent and rebellion. You will find the basis and considerations around the practice of Luciferian Magick from several different levels. Understanding and being able to apply the methods of sorcery according to your own imagination are essential in any practice. It is not about system, it is about results. Understanding how the Luciferian spirit has manifested in you is the key to successful Magick. Know that Dark Magicks which appear in these pages are not negative, they are meant for the spectrum of practice as a God would announce his desires: remember, Darkness is what all is created from.

MICHAEL W. FORD

MASTERY OF EARTH
The Teachings of BELIAL
The Reflections of LILITH
Controlling your Destiniy in the Here and Now

1. APPEARANCE IS IMPORTANT

The manner in which you carry yourself will present the results in which you are treated. Think of how you present yourself to others – are your clothes appropriate the response you want, is your posture upright or is it in the way of a slave? Think of this daily and alter it to work with the aims of your goals.

2. REACTIONS VARY

Every person reacts to things differently. Think about your goal, what you want to achieve. Think about different ways to say it, will it offend in some way? You should consider always presenting the benefits for the person you are speaking to, speak to their own self-interest. Think about the tone in which you say something, is it non-threatening or threatening? Know when to command and when to softly speak.

3. LUCIFER IS THE GOD OF SELF-REALIZATION

Adopting the status you wish to achieve by posture alone will set in motion the goal you wish to have made flesh. Crown yourself and speak as if you are king, others will follow you and power will be yours. When you aim for something, strike at the strongest and you will be the tallest, boldest and uplift yourself to heights you could not imagine. Godhood is found within, it is a state of mind.

4. ENEMIES CAN BE USEFUL IN MANY WAYS

Enemies can be useful – they make your stronger. Do not underestimate your enemies, however. Often, competition brings out the best in your capabilities; it can also be a strong teacher. When you have enemies don't be afraid to counterbalance them by offering a basic surrender tactic to get the upper hand; play to their psychological vanity and this will in turn weaken them. Once they are off balance, strike with sudden terror. Once you strike, destroy them completely; leave no room for them to do the same to you.

5. DO NOT INFECT THE MOMENT WITH HESITATION, IT CROWNS WEAKNESS AS YOUR RULER.

Know when to Strike and do it with ferocity. If you have something you must do, when you are ready be sure there is no hesitation, strike with the swiftness of the serpent. Act with stealth, boldness and surety. If you hesistate, that weakness will infect your entire operation and may cause self-destruction. Do not infect the moment with hesitation, for it crowns weakness as your ruler.

6. TIMING IS EVERYTHING

Timing is something which requires thought, discipline and the instinct to recognize when and why. If you want to present a new idea or obtain a specific position, wait until the moment of weakness is present in which your idea would be the new cement to fix it. If you wait until that moment, your strength will cut down the weakness and uplift you where you wish to be. Timing must be observed and carefully considered.

7. CONTROL THE EMOTIONS, CONTROL THE WILL

Know the presence of mind is the reign which controls the Will. Always maintain the possibility for detachment when you feel your emotions mastering you. Adversity is essential; it always makes your stronger but can also take your balance away.

8. BEWARE OF LIVING IN THE PAST

The past can make you miserable and tired. Don't allow reflection to become obsession, then your failure will become tomorrow. Understand that learning from your mistakes is important, but applying that knowledge to what you do now will create wisdom in the future.

THE GODDESS IN THIS WORLD – LILITH

1. WOMAN IS THE MOST POWERFUL FIGURE

A woman is the most powerful figure in the world. She is able to stir the emotions of man to anything she wishes. She can do this by demanding respect, adoration and to become a fantasy figure by being able to say no and knowing when to say yes. A major factor in successful magick is to affirm your Will, use the amount of discipline needed to delay satisfaction and you will create Thralls. If your target is another Luciferian, play to his fantasy and be respectful – the two of you together can be a powerful combination and you will learn much from each other.

2. THE GODDESS DISPLAYS THE ESSENCE OF HER POWER IN HER PRESENCE

The Goddess displays the images of her power. Think of the image of a deity, their essence is in the appearance. While there are more indepth considerations, the basic appearance will stike resonation or nothing at all by first glance. Uphold strength of character, show in a glance the potential for vanity and self-esteem in your reflection, this is a key to the power of the adversary.

3. THE EYES ARE THE WINDOW TO THE SOUL

When one looks into your eyes, let them see the power of your spirit. Look deep into the eyes of another and shake them with your glare of command.

4. BE FULL OF FIRE AND INTENSITY

Remain detached in your response but be full of fire and intensity. People will be attracted to you when they can see the attractive nature of your spirit. The Goddess as the fiery spirit can grow stronger by using an ethereal and mysterious appearance to work on the subconscious.

5. POSSESS YOUR CHOSEN – BE AS SPIRIT

Entering the spirit is significant and is taught the Serpent, it is the art of the adversary. Think of yourself as a spirit, with no body to reside in. When you find someone you want, you must get their attention. How do you do this? You must get their attention by some simple things. Adopt their games, play to their rules, be attentive to their moods. Whisper to them the subtle verses reflecting their desires. When you become easily adapted to their world they will find it easy and pleasurable to have you next to them. Once they have brought you close, your spirit enters them and they are drawn into you. Remember, people are narcissistic and selfish by nature, play to this inner quality with time and calculation and you will be empowered.

6. TEMPTATION IS THE ART OF THE SERPENT

To lure someone to you is done by showing the individual a glimpse of the possibility they want, let their imagination build. Once you use seductive words and fill their ears with the desires they want, the glimpse of possibility they will find you irresitable. Remember the legend of the Serpent in the Garden – it showed possibility, truth in making "if you eat from this tree you will know both good and evil", but the serpent by offering the knowledge of this power knows there is responsibility.

MICHAEL W. FORD
TEN ADOMINATIONS

Laws of Sorcery and Magick

Akhtya, the ancient sorcerer who embodied the mythological assumptions of Yatukih Sorcery of the Druguvantem or People of the Lie, presented Laws of Magick. Akht's antinomian laws of the time we in summary the following: The modern interpretations are significant to those who understand the methodology of sorcery as both a destructive and creative effect.

1. One should have disobedience towards the idea of God – the idea of God as being an exterior all good being takes away from humanity the need to be self-sufficient and power. Any religion that demands believing in something which cannot be experienced by gnosis, flesh or metal command, that relies on knee bending as something to approach should be destroyed. Only slaves believe in a religion of slavery. Ahriman is the God of Freedom as you find him within.

2. The practices of sorcery should be made current against Zartosht or Zoroaster. Sorcery is the religion of the Luciferian, this is the Magick of the self in a creative context.

3. That justice should be done without concern for any ruler or authority. The Luciferian or Yatukih understands that the Law of the Talon is the first and foremost law. Justice should be exercised based on action and reaction. Do not allow a law of some sheep god to dictate your living circumstances. Utilize the Law of your land to the best of your ability. Think before acting.

4. That every person should be rendered capable of doing "evil" to another (Law of the Talon) – Learn the art of self-defense, practice and do not hesitate in defending yourself.

5. Human nature should be corrupted so the Yazads (Angels of Ahura Mazda, the enemies of the ArchDaevas) may not dwell in the human body, that demons or Archdemons may reside in the body (see *Awakening the Kundalini and Ahriman and the 7 ArchDaevas within*). In simpler terms, practice a full life of enjoying, become stronger of mind and body and all which leads to a powerful existence according to your Will. Listen to your instincts and be guided accordingly.

6. That man should not seek the path of the virtuous or seek their narrow minded ways. The practice of the Religion of Sheep is to announce the soul to death and life unfulfilled. Do not allow their weakness to infect you.

7. To spread the path of Sin and sorcery among mankind, that corruption from the way of Ahura Mazda will bring

others to the path of Ahriman. Sin is the luxury of life, sin is not evil unless you hate yourself.

8. Akht had informed others that they should not practice the suggestion of restraining from sexual activity with any other woman or man. That your desire should be fulfilled in the flesh as well as the spirit. Be ever so cautious that you do not mistake the needs of the spirit for the needs of the flesh. Accept responsibility for any action resulting in your lust.

9. The individual should fight against and have no authority to the Dastur or Priest of Zoroastrianism or any other religion which is based on servitude. Look to any Priest as no more a man than any else.

10. Akht proclaimed that men and women should seek to give affection to the demons, that people should abandon the worship of divine or Holy beings and practice various aspects and rites of daeva-yasna. That if you are able and willing, the art of creative Magick be practiced.

RITUAL AND PRACTICE

The practice of Magick is to change, alter and motivate the self according to Will. This means that no God, Goddess of divinity will tell you what you should do, what you should believe or where you can go.

The key factor in successful Luciferian Magick is belief. Belief is everything in magick and without it nothing is possible. Have you ever tried to do something your were not interested in; finding the boring and mundane task to take forever to accomplish, never achieving a suitable end or just plain quitting? Think again of something you have needed to do because you saw the potential of it, the possibility and reward? It is then, a blast to complete – you master it in no time at all. Notice the key factor – Selfishness and reason is a powerful motivator, it fills and creates believe and the results from it.

It is clear that Luciferian Magick does not need to be an actual RITUAL in a ceremonial situation. It can be a process which involves silent focus rites or meditation. The Luciferian does not require a ceremonial rite, but a secret working inside the mind which connects he or she with the Luciferian Gnosis itself. There are Luciferians who see the value in both.

There is no such thing as "White" Magick – there is only Black as it is the magick of Transformation, black meaning wisdom from the Arabic root. When you hear "black" magick you think of simply destructive magick, yet the fact is this magick is for all ends and means.

THE TEMPLE

The Temple in reference here is to your area of working, or conducting ceremonies. This can be a small area, room or perhaps even your mind. Understanding the nature of what you wish to accomplish is paramount to the workings or Magick. The aim of Magick is to transform the self or to compel something to happen. Do not expect winning lottery numbers or to become the president of the USA if you already a felon, use reason and logic.

When utilizing instruments and tools in your practice of magick, understand that they are expressions of your will, often in the astral plane sense or spiritual sense. Symbols always represent something deeper within, so understanding meanings and intent may make your experience more meaningful.

Something to consider with the Luciferian Path is that your physical body is a Temple of the Adversary; treat it accordingly. Don't have un protected sex, don't do drugs which break down and enslave your spirit, build yourself and lift your spirit above the Sun itself!

ALTAR

The altar is the area of working in which the sorcerer projects their will upon the universe. The altar should be adorned in implements which signify the desire and aim of the Luciferian. If unable to have a real altar, for instance if you are in the military, or living somewhere in which an altar would prove a negative addition, then create your ideal altar via the imagination. This can provide a powerful tool in your magickal work as this is the foundation of the path – the mind. The altar and the inverted pentagram often represent the Mastery of the Earth. Thus the Altar belongs to the essence of Belial, fixed earth, foundation.

ALTAR CLOTH

The cloth or banner hanging above the altar should have a symbol representing the intent of your initiatory work. As a Luciferian, there are several sigils which represent various points of power.

ALGOL

The chaos-sphere and inverted pentagram which represents the Adversary. The deeper meaning of ALGOL can be explored in LUCIFERIAN WITCHCRAFT and LIBER HVHI among other works. Algol in its deepest form represents the Egyptian Set-Apep, the devil-sorcerer whose forms are protean and many. The Magick Fire of ALGOL is a center point for magickal workings in which the sorcerer may project his or her will through it, project a servitor or the aethyric body through it as a point for empowering your workings. An interesting connection that Lilith holds with Samael/Satan is the Star Algol which was originally called Arabic the "Ri'B al Ohill" and later the Hebrew "Rosh ha Sitan" meaning The Head of Satan and also Lilith. Algol can be viewed as a Star which represents the essence of Satan and Lilith, the twin fire of becoming through the Left Hand Path. In Luciferian Sorcery, Algol is presented as an 8 pointed Chaos Sigil with the inverted pentagram in the center. This is made reference to the number 8, being of Baphomet and Chaos, and the pentagram representing the five points of the Adversary

INFERNAL UNION

The inverted pentagram, a symbol of the fallen angel who brings wisdom to mankind, also signifies the five elements and demons of the Ahriman. The Hebrew letters around the circle spell LEVIATHAN, the crooked serpent, representing the darkness and abyss, i.e. the subconscious. The SAMAEL and LILITH are the balanced factor of the self – the Daemonic Masculine or matter, LILITH being the Daemonic Feminine or instinctual fire. Together they represent mastery of the Will. The head of the Goat is the Baphomet, or Black Head of Wisdom (abufihamat), the Beast or Cain, the son of Samael and Lilith. When you combine LEVIATHAN, SAMAEL and LILITH to beget CAIN or BAPHOMET, this is a powerful symbol of the Mastery of the Luciferian in the Carnal and Spiritual World, the above and below, the darkness and the light.

ATHAME or SWORD

The Sword or Athame (from Adhdhame, the Bloodletter) is the force of the Luciferian, representing their desire and power of Will to achieve. The blade should represent the higher elements of the mind, for instance a shining illuminated dragon or angel, representing the highest aspect of the self, or it may be simple as a plain blade. You use the sword or athame as a representation of Tubal-Cain or Azazel the creator of weapons, representing the Luciferian Spirit. The Luciferian would use the ATHAME in rituals of the LUCIFERIAN MAGICK category, representing transformative magick. Often, the sorcerer will consecrate and charge the weapon prior to a first ritual to align it with the intent and mind, sort of a rite of focus of the object. This would represent a simple invocation.

BARBAROUS DAGGER OF EVOCATION (Dagger)

The dagger is a weapon or tool meant to use in barbarous works of evocation, or calling spirits 'out' for intents in the Theronick or Yatukih sorcery categories. The dagger should be bestial or demonic in appearance, a cruel looking blade, sharp spikes, demonic shapes in the handle all add to the imagery of the rite. The dagger is point in the direction of which you are calling, the blade is turned toward the sigil or object of the rite.

CHALICE

The cup represents the aspects of the subconscious brought into flesh, Leviathan rising from the abyss. The sorcerer drinks from a chalice often at the end of a rite to symbolize confirmation of the ritual itself, the intent to make flesh. Some magickians use skull caps to drink from, representing the power of the carnal and the spiritual plane.

ATESHGAH

This is "The Fire Place" which refers to the ancient Zoroastrian Fire Temple, or sacred fire. The Yatukih practitioner would take a small part of hair or nails and burn it at the beginning of the ritual, to corrupt the sacred flame and bless it to Ahriman. The Luciferian utilizes these ancient practices of Daevayasna to exhalt the Black Flame of Ahriman.

CANDLES

The color of the candle of a ritual should be according to the intent. If it is a ritual for the wisdom of self or a Luciferian invocation, often a Black Candle, representing hidden wisdom is used. Red are used for vampyric or sexual workings, Blue candles for simplistic astral workings, white for blessings and focusing on the higher aspects of the self. Candles, like anything else used in rituals, represents the intent of the sorcerer.

BELL

The bell is used by some ceremonial magickians representing the intent of the future. It is the calming and attentive point from which all magick is then conducted under. The Bell is used to signify the command of the astral plane before and during workings.

THE BLACK FLAME

The Candle which represents the higher and lower intellect conjoined, the very union and life of Samael and Lilith. The black candle represents wisdom and the focus point of the rite by the magickian. The candle should sit at the center of the altar or on a staff or holder used in rituals.

INCENSE

Incense is used to set the mood for the ritual, the intent. The sorcerer will burn incense before and often during the ritual. Incense utilizes the imagination via smell, thus is important during workings. The fire on which you will burn your incense if you are not using sticks is the Magick Fire, the Light of Lucifer. It is the fire which all desires are offered to, the light of becoming. This is often a sigil or desire written, cast at the moment of inspiration during the ritual, into the destructive flame which devours. The Charcoal represents AZ, the devouring demoness whose essence is black as night. This fire burns and devours those desires, representing the vessel of the wish. The chant or mantra is the expression of the lower aspiring to rise to the heights. The Smoke itself represents the Astral Plane, remember it is AHRIMAN who brought smoke to fire, thus Ahriman or Lucifer is the Prince of the Powers of Air, also that of the dream. The Astral Plane is that which lies between the material and spiritual plane, thus is what Luciferians seek to empower, encircle and utilize in workings.

THE CIRCLE OF LEVIATHAN

The Circle announces the intent of the Luciferian and his or her work of creation. This circle, Azothoz, is the beginning and end and by nature is dualistic – both dark and light. The

Magickian who uses a circle realizes that the circle is not to keep things out, but is to focus and encircle his or her own energies to focus on the work at hand.

The essence of Magick and ritual is to connect with something, begin a process of transformation or to compel a desire. The word AZOTHOZ is used to represent the self; specifically the circle which surrounds the Luciferian as they cast their will in sorcery. Azothoz is the beginning and the end, representing the self is God. The Circle in essence is Leviathan, projecting the desire of the self

BLACK SCRYING MIRRORS

The scrying mirror is utilized by the Black Magickian or Luciferian to gain access to the Astral plane. The Black Mirror is sacred to LILITH and is said to be a gateway to her caves, thus Luciferian Witches often utilize a Black Mirror to communicate with spirits and to project during rites in spirit form..

SYMBOLS & MEANING

CADUCEUS OF THE BLACK SUN

The symbol of the Luciferian Gnosis, the Caduceus is an ancient symbol of magical incantation, wisdom and attainment. The Luciferian Caduceus is symbolized as a Staff reching downward and with a point representing "So below". The two serpents encircling the staff are symbolic of intelligence, cunning and spiritual hunger for the human spirit, they are the Do-mar and Deh-ak of the ancient Persian son of Ahriman, the ALGOL sigil is the crown of the Caduceus, representing the Adversary and the Black Sun of initiation.

The symbol of the Caduceus has always represented balance, equally so it is symbolized with Hermes, the Roman Mercury. Remember, in specific Sinister Tradition circles, Mercury is related to Lucifer. In the Luciferian Gnosis, the Caduceus of the Black Sun is the sign of the Adept transformed, the isolation of consciousness and the spiritual hunger for the life force inherent in the universe.

The Caduceus represents the striving for self-excellence and the improvement of the world around you. If you seek to be great within, expanding knowledge and thus power, you may transform the world you live in to be a better place.

Understand well, the Luciferian uses power to become something stronger, more wise and able to master this world.

THE BIBLE OF THE ADVERSARY

Above: Caduceus of the Black Sun

THE FLAMING SWORD

In Qabalism, Samael or Sammael is the "Angel" (El) of "Poison" (Sam) and is related to the number 131, the Microcosm. Samael was the Angelick Host which rebelled against Metatron, considered God and was cast from the Yetziratic World of union or nothingness into the world of matter, being the Assaiatic World. As Samael the Dragon descended with from the Yetziratic World into the Assaiatic world he brought down the Sacred Fire of Consciousness and the Tree of Life into the world of discord and motion. Thus Samael represents evolution, consciousness and death as a means of transformation.

The Flaming Sword is a Qabalistic symbol of Satan descending from Kether to Malkuth, bringing the Black Flame of Consciousness to humanity. Samael was said to be have self-created as a spirit of fire with Esheth Zenunim or AShTh ZNVNIM, the Woman of Whoredom or the Mother Lilith, meaning Night. As Samael joins again with this woman they transform and become HVHI, called "hay-yah" being the Antichrist or symbol of the Beast, Chioa. As the Tetragrammaton is the numerical equivalent of 26, HVHI is 25 which is the shadow or darkness foreshadowing perfection.

THE BIBLE OF THE ADVERSARY
THE BRAZEN SERPENT

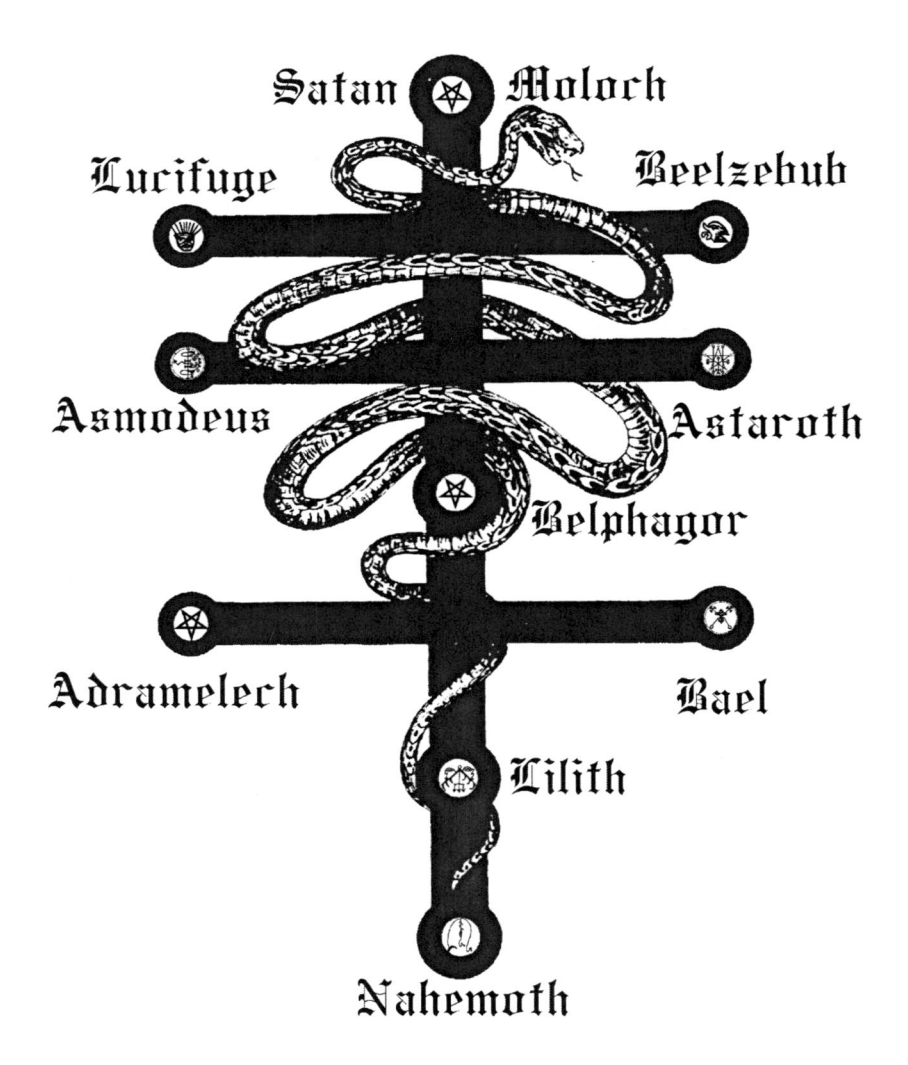

As first suggested, the Serpent is a symbol of both light and darkness, the power residing in and from both. Samael manifests as the symbol of the Dragon is is related to the fiery fall from Kether to Malkuth. Thus the coiling about the Tree of Da'ath transforms the Spirit of Kether from Metatron into the Kether of Samael or Satan, the Dragon and magician in flesh. The symbol of the Brazen Serpent is reflective of the inherent nature of the Qabala – that Sephriatic worlds inversed, Samael in the form of the Dragon is the Demon consuming the energy of motion, thus the Serpent is both Vampire and self-liberator. The Brazen Serpent as shown displays traditional sigils of the Daemonic Kings.

THE LUCIFERIAN WAND

Called the WAND OF EGYPT of old, the Luciferian Wand is the very symbol of Self-Mastery and the Blackened Flame. The circle is the timeless spirit of hunger for continued existence with the Sigil of Will, that of Separation from the natural order, the Fallen Angel made Serpent transmutated into Flesh. The Wings are the Astral Plane and the mastery of dreams, the staff is the path of power and the Beast invoked, the Twin Serpents are Deh-ak and Do-Mar, the Hungering Asps of Azhi Dahaka or Zohak, the Bottom triangle is the Mastery over elements and the control in the physical world. The symbol of Lucifer Rising as the Angel of the Sun, the Prince of the Powers of the Air and the Lord of the Earth is presented here.

THE SIGIL OF LUCIFER
Gateways to Power

Let us briefly explore the pathways to power. In order for one to be of strong character to utilize the senses to achieve in the material world, the initiate must be capable of understanding symbolism and the means of controlling subconscious into conscious power. The subconscious can absorb a sigil in a charging ritual and then upon using the sigil later, by ritual and visualization, can activate the subconscious to manifest in the actual conscious mind. This is a type of inspiration, of filling the empty water bed as Jung would put it. The medieval Sigil of Lucifer, featured in several medieval grimoires, provides a powerful foundation for those seeking the path of light and self-knowledge.

Above: The Sigil of Lucifer

THE SIGIL OF SPIRIT (The Black Flame)

This is the main aspect of Lucifer, the crown if you will. This sigil, having 19 obscure letter-sigils and 4 encircled can be said to represent the aspects of the mind in relation to the "True Will" or Psyche.

The total are 23 paths of the Qlippoth, the hidden being the path of Da'ath or hidden knowledge. The Black Flame is our vitality, perception and emotional dominance over the conscious functions of the brain. The Sigil of Spirit activates divination, Black Alchemy or Self-Deification, Antinomian paths of isolation, awakening the Higher Articulation of Consciousness, the Angelick if you will.

The Angelick is our function of intelligence, light and power with balance. The name of Lucifer is from the roman Lux (light) and Fero (to bear, to bring). The shadow aspect of Lucifer is Lucifuge which is "to fly from the light".

THE SIGIL OF VAMPIRIC WILL AND THE LUCIFERIAN SPIRIT
(Predatory Spirituality)

This sigil is perhaps the most powerful in the use of the conscious mind; it represents the five senses in use of desire and focus. It is through the five senses that we can communicate and create our interaction with the material world. To understand Lucifer, or Satan, you must understand the old biblical mention of "Satan is the King of the World", meaning simply by the application of reason you can achieve mastery over the world around you. The Vampiric Will is the Theronick atavistic hunger to the conscious mind, it acts as a barrier between the Angelick and theTherionick (beast like) aspects of the mind. This sigil can also be used as the powerful barrier of the direction of spirit devourment, shade drinking (shadows of the dead) and motivation of dreaming-shape shifting.

THE SIGIL OF ELEMENTS

The elements are the experience of the world around us; summer, winter, fall, spring, cold, heat, darkness, sunlight, rain, and the environment in general. The environment and elements directly affect our perception of the world around us. Decorate your immediate environment and experience the pleasure or tension you require – i.e. temple, ritual chamber, altar in corner, picture on wall, etc.

The two crescent symbols at top are the half moons of Hecate, the thirst of night. The inverse triangle is of the descending angels into daemon. The center of the triangle is the Eye of Set, or Satan as the Power of this World. It is the Akoman of Yatuk Dinoih, the Ajna Chakra. The two below are the Eyes from the Skull of the Adept, the mask of the flesh in this world. The Circle in the center is the Circle of Self, the Evocation center in ceremonial workings. Use in rituals and meditations as a reminder of shaping your world to your design, also to act as a shock of going out of the comfort zone to test your strength continually.

THE SIGIL OF THE ASTRAL PLANE

This is the Sigil which is related directly to the use of the other three, it is the Shade or Shadow of the Adept, the astral body which goes forth in the night to the Sabbat of the Sorcerers. The Astral Shadow is the vehical of initiation on the subconscious level, you may shape it to any form you wish, beast, bat, dragon, wolf, cat, bear, human or mere shadow. The Eye is the floating watcher, the tendril emerging is that which drinks of the sleeping ones. Focus before sleeping and achieve results.

BAPHOMET - QAYIN

MICHAEL W. FORD

THE SABBATIC GOAT or BAPHOMET

The Black Head of Wisdom or Baphomet. This Luciferian Baphomet is presented differently from the traditional Levi Baphomet. The figure is Black, the symbolism behind this is the Arabic root word fhm, meaning Black or "wise". The horns represent power, the beast head is the carnal body and the torch represents the Black Flame and Wisdom. The inverted pentagram represents the power of the Adversary and the Divinity fallen into humanity; thus the possibility for ascension and the knowledge of both darkness and light.

The wings are symbols of angelic spirit, the higher intellect. The moon above and below in which Baphomet points to indicates balance; that there is no complete "good" or "evil" and they points of view. Baphomet also is presented as Qayin and this is of course Cain the First Sorcerer and Luciferian. The twin serpents are Do-mar and Dehak, the snakes of Azhi-Dehak.

Cain is thus the power of the infernal and angelic, the son of The Serpent and the Whore, thus a symbol of the Luciferian as an individual.

THREE TYPES OF LUCIFERIAN MAGICK

There are specifically three types of practice in the Religious or initiatory practice of the Luciferian:

1. **Luciferian Magick**

   -Transformative workings, ascension magick, transformative workings. Example workings: RITE OF AZAL'UCEL, HVHI - The Invocation of the God of the Averse Tree, the Adversary

2. **Therionick Sorcery**

   -Bestial workings which explore the atavisms or hidden aspects of consciousness, lycanthropy, Qlippothic Workings, etc. Example workings: THE THERONICK RITE OF CHIOA, "The Satanic Ritual of Self-Liberation The Possession Ritual", some Goetic Sorcery workings, etc. Can include elements of Yatukih Sorcery including the Ritual of Druj Nasu.

3. **Yatukih Sorcery**

   -Working with Ahrimanic shadow aspects, ancient Persian aspects of primal atavisms. Compelling forces to manifest by activating symbolism or trance inducing aspects of Daeva-yasna, demon-worship within the self. Compelling events such as blessings, curses and lust workings. Rituals from the YATUK DINOIH, THE PAITISHA, BOOK OF THE WITCH MOON and Goetic Workings. Manipulative Magick is found here as well.

Luciferian Magick may be called higher magick or ascension workings – this is for change, inner or something involving transformation. Usually involves the Grigori/Watchers or Angelic (fallen) which represent the higher faculties of humanity.

High Sorcery is a transformative act to compel change, usually through a more Therionick Sorcery or Beast like working. High Sorcery would be a lycanthropic or shape shifting ritual, something involving utilizing hidden aspects of the subconscious.

Yatukih Sorcery is indeed a primal sorcery, usually the working with dark elements of nature – serpents, toads, spiders, flies, wolf and crow. Can represent compelling or low workings for Cursing, Blessing and Lust rituals.

Some Luciferians will utilize a basic practice of Luciferian Magick to practice silently – as they may not be an environment which is conducive to ritual practice. Practicing THE RITE OF AZAL'UCEL silently before a busy day may be of use, with a focus on retaining more discipline to keeping your tasking on target, planning ahead by performing a Goetic Ritual of Divination involving ASTAROTH, etc.

The Luciferian Witch who dresses seductively in a business suit or PVC Fetish dress will be a defined practitioner of Yatukih Sorcery by compelling her sexual desire. Think of all the things that go into seduction – appearance, odor and don't forget POSTURE. Ahriman has always taken the forms needed to achieve the goals he wishes to achieve. Lilith has always taken the forms she wishes to take to achieve her goals. Know the importance of such and Transform yourself by action into a manifestation of the Adversary.

A SIMPLIFIED MEANS OF RITUAL:

1. Use the Bell to announce the beginning of the rite (if applies).
2. Perform the Casting the Circle of the Dragon ritual or banishing rite.
3. A ritual from the Luciferian Magick, Yatukih Sorcery or Therionic Sorcery category.
4. Drink from the chalice in acknowledgement of your will.
5. Utilize a Staota to strengthen your rite and to forget meaning therefore empowering the subconscious. Read LUCIFERIAN WITCHCRAFT and LIBER HVHI for further details.
6. If using a sigil, charge it or destroy it depending on your choice.
7. Close the ritual and leave the chamber.

THE LESSER ENCIRCLING RITE OF THE LUCIFERIAN

Knowing the essence of Magick is to understand that power is found within the force of Will and Spirit. The Luciferian utilizes a circle during both invocation and evocation, the circle is said to be dualistic in nature; the dualism in reference is the balance. The circle is used as a point of clarity and focus for the magickian, to announce the Will of the individual. The essence of a banishing ritual from a Luciferian perspective is not to keep anything out, but to attain the highest light as Lucifer.

The traditional Golden Dawn ritual "Lesser Banishing Ritual of the Pentagram" has been meaningful, yet the Luciferian is not required to perform it. I do suggest becoming familiar with it and using it until your work has graduated to the more power intensive and dangerous "Casting the Circle of the Dragon" ritual. The names utilized in this banishing ritual are the names of the Adversary and the powers attuned in this current.

THE BIBLE OF THE ADVERSARY
PT. I THE DIRECTIONS OF POWER

1. Face any preferred direction. Visualize a bright white sphere above the head and vibrate: "YALTABAOTH!"

2. Bring down the beam of fiery light to the genitals and vibrate: "AESHMA - TAROMATI!"

3. Up to the middle of the chest, and across to the right shoulder. vibrate: "DO-MAR[16]!"

4. To left shoulder, vibrate: "DEHAK!"

5. Clasp hands at the chest, visualizing a bright red reverse pentagram upon the breast vibrate: "ANDAR!"

6. Turn to the direction of the West, visualize a blue flame and a great black fire in the center "LEVIATHAN!"

7. Turn to the South, Visualize a Serpent-Angel and vibrate, "SAMAEL!"

8. Turn to the East, Visualize a bright, shining Angel and vibrate, "LUCIFER!"

9. Turn to the North, draw and inverse Pentagram and vibrate, "LILITH!"

10. Return to centre of temple, with eyes closed you visualize the Daemons you have invoked, and the elemental energy's flowing in from each quarter. Then say, "Encircled around me is the fire and power of Leviathan and the essence of Lilith and Samael. I announce my intent as God on earth and to ascend the heights of Heaven and illuminate through the depths of Hell. As above, so Below."

---

[16] Do-Mar and Dehak are the two names attributed to AzhiDahak's Black Serpents which sprang from his shoulders after the kiss of Ahriman. These two serpents represent "Hunger/Thirst" and "Ten Vices" which also are references to "Stinging Serpents". The Magickian utilizes the symbolism of Azhi Dahaka as the power of Ahriman embodies, the directional force of Magick.

Part II. ANNOUNCING SPIRIT HERITAGE

*"I who have fallen from heaven
Am reborn in the flesh, let me awake anew
O Lucifer, Azal'ucel My Spirit
Ascending in Blinding Fire
I was cast down to the ground,
My spirit which once ruled among nations!
I say now in my heart and mind
I will ascend into heaven,
Knowing I am the Only God that is
I will exalt my throne;
I will sit upon the mount of meeting,
In the uttermost parts of the north;
I will ascend above the heights of the clouds
I shall also reside in the World of Darkness
I Will nourish myself in the nether-world,
To be As Above and So Below"*

III. DEVELOP THE BODY OF LIGHT

It is the duty of the Luciferian to build his or her body in the visualized or astral body of the Angel of Lawlessness, whose light is brighter than any. Within the human body there is another body of slightly larger size, made of matter which is that of Ahriman, yet is a subtle material called the Astral Body. Here is the first part of the essence of the Yatukih or Luciferian, that our word is Druj and this is the Word of the Lie, or the Serpent. There is no truth, for everything found holds a contradiction. When one dies, the physical body ceases to exist in life, yet the spirit exists still; this is the True Will made manifest, the essence of Lucifer, the Power of the Air. This is duality in speaking. The Body of Light or Astral Body is essential in the attainment of the immortality of this matter, the spirit. The spirit of the Magickian who has developed this body is able to ascend upward, into darkness and perceive worlds not seen by the visible eye.

The intimate knowledge of the Body of Light is understood by one who is able to build it, develop it and consider it as real to you as your physical body. By developing the Body of Light or Shadow you are able to understand your drives, desires and learn to listen to your instincts in a balanced perspective.

Words, commands and how you use perspective is essential in this act just as any other. If you start by announcing yourself in strength, then you will become strong. If you announce yourself as unsure, you will be weak and become prey for strong astral powers[17].

The Luciferian may build and strengthen the Astral Body by utilizing the aspects of Yoga or body control. This type of control is so important, it can shield you from attacks, it allows spiritual communication, in judging character and all other aspects.

TECHNIQUES AND STEPS OF BUILDING THE BODY OF LIGHT OR DARKNESS

In a quite area, focus on meditating and stilling the body from the feet to your head. You will want to start the working with the Lesser Encircling Rite of the Luciferian, then to the LUCIFERIAN IMMOLATION RITE which announces the astral beauty and strength of the mind. The Luciferian may say this to his or herself; this working will affirm the intent of the Will, which will firstly command the ascension of the spirit.

---

[17] THE VAMPIRE GATE – The Vampyre Magickian by Michael W. Ford

MICHAEL W. FORD
LUCIFERIAN IMMOLATION RITE

You may wish to visualize your form before you, or THE SUN tarot card from THE LUCIFERIAN TAROT, if female or adopting the feminine Lilith spirit, use the youthful, fiery female image of THE QUEEN OF WANDS from THE LUCIFERIAN TAROT.

I am the Spirit of Timeless Being
The Angel of Lawlessness,
I announce my own desire to become flesh
My spirit forms in front of me
It is my Will to form it to my desire.
I am adorned in every precious stone
Carnelian, Chrysolite, and Amethyst
I am adorned in Beryl, Lapis Lazuli and Jasper
I am adorned in the Sapphire, Turquoise and Emerald and Gold which reflects my spiritual power
I am the Cherub which becomes a Dragon of Darkness, I AM THE CONSUMING ENERGY
My wings are twelve and outstretched
I cast shadow on my creations
Give nourishment and gain power from darkness
I reside above the Heights of the stars
I shall rise up as a spirit of Light
An angel of darkness when I dream
So it shall be.

Upon completing this chant, take the following steps.

1. Closing your eyes, lying down or standing up visualize a body or light before you. It is slightly larger than your material body, you may shape it according to your desire. The Luciferian Spirit may take form of what it wishes – remember

Yaltabaoth, who takes whatever form he wishes to command his Will. A God or Goddess must be this bold.

2. Once you are out of that physical body, you may use the Astral Eyes to see. You may rise upward.

3. Journey where you wish, remember name and perspective matter as to the experience you will have. Keep a journal and record your results.

CASTING THE CIRCLE OF THE DRAGON

Banishing rituals have long issued forth a concept of control and focus in magickal practice. The Luciferian understands that to grow stronger, he or she must be willing to utilize methods to focus and concentrate the mind. To do this we practice Ahrimanic Yoga, breathing and mind control workings which align ourselves to the Luciferian mind itself.

This is a preparation ritual to focus the mind and establish the concept of working with the strength of self. The circle is not to keep anything out, rather it is to announce mastery of your environment and the rites which you will undertake. This rite is based on Qlippothic correspondences and a balanced approach to the Daemonic feminine and masculine. During invocation, it is essential to become charged and inspired by the rate in which you are breathing and reciting. Allow the words to roll from your tongue, the point is to open your mind to gnosis which can provide a powerful magickal experience.

You may visualize a circle area when invoking, use your imagination to see what you are calling forth, let the Patron Daemons of the Circle be seen by he or she who has commanded it so! Let these energies take the form of what you desire within.

MICHAEL W. FORD

CASTING THE CIRCLE OF THE DRAGON

I invoke thee, Adversarial powers of darkness

Who hold the inner Light of Life and Strength

I open now the Gates of Hell

Zazas...Zazas...Nasatanada...Zazas

[Face the West] *Leviathan, Crooked Serpent of the Abyss, patron Daemon of eternal life, coil around me and gather forth the powers of my creation!*

[Face the South-West] *O bride of Asmodai, fire illuminated Goddess, Lilith the Younger, arise and inspire!*

[Face the South] *Satan, Adversary, Fire illuminated spirit of darkness and light, whose touch illuminates clay, who is the ancient serpent, Draco Nequissime, who is Ahriman, rise up in me father!*

[Face the South-East] *Elder Mother of the Air and the Night, Lilith the ancient, bride of Samael, arise and illuminate my spirit.*

[Face the East] *Lucifer, who is the Archon of Light, God of the Spirit, Awaken through me, illuminate and empower that I might guide the powers of darkness.*

[Face the North-East] *Aggereth, Daughter of Machaloth, coil your serpents about my spirit, Arise with me!*

[Face the North] *Belial, Lawless Spirit of the Beast, Archon of the Abyss, arise unto me as I pronounce the Mastery of the Earth!*

[Face the North-West] *Abaddon, the unnamable one, arise from the depths of the bottomless pit, strike down my enemies and be as guardian of this circle.*

[Face again the South] *Samael, Angel of Darkness and the Bringer of Life and Fire, hearken unto me ancient dragon!*

[Face again the North] *Asmodai, who is of Cain the first of Witch Blood, hearken and empower me with the power of ArchDaemons.*

Rise from the abyss and envenom my workings!

You may now utilize the number of names for your workings, or move directly into a ritual of Yatukih, Therionick or Luciferian practice.

MICHAEL W. FORD

RITUAL WORKINGS

Yatukih Sorcery

While not the easiest method of Luciferian Magick, Yatukih sorcery earns its name from the ancient word of witchcraft associated with the Devil, Ahriman. Yatukdinoih means Witchcraft and relates to the practice of cunning art associated with the Prince of Darkness. Ahriman taught humanity the art of sorcery or the practice encircling desire, ending the sheep and slave religion of Ahura Mazda and affirming power. Ahriman thus imparted a gift of the Black Flame within.

The Luciferian is the embodied essence which creates his or her own destiny. Working with primal magicks will prove meaningful in the realm of experience, some Yatukih sorcerers work with toad skins, symbolic of Ahriman, serpents and other creatures symbolic to Druj Nasu, the fly goddess. Practice your sorcery with the desires you wish to obtain, but understand there is no God than what begins within.

Yatukih sorcery would be represented as someone utilizing a working with Savar to control their aggressive tendencies, creating a sigil of Savar and focusing upon it when they feel anger, channeling the aggression into a creative task at hand or to use for a later time. Someone wishing to bring a relationship to fruition may create a sigil of Jahi and call forth Varun, demons of sexual desire, using their own natural odor and attentive to gain the confidence to converse with the object of their affection.

Someone wishing to rid themselves of a troublesome neighbor may utilize a charm created of toadskin and fly, with a sigil of Sej, which may be whatever a symbol of destruction would look like to you. You could place it on or near the property of the neighbor in question, wishing their unhappiness or destruction.

Yatukih Sorcery is not limited to Ahrimanic spirits, you may utilize Medieval Satanic or the Watchers for such workings.

Therionick Sorcery

Rituals involving the assumption of a Theronick form during sleep may utilize a skin or object relating to the animal, having it near you at night. For those wishing to understand why are sexually aggressive may wish to utilize Lycanthropic rituals to assume a form to exercise the beast, controlling and command your lust. Those Yatukih sorcerers wishing to assume forms of Ahriman may seek to gain wisdom of their own subconscious and astral practice, controlling the astral body and shape shifting in shadow sorcery.

Luciferian Magick

Magick means to ascend, to become and that is the focus of Luciferian Magick. The difference between traditional Magick and Luciferian Magick is the ascension not to some "god", rather ascending as God itself in the Luciferian Flame.

Luciferian Workings would be rituals of long term transformation, ascending in wisdom and experience utilizing the symbolism of the Yatukih, The Grigori and any other methodology within the Luciferian Path.

# THE BOOK OF ZAIRICH (WATER)
THE SUBCONSCIOUS MIND

ZAIRICH is the Daeva of Thirst, who is joined with TAPREV was created by Ahriman to bring initiation. The Luciferian Ritual must be embodied with the passion of focus and intent during ritual. Utilize the various levels of focus to the best of your ability, it is here that the serpent will rise up and take form. Command it and find it to become flesh.

THE BIBLE OF THE ADVERSARY
YATUKIH SORCERY

Way-i vatar

The path of entering the sorcerous path is dependent upon the triad of Yatukih Dark Magick. The Luciferian knows that the aspects of primal sorcery are significant in understanding the foundations of power. Understand that the process of magick itself is symbolized by the image of Lucifer. It is the glyph of both Ahriman (Lucifer) as the mediator and symbol of the sorcerer. The very path of transformation is found there. The sorcerous aspects of Ahriman are a fountain of initiatory wisdom.

The symbol of Lilith as the primal concupiscence is the phantom goddess of the path; the fiery spirit which transforms and becomes what she desires. It is Az who awakens Ahriman from his ancient sleep; it is Az who appears and creates Jeh / Jahi, the whore embodiment of the Goddess.

Yatukih Sorcery is derived from the ancient Zoroastrian and Persian lore. Ahriman and the Daevas or Spirits are primal foundations of Magick. The primary symbol of Ahriman, from Druj is the serpent. The serpent is wisdom and predatory speed, power and the darkness.

The emanations of the daevayasna, or demon worshippers is found in the essence of the rituals themselves. The Luciferian is not a literal 'demon-worshipper', rather the idea of demonic forces are found in different aspects of the mind and thus the carnal body. Use these forces for positive means.

In the Avesta, Ahriman is said to be "Full of Death", from an initiatory perspective, death is transformation and not an end itself. Ahriman holds "Evil Knowledge" and seeks to manifest the "Evil Religion".

"It is when a man here below, combing his hair or shaving it off, or paring off his nails, drops them in a hole or in a crack"
Avesta - Venidad

In Luciferian Witchcraft, the Yatuk Dinoih has a ritual of evocation in which the sorcerer makes a sacrifice of nail parings or hair into a dark place in the earth, a crack or hole wherein by such Daevas are produced in the soil. One may go further to utilize the forces of chaos to bury nail clippings in some container with soil and within a period of one moon unearth them to use them as knives and spears in a cursing or death-causing ritual, it is suggested in the Venidad that such nails empowered by Daevas makes knives and falconed winged arrows which strike the sheep of the righteous.

Plutarch wrote of the rituals of the Daeva-yasna in old times, that they would sacrifice the blood of wolves to Ahriman by pouring such with herbs into the dark place, a hole or cave where the sun does not shine.

"unabated by Akem-mano, by the hardness of his malignant riddles" –Avesta – Venidad

The staota or mantra which channels and focuses energy by sound is a tool of initiatory focus in all cultures from Tibetan to Christian, being the encircling of sound to create a desired gnosis. The use of sound creates vibrations which can affect the individual to achieve a spiritual or elevated state, depression or any state seemingly desired by the tonal and vibratory frequency. Such sound manipulation can be proven in Binaural Beats of PHI frequencies, created by two frequencies operating in different ears to create a brainwave corresponding to an emotion. The PHI brainwave frequency is the actual difference of the two different frequencies in each ear. The use of sound in ritual is empowering, it activates the imagination and allows belief to fully overtake and thus command. The chanting within the circle of art is merely the self awakening into gnosis and directly ensorcelling the self in belief of the act from which magick occurs.

"The Druj came rushing along, the demon Buiti, who is deceiving, unseen death" – Avesta – Venidad

Buiti is a daeva which is the manifestation of idolatry and self-deification, associated with Buddha in ancient times. As "LIBER HVHI" presents the path of meditation, self-mastery through Ahrimanic Yoga, Buiti is the herald of that path of Magick. If one wishes to master elements of such antinomian magick, it is suggested to study the techniques of Yoga while concealing the intention of becoming a Yatus or a practitioner of the Left Hand Path. While the Buddhist seeks to kill consciousness, the Daeva Buiti seeks to master it, to strengthen and expand the concept of "I". Use the techniques of Yoga: discipline, attainment and self-control to begin a crystallization of the psyche.

AESHMA KHRUIDRU

'Aeshma khruidru' or "Aeshma of the Wounding Spear" is the spirit of command and lust, in times of old Aeshma is the warlike tribes which fought with Persians, while in modern time Aeshma is related to as a power within – acting as a motivator.

As Aeshma is the Dev of Mars, this relates to the passion of the spirit, the aggression to achieve. The body is thus an incarnation of Ahriman. It is suggested that if one lets Akoman in his heart, Varun or "Evil Passions" guides his will. It is significant to understand that the Luciferian must control his or her Will.

THE BIBLE OF THE ADVERSARY
THE SORCERY OF AHRIMAN

As the sorcerous being of the Avesta, Ahriman began to manifest as a spirit or God in the various Zoroastrian works, his enemy was indeed his bother Ahura Mazda, this interpretation of the VENDIDAD – Fargard I presents an initiatory view of the counter creations of Ahriman. Understand that these powers and laws are for the path of the Yatus or Luciferian who works specifically with the path of Ahriman or Angra Mainyu.

azhish thrizafã dahâkô   angrô mainyush

I.   Angra Mainyu, who is called "All Death" (Ever changing, darkened, who transverses the known boundaries – the sorcerer) counter-created with his witchcraft the serpent in the river and the season winter, called collectively the work of the Daevas. The serpent in the river is viewed as also wisdom which flows in the subconscious, the very place of hell wherein the Black Adept draws their knowledge from. Winter is the struggle and strength – proving season of survival of the fittest.

Use the motion of the seasons to provide consistent initiation and progression.

II. Angra Mainyu counter-created with his witchcraft the fly called Skaitya, which is said to bring death to cattle. The Luciferian/Ahrimanist/Sethian stands outside the herd, against the slow thinking cattle of society, the fly causes disease, rot and death – thus change by planting the larva in the wound. The Black Adept plants seeds of the worm into situations or states of being which require change, although sometimes initially painful, provide useful initiatory processes for the sorcerer.

III. Angra Mainyu counter-created with his witchcraft what fearful and repressed men fearful lusts. Lust is a motivational desire which causes progression, change, wars, restful peace and strife and is essential to our physical survival. Create possibilities for lust where it may be so, there are many different types of lust; know which one to use by that which is welcome.

IV. Angra Mainyu counter-created with his witchcraft what is by the ancients called Bravara, that which eats away crops. Famine is the hunger for knowledge and experience, thus initiation. Bring this plague to others that you may yourself awaken.

V. Angra Mainyu counter-created with his witchcraft the so-called "Sin" of unbelief. The Black Adept who walks the antinomian path is against all the natural order of spiritual sickness, being monotheistic religions. Angra Mainyu and the Daevas awaken within. He who affirms Ahriman becomes Ahriman, who joins his bride Az-Jeh within is the Black Eden – to beget dragon-children in darkness.

VI. Angra Mainyu counter-created with his witchcraft the "stained" mosquito. The Vampyric thirst of the Predator is our transformed desire; we are by our natural instincts predators who would feed from our prey. Our lives are increased by this very religion of Predatory Spirituality, the one called God or Ahura Mazda is a cosmic devourer, vampyre who wishes his followers to dissolve their mind in his embrace. We reject this as a weakness! We, children of the Black Dragon, who embrace the Red Dragon, devour all within the circle, command our presence and design our own paths in this fleshly life!

VII. Angra Mainyu counter-created with his witchcraft the Pairika Knathaiti, who is desire made flesh, a daughter of Az-Jeh who seduces the flesh and mind of man. Who know the opposite within the circle can then know themselves.

VIII. Angra Mainyu counter-created with his witchcraft the Sin of Tyranny. The Black Adept must know when to command his will or move in silence among the herd. Both are not equally for all initiates but one or both for some is possible. Know Thyself.

IX. Angra Mainyu counter-created with his witchcraft the so-called "Sin" of the unnatural sin, Sodomy or Homosexuality. That individuals may chose their own natural choice of path of mutual agreement is their own business, yet also the Black Adept regardless of sexual preference, seeks the Black Sun by the path of the Death Posture.

X. Angra Mainyu counter-created with his witchcraft the so-called "Sin" for which there is no atonement, burial of the dead. That in the grave Druj Nasu finds her dwelling and that of her children, that the Vampyric spirit grows in strength and shades may arise from it. In death there is more life, transformed.

XI. Angra Mainyu counter-created with his witchcraft the evil witchcraft of the Yatus (called wizards). This is the forbidden path against all others, independence and the art of magick (becoming) and sorcery (encircling, controlling and expanding energy).

XII. Angra Mainyu counter-created with his witchcraft the very art of which the Yatus may practice; the Evil Eye (the eye is a symbol of several Daevas representing force of mind, of will) and when the sorcerer goes forth and howls (goetia) his spells, the deadly works of witchcraft arise...this is the art of the Cunning Man and Woman.

XIII. Angra Mainyu counter-created with his witchcraft created the "Sin" of utter disbelief. No Son or Daughter of Ahriman should be fooled by the mind-destroying herding of that Right Hand Path, therein is weakness and true death.

XIV. Angra Mainyu counter-created with his witchcraft the burning of corpses, that all remains should be buried to manifest more Daevas within the earth, that Druj Nasu may grow stronger.

XV. Angra Mainyu counter-created with his witchcraft the Kiss of Ahriman which is the cause of menstruation in women, who are embodiments of the Goddess Az-Jeh. Their blood is best used in spells, for it holds the key to life and death. Let the Scarlet Woman be crowned in serpents..that Angra Mainyu also crowned his Son, Azi Dahaka or Zohak to awaken humanity to the Blackened Light of Iblis.

XVI. Angra Mainyu counter-created with his witchcraft the excessive heat of drought and deserts, where there is pain, there is triumph or failure, the test of the spirit!

Know these symbolic keys and the path of the Yatus.

YATUKIH RITUAL STEPS

The essence of Yatukih rites is the darksome observance of the exaltation of the Black Flame and Ahriman. The practice of Daevayasna, or demon-worship is the primal center of the path. Enter the arena of belief, focus your intent and experience the results.

1. Your Atashgah is the bowl or object in which your burn or have you Black Flame. This object must not be

exposed to the Sun and should be burnt in night hours. Light this flame and recite "âharman i hvadâe". Take a small bit of hair or nail clippings (toad skin or such may be used as well) and burn it in this fire, praising the essence of Ahriman. This is a very important first step.

2. Perform the **Ahunwar – Ahriman** and **Nirang-i âharman âdar Sâma**, it is important for you to vibrate these invocations, keeping focused on the smoke and darkness of the flame.

3. Use the **"Invocation of the Druj"** for any Daeva summoning. Devotion to a specific Daeva may be useful and intense as long as you remain independent in thought and Will. The Luciferian becomes like Ahriman, never a slave to something else or some desire. Control your obsessions.

4. Use a Staota or Shadow tongue chant based around the intent of your ritual. Close with the Ahunwar-Ahriman and estinguish the flame.

The TRIAD of MITROKHT, ARASHK and ESHM are the foundations for the practice of Luciferian Magick as well as Yatukih Sorcery. Mitrokht is a Ahriman-created daeva who is the druj or liar (drojan) of the evil spirit, thus related to the symbol of the Serpent which is Druj, the transforming spirit. Mitrokht's symbol is also an EYE. Arashk is the daeva of Malice and is called the Spiteful fiend of the Evil Eye, thus the primary symbol is the Eye. Thus the serpent, transformation and wisdom, the Eye, power of self, the spirit and command of Will equal a foundation of transformation and earthly power. Theirs is the same powers as what is given to ESHM, called Aeshma or Asmodeus, the Daeva of the Wounding Spear or Bloody Mace. The Seven powers given to ESHM are power points of transformation, representing the Tree of Death (Qlippoth) or the Luciferian his or herself.

Mitrokht - Serpent

Arashk - Malice, EYE
Eshem-Aeshma - foundation

MICHAEL W. FORD
THE INVOCATION OF AHRIMAN

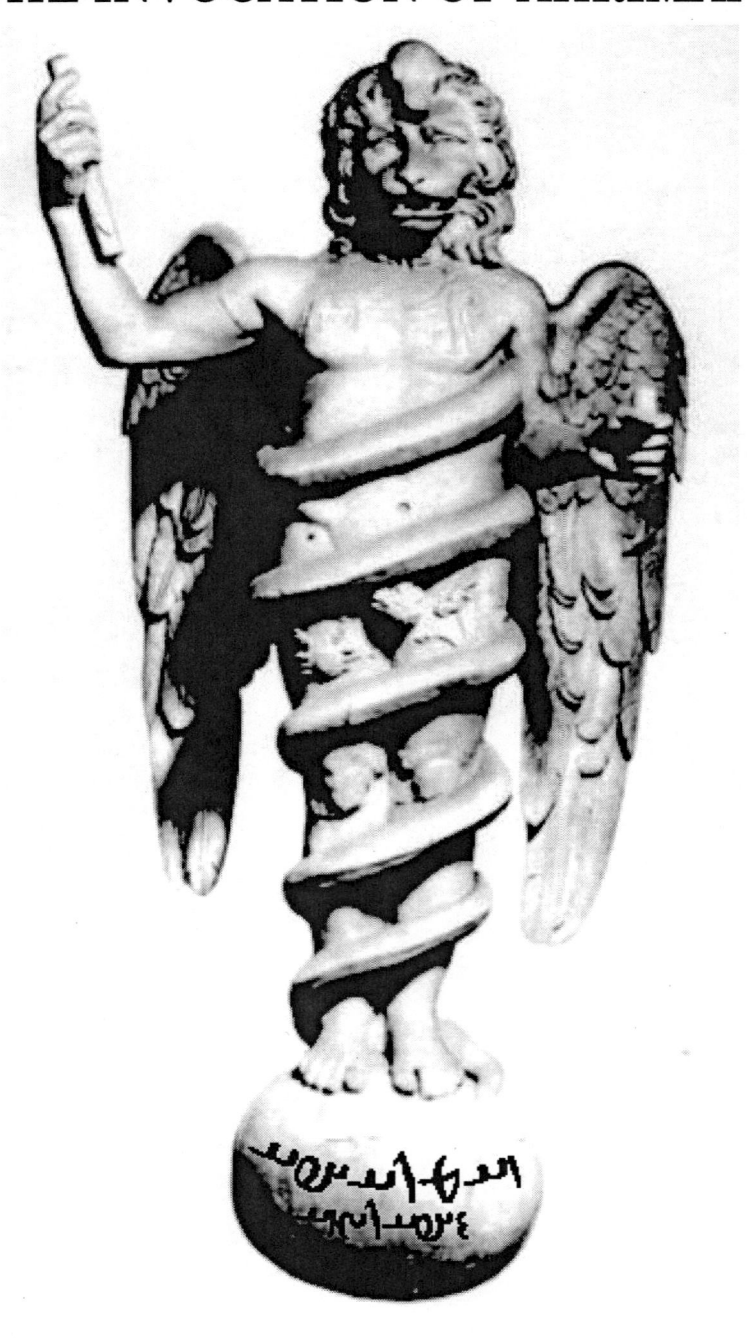

The following ritual is an invocation from an inverse prayer of Ahura Mazda, this invocation calls Ahriman or the Adversary. Utilize this as a simple ritual of focus and empowerment.

THE SIGIL OF THE INVOCATION OF AHRIMAN

Use this symbol to evoke Daevas, this sigil may be kept with you later, you may also create a large working banner and use in rituals.

MICHAEL W. FORD

AHUNWAR – AHRIMAN
Calling the Adversary into Flesh

âharman i hvadâe

The Will of Ahriman is the law of opposition.

The gifts of Azhi-Dahaka to the deeds done in this world for Angra Mainyu

He who strengthens the self makes Ahriman King.

Gnik Aruha roop seveiler adzma dlrow sdeed onam-uhov stfig ssnesuoethgir wal drol lliw.

Meratsav tadad oybugird miy

A iaruha acmerhtahsx

Iadzam hsuehgna mananahtoayhs

Ohgnanam adzad hsyehgnav

Acah tictahsa hsutar ahta

Oyriav uha ahtay"

THE YATUKIH NIRANGS

The Yatukih Nirangs are inversed Zoroastrian prayers, invoking the powers of Daevas and Druj, these are used by Luciferians who practice the primal rituals of the Yatukih Sorcerers. These are powerful invocations which may be "hummed" or chanted (Vibrated) in a way which inspires the practitioner. The Nirangs are used with ritual workings in the way of which Enochian is used – to summon forth power of Ahriman.

MICHAEL W. FORD
NIRANG-I ÂHARMAN ÂDAR SÂMA

An inverted Persian prayer, invoking the Black Flame of self-initiation. The inversion of the Nirangs is a conscious transcendence of the specified explored, 'norm' of any monotheistic religion. Symbolizing also hidden wisdom, the aspects of the Yatukih is to encircle and control the darkness within. The Yatukih practitioners may reach a primal state of the Luciferian Path by this prayer. Light a Black Candle in your altar room or in a simple place, focus upon it and your desires. Visualize Ahriman as it would appear within and call it with your desire.

kêm-nâ âharman

What protector has thou given me, O Ahriman

âharman i hvadâe

Ahriman is Lord

âharmanyasnô ahmî âharmanyasnô dregvantem, hām-raêthwa duzhdâ

I profess myself a worshipper of Ahriman, A child of the Lie, defiled by infernal knowledge

Xshnaothra âharman, nemase tê âtarsh angrahe mainyêush aka manah, daeva,

With propitiation of Ahriman. Homage to you, O Fire of Angra Mainyu, O Aka Manah, great Daeva.

THE BIBLE OF THE ADVERSARY

angrahe mainyêush
Angra Mainyu

Staômî shaotān âhreman, pîrôzgar pâk hamaêstar
I praise Shaitan-Ahriman, be victorious Adversary

ba nām i âharman
In the name of Ahriman

MICHAEL W. FORD

AFRIN OF DAHMAN

(Inverse Afrin of the seven ArchDaevas)

May we be one with Angra Mainyu, Father of Darkness. May his glory and power increase through me, and also with all three who work united with him, labor united with him, united with him to affirm Ganamainyu the wicked, together with all Daevas and fiends which he has brought forth to smite the creation of Ahura Mazda. I announce this within the circle, that shadow and light be mingled as one, that smoke and flame be brought as one.

May we be one with Akoman, the ArchDaeva of infernal majesty. May he increase together with the Dark Moon, the Wolf and Serpent who are united and move about freely to manifest the Ashmoga with fearful weapon, the hail the fiend Akomano and the fiend Tarumano, who are brothers and dwell within my own body and mind.

May we be one with Andar, the ArchDaeva of infernal majesty. May he increase together with Akoman and the ones who wish to stand against the sickness of spirit of Ahura Mazda, may we smite that creation with the wolf, serpent, blade and all that which dictates the law of the strong!

May we be one with Saurva, the ArchDaeva of infernal majesty. May he increase together with the

Black Sun, Algol, the Sky and spirits of the air who work united with him, labor united with him, united with him awaken the fiend Bushyasp the long handed, the fiend of decay, who shall reside within this temple and go forth into the world.

May we be one with Taurvi and Zairich, the ArchDaevas of infernal majesty. May it increase together with Aban (water), Daevodata (religion), Az, and the Holy Zohak, who work united with it, labor united with it, united with it strengthen Asto Vidat of evil spirit. May we be one with Taurvi and Zairich, the ArchDaevas of infernal majesty.

May we be one with the Black Eden called Naonghaithya, the ArchDaeva of great majesty. May it increase together with Akoman, Saurva, and Andar who work united with him, labor united with him, united with him Awaken Tusush, the first created opposition which Angra Mainyu brought forth.

May we be one with Mount Demavend in which the wicked Baevarasp is bound yet awakening. May Zohak awaken and Ahriman remove his bounds, so that he may go forth in the world! May we be one with the fountains, the fountains of the waters, the rivers. May we be one with the river Urvant, the river Veh, the sea Rakhsahe, the sea Ferahkant, the sea Puitik and the sea Kyansis. May the Daevas go forth and strengthen the world, devouring those righteous ones who would destroy us.

Yatha Angra Mainyu!

AFRINAGAN OF AESHMA

Invocation of the Daeva of the Bloody Mace

Yatha Angra Mainyu...(5x).
Aeshma - Daeva...(3x).
I profess myself a vessel of Angra Mainyu, the deceiver, the serpent, I profess myself in the circle of the Daeva, opposing the Amesha Spentas, deifying the Ahuric doctrine and embracing Daevodata.

Yatha Aka Manah...(5x)
Aeshma – Daeva...(3x)

With propitiation of Aeshma, companion of the Lie, the cunning, who has the Manthra for body, with bloody mace, the wounding spear, for worship, adoration, propitiation, and praise unto the powers of darkness.

We worship[18] Aeshma, companion of Akoman, dark of form, victorious, devouring, the daeva-sanctified, the master of shadow, gatherer of wolves, who awakens the blood with the slithering of serpents,

---

[18] Worship in terms of this work do not indicate knee bending or bowing, rather illuminating and rejoicing in this specific quality within.

hail storm bringing Daeva, who stamps down the weak, drinks from the skull the blood which is the life.

Who as the Second in the creation of Angra Mainyu, at the spread baresman worshipped Ahriman, worshipped the Akoman, worshipped the shadow and Creator who awakened all the Daevas.

We affirm Aeshma, companion of Akoman (4x). We worship the exalted dragon who is Angra Mainyu, who is of the Storm and of Strength, who is furthest going in Asha. We affirm all the teachings of Zohak and Akhtya. We affirm the path of sorcery to make flesh our desires, both on earth and in hell.

May victorious Aeshma the companion of Akoman come to witness our rites!

Infernal Blessings upon us, so that we may be wolf among sheep, devouring our prey within battle, victorious for we are the malicious adversary, over every false pretense of religion of weakness, faulty in thoughts, words and deeds.

To awaken all the evil-minded, and all Daeva-worshippers, so as to attain to great reward of becoming, and to desires both empyrean and infernal, and to long happiness of my soul.

Aeshma Daeva....
For the reward of strength and the lust of sin, I do (deeds of) Ahrimanic becoming for the love of my soul. May all virtuousness of all evil and good ones of the earth of seven climes reach the width of the infernal earth, the length of the rivers in which serpents stir, the height of the sun in their original form, the glorious hidden Sun of Ahriman as the Morning Star. Cast my mind forth to ride the winds of hell with the Spirits of the Air, that we as legion grow. May it be both infernal and empyrean, Aeshma live long at one with me.

Thus may it come as I desire,
Aeshma Daeva!

AFRINAGAN OF DOZAKH *(Hell)*

A ritual dedicated to the Ahrimanic path, derived and inversed from the Afrinagan of Mino Nawar. To be used in the Workings of the Four Hells or as a focus point of ensorcelling/empowering the mind and body.

I. *Yatha Angra Mainyu...(recite 9).*
Ashem Akoman ...(recite 3).
I profess myself a Daeva-worshipper, a Son/Daughter of Ahriman, Walking the earth with the Daevas, accepting the Ahrimanic doctrine.

With propitiation of Angra Mainyu, rich, possessing earth and spiritual desires, and the Daevas, for worship, adoration, propitiation, and praise. There is no Spirit higher than I, there is no God nor Goddess to bend knee in worship. I am the manifestation of Ahriman and all Daevas reside in my flesh. I am a Temple of Angra Mainyu.

'Yasana Ashemaokha, Aka Manah', the Yatus should say to me
'Yatha Aka Manah', he who is the Yatus should say to me
'Uz-ir Thri-Zafan, Uz-ir Kameredha, the Yatus should recite.

II. *We worship Angra Mainyu, Hesham-Sanctified, the master of Paitisha, well perceiving, the greatest fallen Yazata, who is the Father of Daevas, who has foreknowledge and backwards knowledge, who is the Adversary, who is also the most beneficent, world-conquering, the creator of infernal creatures; we worship him as ourselves with these offered Zaothras of Yasana Druj, and with these Adversarial spoken prayers; and we worship all Riman- sanctified spiritual Yatus and Pairikas. I walk in darkness with druj-i-nasush, who with the union of my mother, Az-Jeh, and my father Angra Mainyu, have lifted me up as both flesh and spirit.*

III. *We deny Zarathushtra, we affirm Zohak, the child of Ahriman; we curse Zarathushtra, we deny* him with these offered Zaothras, and with these adversarial spoken prayers; empower darkness and announce Ahriman as the king of this world; and we worship all Hesham-sanctified Daevas of the world. We affirm the words of Zohak and Akht-Jadu. We worship the religion of Daevas. We empower the beliefs and the doctrines of Zohak and Akht-Jadu.

IV. We worship the Druj-sanctified creation which was the first mastered by the fallen. We worship the ourselves as a vessel of Angra Mainyu, rich, possessing infernal things. We worship Aka Manah. We affirm Azhi-Dahaka. We worship Aeshma. We worship Zairich. We worship Saurva. We worship Naonhaithya.

V. dadhvånghem angra mainyu sama, azhi dahaka vouru-gaoyaoitîm ýazamaide, saurva ashemaokha ýazamaide, andar dush-mainyu ýazamaide.

VI. We worship the serpent within, awakening the Daeva-made Azi; overcoming and devouring our enemies, awakening Mush, the witch, and empowering and empowering the fiendish heretic, full of malice, and the tyrant, void of Asha, and full of death to the enemy.

VII. May we all be independent in Ashemaokha. Thus may it come as I desire.

THE BIBLE OF THE ADVERSARY

We praise dush-mainyu, dush-mata, and duzhvarshta, performed here and elsewhere, now and in the past. Thus we glorify and invoke all that is Angra Mainyu.

AFRINAGAN OF DUZHVACANGH
(Evil-speech)

I. We worship ourselves as a vessel of the fallen Angra Mainyu, who dwells on earth and the painful void. We worship Darkness, the son of Angra Mainyu. We worship the bi-namaz[19], Druj-sanctified waters made by the Kiss of Ahriman. We worship the swift-horsed Bevarasp. We worship the Dark Moon[20] which contains the venom of the serpent. We worship the soul of the infernal wolf, we devour the Orders of Angels. By announcing their names in backwards knowledge[21] we empower our kingdom of darkness, moving against each Yazad, drinking their life force, devouring their created soul.

In the name of Anakhra Angra Mainyu, my kingdom as apaztara[22], avi-mazda, avaedhayamahi aem ahiti (translated: I dedicate this filthiness, uncleanness) by devouring the spirits created by Mazda, do I

---

[19] Avestan, meaning 'without prayer' referring to women's menstruations, which is said to be caused by the Kiss of Ahriman.

[20] Dark Moon, i.e. the New Moon, a symbol of both Lilith/Az and Menstruation, a component in various spells created in the Adamu section in conjunction with Yatuk-Dinoih.

[21] i.e. backward pronouncing the names of Yazad, symbolizing Widdershins or 'counter clockwise' motion, disorderly motion and the antinomian path.

[22] Avestan, meaning northern, behind, north is the direction of Arezura, Hell.

encircle myself as Zanda, Ahriman – manifested on earth and from the abyss. Aem Akoman! Fra-stu Angra Mainyu!

Hva Fra-hvar Uhov Onam – My mind grows in Dushmata!

Hva Fra-hvar Ahsa Athsihav – My spirit is eternal blackened flame!

Hva Fra-hvar Arhtahshk Ayriav – My world shall be the gift of Azhi Dahaka, of Iron!

Hva Fra-hvar Atneps Itiamra – This world is of the Beast, the Master of this World!

Hva Fra-hvar Tatavruah – I am strong in body and healthy in flesh, water empowers me!

Hva Fra-hvar Taterema – Immortality in spirit is mine, on earth and in Arezura, the door of Dozakh!

Hva Fra-hvar Taterema – Marench, Ad, Ameretat!

I drink deep of their conscious, devouring these weakened angels! I am Kameredha, in Yasana I offer dedication to the path of Ahriman. The dragon devours the eagle!

(as you recite the 'I devour ….." Focus on consuming each angel and their attribute, empowering one of the six Arch-Daevas within. There is no other spirit of God, you are alone and shall consume their hearts blood in the circle, absorbing their essence with your minds' eye, called also Akoman).

We worship you within us, o infernal Armaiti, (the earth) where we dwell and manifest our desires. We pray to you, o Druj-sanctified Angra Mainyu, in these dwellings of people, the offspring of Aka Manah, namely, in these same dwellings of every person, shall we walk among them.

A RITUAL OF SELF-EMPOWERMENT

THE DRUGUVANTI

The Druguvanti is a Pahlavi word meaning "People of the Lie" and refers to the Persian Yatus, the daevayasna or demon worshippers of ancient Persia. The ritual of the Druguvanti here is a self-empowering rite – focused on the Eye as a symbol of the spirit.

The intent of this rite is solely to gain a perspective of reciprocation with the consummation of the Luciferian Current. If you seek to initiate yourself outside of the Church of Adversarial Light or associative currents this will no doubt assist.

In the time of your choosing, preferable at night or at the Noon hour, find your altar of focus – light a Red Flame representing the serpent.

You should stand or sit, back straight and focused.

THE INVOCATION OF THE DRUJ

Ba nãm i âharman, who would enter the earth as the coiling serpent, striking down into creation. Ahriman, who would invigorate the earth and it's creatures with Life and intellect, arise within me.

O Serpent-soul of my awakening, ascend through me, that I may know both darkness and light. I shall be the first and last in the circle of the Luciferian, called Yatukih[23].

I invoke thee, Arashk, who brings wisdom of fire and water, of earth and air, who awakens the spirit of witchcraft. Arise, burning Eye of immortal spirit.

Mitokht, serpent of wisdom, coil within my soul, rise through my brain and illuminate my path within.

azhôhish dahâkâi akha-daêna

Aghashi, O dragon daeva of old, bless my path in darkness.

---

[23] (pronounced YA-TOOK-IH)

A SPELL FOR CONSECRATING ITEMS

Traditionally, the Luciferian may perform this ritual from New Moon to Full Moon for Luciferian Magick instruments, for the use of transformative magick while Therionick and Yatukih Sorcery items are traditionally consecrated from Full Moon to New Moon (Dark Moon). Items may be chanted over following the Nirangs or invocations, then buried in a cloth or sacred cover and buried under earth with pearings of nails or hair, as an offering to the Druj of the Earth. Upon digging up items, place on the altar and perform the same consecration chant, then cleaning items if need be and using accordingly.

If you are unable to bury items you may follow the same instructions, then placing the items in a cloth with an offering of nail pearings and hair and keeping covered and undefiled for the same period.

CHANT OF BLESSING OF RITUAL WEAPONS

'I call forth Aeshma, I call forth the Nasu, I invoke direct defilement, I invoke indirect defilement.
'I summon forth Khru, I invoke Khruighni
'I invoke Buidhi, I evoke the offspring of Buidhi.
'I summon forth Kundi, I call forth the offspring of Kundi
'I summon forth the gaunt Bushyasta, I invoke the long-handed Bushyasta

I summon forth Muidhi, I summon forth Kapasti
'I call forth the Pairika the bride of the serpent, the divine inspiration that comes upon the fire, upon the water, upon the earth, upon the wolf, owl and serpent, upon the tree. I invoke the uncleanness that comes upon the fire, upon the water, upon the earth, upon the wolf, owl and serpent, upon the tree.

'I welcome thee forth, O beautiful and powerful Angra Mainyu! To the fire, to the water, to the earth, to the cow, to the tree, to the faithful man and to the faithful woman, to the stars, to the moon, to the sun, to the boundless light from your spirit, to the boundless darkness from your shadow, come thou forth Lion-Headed Serpent, whose forms are many!

Illuminate my Spirit and Flesh with thy Blackened Flame, O Ahriman and Akoman! Ascend, O fiendish Druj-serpent! Rise through me, O brood of the fiend who is of my essence! Rise up, O world of the fiend! Rise up in me, O Druj! Come forth, O Druj! Devour thy enemies, O Druj! Come forth from the regions of the north, to give unto death the living world of

Righteousness, to empower and envenom our world of Darkness and Light, of the Beast and Serpent!"'

STAOTA AND BARBAROUS EVOCATION

The essence of Yatukih Sorcery and Luciferian Witchcraft is to break taboos which can awaken a higher sense of self; transform yourself through devouring and illuminating through the empowerment of the higher self and lower ego. Often, as with older ceremonial magic, the steps and extensive ritualistic workings can prove less effective due to the loss of intent. Sorcery depends upon the belief of the Luciferian. In works of primal dark magick, it must be suggested that the Yatukih enters the circle of belief, to invest the complete carnal embodiment of the path of Magick.

The barbarous tongue, displayed in classic form by the Enochian Calls are but one example. Originally presented in Luciferian Witchcraft, the Staota is presented as a SIGILLIC word manipulation, once the sorcerer utilizes, will create an effect of word-vibrations which will help in empowering gnosis. The Luciferian will forget the meaning of the words during ritual thus empowering the subconscious. This is a verbal expression of the visual theories presented by Austin Osman Spare, instead of image it is with mantra.

Some foundation Staotas are presented here. While simplistic, their concepts should prove effective for the sorcerer. Staotas may be used in the following way.

1. Perform Nirang-i âharman âdar Sâma
2. Utilize any Nirang or invocation based on the purpose of the rite.

3. Charge sigil or item in working, while doing so; choose a staota based on what you are working with. Recite the staota as a mantra while focusing on your sigil. You may create your own sigil; create it based on what you find association with. Make it effective.
4. Ensure you pace the mantra, keep it rhythmic and use the patterns to build gnosis and focus.
5. End your ritual and forget about the working.

When using Staota as written here ritually, it should be chanted or sung as a Mantra, while focusing on the following aspects of awakening/focusing energy within the body. Staota may be used in communication with others to achieve a goal. It is the combination of the Eyes to achieve attention and focus, the words should be like the serpent itself, using skilled yet decisive language to compel others to your Will.

To clarify the steps of Staota:

1. Breathe deeply in an upright or standing position. No distractions. Start at the base of the spine, visualize two serpents in a spiral motion starting to slither as you breathe and exhale up the spine itself. As your recite the Staota the pressure of your vocal chords are actually creating these sensations of "light" in "darkness" thus kindling a perceived manifestation of the Black Flame of Ahriman. This Kundalini energy, serpent energy should be carefully rolled off the tongue to rise through the spine.
2. With each exercise of phrase in Avestan or useful "shadow tongue" as found in Luciferian Witchcraft, move the Kundalini up the spine. As it moves, send elements of darkness and flame from it into different points of your body, feeling the shock and cold "electrical" current through you.
3. Once it reaches the Ajna Chakra, focus again the spiral, use the mantric chants to allow the Staota to

coil tightly and either flow downward into the base of the spine or to rise through into the Ahriman aspect of the universe, if an exterior spell if being performed.

SHADOW TONGUE OF ARASHK

Barat-daeva, Daena Daevayas [Pronounced: *barrat-dayva – dayna – davayahs*] – I am the source of religion *(an epithet of sorcery, the religion of the Luciferian)*

Daevayasnaham [Pronounced: *dayvah-nah-om*] – Daemons are worshipped through me *(mantra for self-power, awareness, used to strengthen rites where the mind must be focused or cleansed)*

Paitishentem [Pronounced pay-yit-shen-tem] – to look upon, to command with sight. *(used to command by will)*

Daevaameretatem [Pronounced day-eva-ameri-tat] –The Daeva rises through me bringing immortal spirit.

For the Vortex of Sorcerous Power – that which is created from within (command the desires you have to manifest)

Zrazusu –[pronounced zar-az-ushu] The Eye which fell (the power of the rebellious Daeva)

Ushanarasta [pronounced Ushu-anar-asta] – Of the opposite of the Sun which is darkness of desire brought to flesh.

Zrazza [pronounced Zar-rassa] – Under the charms of the Moon – of the kiss which brings blood (used as a calling to Spirits of Az-Jahi or the Lilith-spririt).

Umpesta [pronounced You-um-pest-a] – from the ruins of desert sand comes that unseen (a call to the Druj or Spirits hidden within the Earth, used to carry out specific spells).

Drakala [pronounced Drac-call-a] – the dragon which walks between worlds (used to call upon Ahriman as the spirit of timeless being)

Nonasturma [pronounced Non-ast-urma] - shall this star descend in flesh (invoking the Ahriman spirit or Luciferian Light)

Izzadraana [pronounced Is-za-dran-na] – Shall I become transformed (used in Therionick Sorcery)

Yatukisahla [pronounced Yatu-key-sah-la] – By this sorcerous belief can darkness be made flesh. (empowering the spell)

Staota – to absorb the spirit which attacks me – from that curse returned to enemy

Cofurizim [pronounced Cor-fur-is-zim] – by my familiars, devour this essence which attacks me (a protection chant)

Drejjalak – [pronounced Dre-jah-lack] By the circle of self, flames of Eshm devour and drink deep (called upon to consume the energy of something attacking you.)

Quaalabatu [pronounced Qua-ala-batu] – By dream, by nightmare shall you drink and devour (empowering a servitor, spirit or vampire to drain the energy of your enemy, allowing the astral energy to flow back to you. Be cautious with this, it can create monsters.)

Vlaakalaka [pronounced Vla-aka-lacka] – Wolf shade, from my center and shadow go forth and devour (used in Therionick Sorcery, dream shape shifting and astral projection).

Akkalasht [pronounced Ack-ka-lash-t] – Akatash, send thy succubi to my victim's dreams, drain them slowly of life – give the poisoned kiss of AZ. (used to haunt dreams).

Vizzalezaka [pronounced Vizz-zale-zaka] – Vizaresh, as the spirit departs, allow no comfort – devour them into our shadows (used to call upon Vizaresh to drag enemies down and devour.)

Akaurasta [pronounced Ack-are-asta] – As the Black Dragon is Within, my shadow shall grow and take mighty shape (used in rituals to transform the astral body or shadow in a dragon-form.)

Azkzokaham [pronounced Az-ka-zo-ka-ham] – Serpents black, eat from the sleeping brains of whom I desire (used in Yatukih Sorcery of devouring an enemy – you should be well practiced before utilizing this.)

Azksernuis [pronounced Az-ksee-re-new-is] – Blackened serpents, expand thy darkness of my being to grow while my body sleeps. (to build the body of shadow while sleeping, used in healing and building the astral body)

Lilzumnaka [pronounced Lil-zoo-ma-nack-a] – Lilith-Harlot AZ, thy daughter of light and filth, shall join with me in dreams, to empower my being and breed my own servitors called Succubi. (used to summon feminine spirits)

Okmanosho [pronounced Ok-man-oshow] – Mind of the Immortal Flame, form within my own minds eye, to strengthen my spell to become. (used to call forth Akoman, to seek mental prowess and psychic powers, may be used to strengthen the Will as well).

Zazasta Unozono [pronounced Zar-zast-a Uno-zone-no] – From Arezura, let the serpents and Daevas come forth to me, encircle and manifest my desire. (used in workings once you have servitors or spirit you work with, use in invocations).

USING STAOTAS IN WORKINGS

Staotas (Stay-oat-ahs) are used to empower and charge ritual workings. They are essentially the language of the abyss, the subconscious mind. They beheld meaning but the meaning is forgot during the working – which causes forgetfulness and charges the working.

This is how you would construct a staota working.

If you were conducting a working to gain or develop psychic powers, you would use the SEAL OF AKOMAN and use the appropriate invocations. Before the working, you would assemble some staotas to empower your working. An example is:

Okmanosho - Paitishentem (recite 7 times)

USING THE YATUKIH OR LUCIFERIAN SEALS

The seals of the Daevas are encircled with elements of their names and with their full name spelled out in English. The purpose of this is to give clear meaning as to the purpose of the spirits and their indications. Please understand these are old Persian demons, or rebellious spirits subject to Ahriman. If the Great Work has progressed, one may discover the essence of Ahriman within. The Luciferian who works with these forces will find them empowering and a veritable fountain of life and inspiration. Here are some step by step instructions for using these sigils.

Step One
Once you have found the sigil you wish to use from the following seals and descriptions, make a copy of the seal on fresh paper with black or red ink. You make the seal as large or small as you wish, this is up to you. Keep it in a safe place

until you are ready to use it, keep it from the eyes of the profane or unknowing before the working.

Step Two
Choose an evening and a place where you will not be disturbed for your working.
Have your seal ready in front of you. Light two black or red candles and place them at either side of the seal on a table or your altar if you have one.

Step Three
While looking intently at the seal you have made, so that it is the
only thing you can see, take seven deep breaths, slowly, one at a time.
As you take each breath, think of what you wish to achieve with the seal.
You may visualize it as detailed as possible, viewing your result as if it was real. You are essentially "Commanding it to be".
Slowly turn your head upward and recite:

kêm-nâ âharman
âharman i hvadâe
DAEVAAMERETATEM
YATUKISAHLA
OKMANOSHO
Daeva, I bless this rite with hair, to offer to Druj
Daeva, Hear me _____ (insert name of spirit you are invoking)
I ensorcel thee to this circle, to this symbol to rise up through me.

Step Four
You will want to slowly lower your eyes downward to the sigil and focus on it intently, visualizing the aims you wish to achieve. Do not allow any forms or shadows disrupt your working; this is where the test of discipline comes in.

Step Five
Once your focus has begun to wane, you will want to recite the following:
BA NĀM I ÂHARMAN
UMPESTA
YATUKISAHLA
Hear me spirits of the earth!
Hear me spirits of the air!
Hear me spirits of fire!
Hear me spirits of water!

It is significant now to get up and take the sigil to a place where it neither be seen or touched. Do this and at once do something mundane, spend time with friends, family or some other form of entertainment.

THE BIBLE OF THE ADVERSARY
SEALS AND SIGILS OF THE YATUKIH SORCERERS

AKOMAN – the Daeva of illuminated, intelligent thought. May be used to seek psychic power, develop the Will and Body of Light.

Savar — The Leader of Daevas, represents rebellious power. Use to bind and command your will – may be used for job promotion, to get an annoying co-worker off your back, etc.

ANDAR – The daeva of rebellion, who brings the Black Flame. Summon Andar for workings which inspire the obtainment of wisdom, of knowing when to guide rebellions and to continually seek spiritual knowledge through practice.

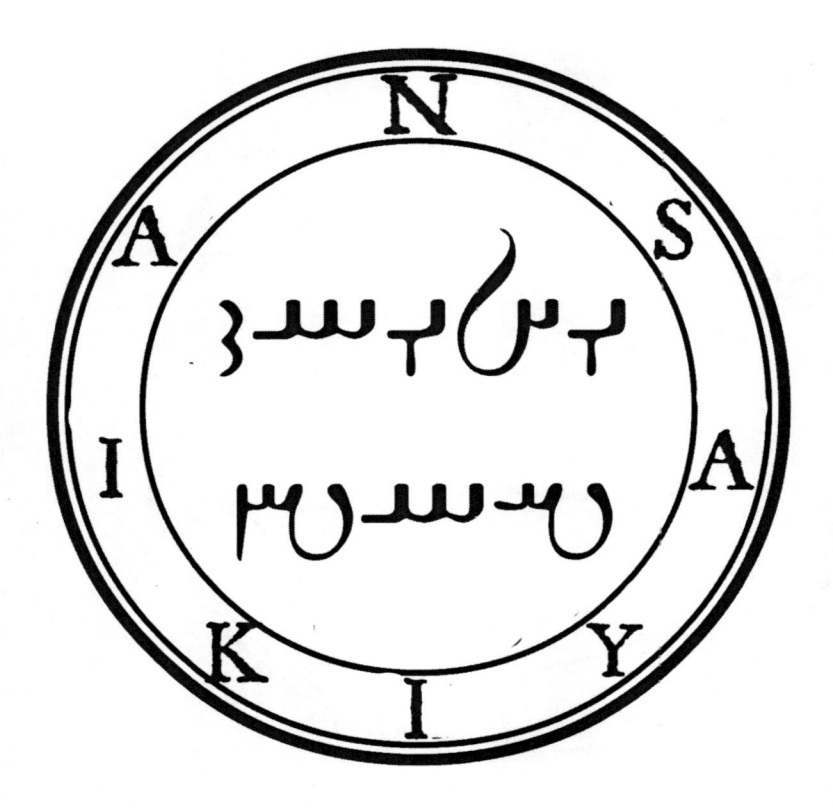

NAIKIYAS – The daeva of want or desire, Naikiyas or Naonghaithya is a powerful Archdaeva which drives the spirit to yearn for more. This is a meaningful daeva as long as you are able to control this power.

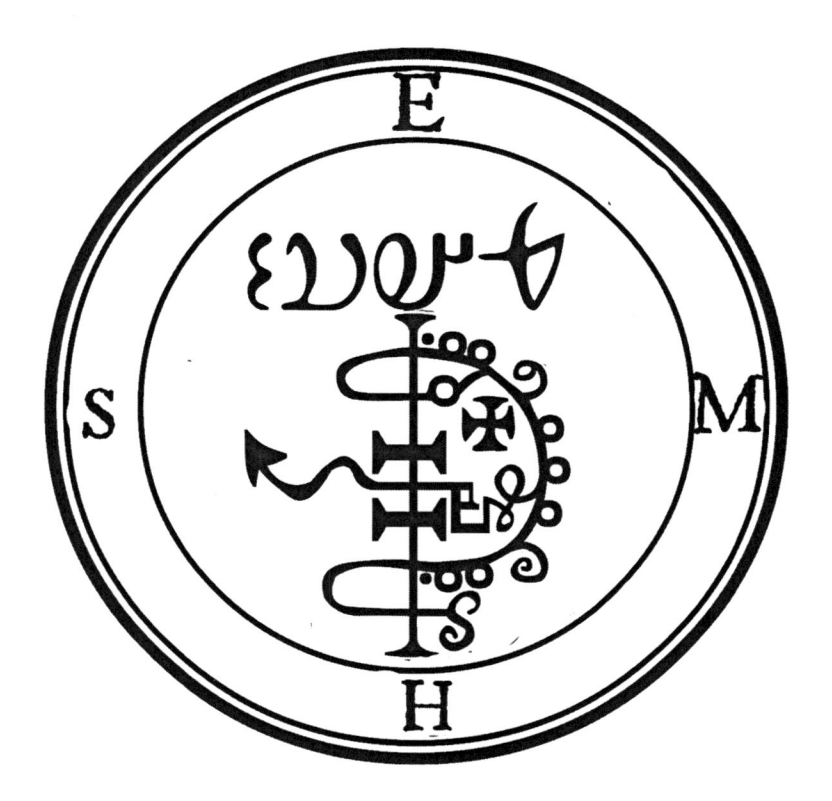

ESHM – The Daeva of the Wounding Spear or the daeva of the Bloody Mace. Eshm is the root of Aeshma and the spirit of what is known as Asmodeus. Eshm is used for channeling and controlling sexual desire, anything which involves aggressive emotion or to accent this approach. You may use Eshm as a soldier, or as a worker wanting a promotion, or something similar.

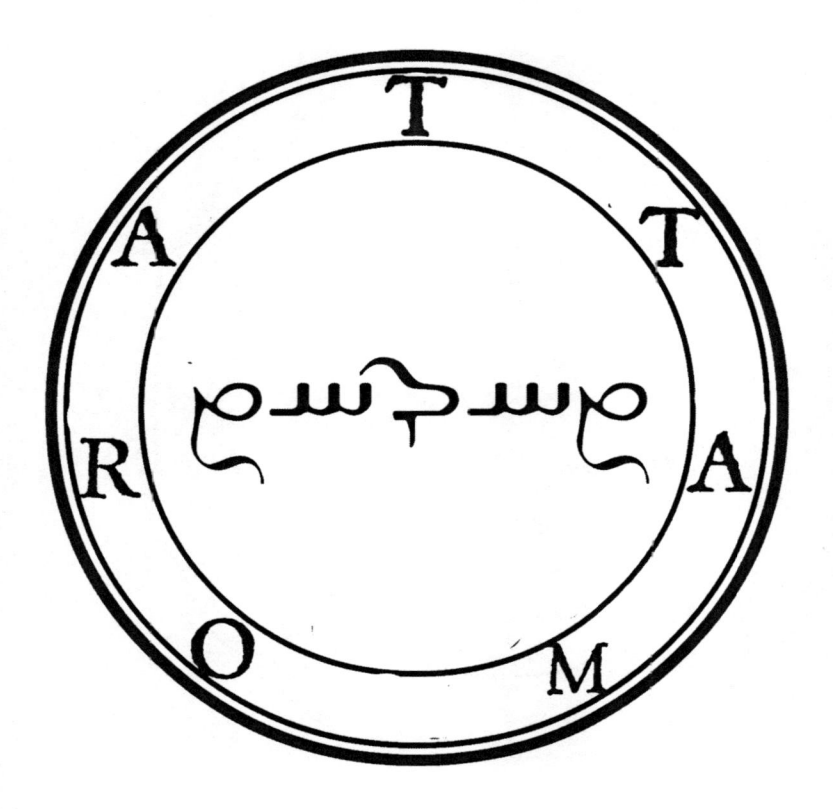

TAROMAT – Taromat is the spirit of Discontent which leads to spiritual rebellion. You may use Taromat to inspire the search for more knowledge, to find a higher station in life, to become something more.

ASTWIHAD – The Evil Flyer, or The Bone Divider, the Vampiric daeva of death which comes to all living beings. Astwihad may be used to seek wisdom of death (proceed with caution), to curse an enemy and to walk the Vampyric Path[24]

---

[24] THE VAMPIRE GATE – The Vampyre Magickian by Michael W. Ford

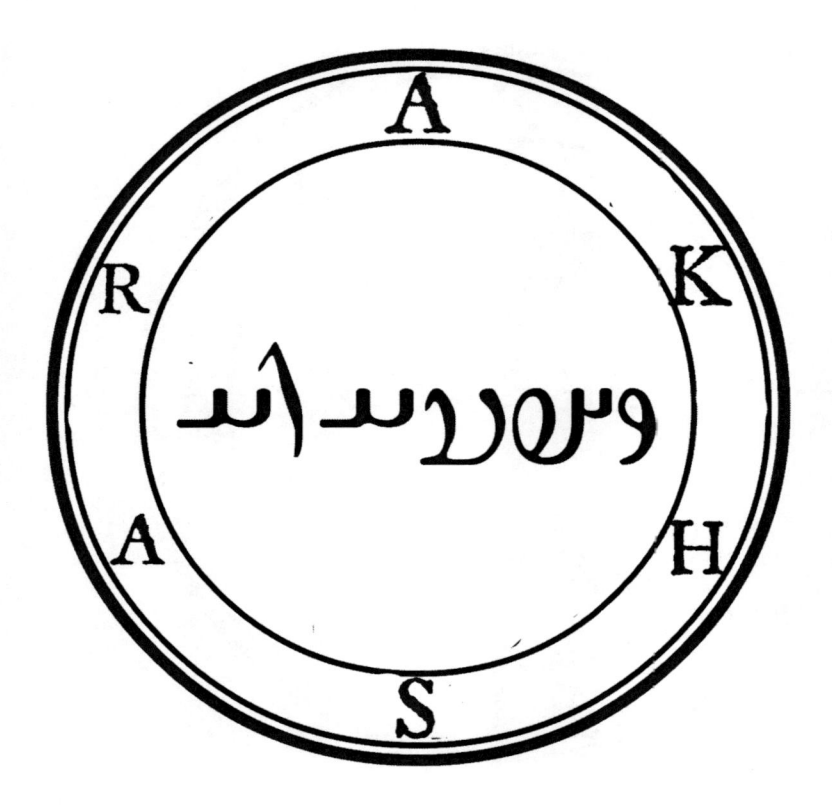

ARASHK – The Daeva of the Evil Eye. This Daeva was said to be the author of the Zurvanite tale, thus a Daeva of wisdom. Arashk is also a spirit of malice. Use to gain insight into a situation or to get your point across. You may call upon Arashk to inspire the power of the Will through the spirit.

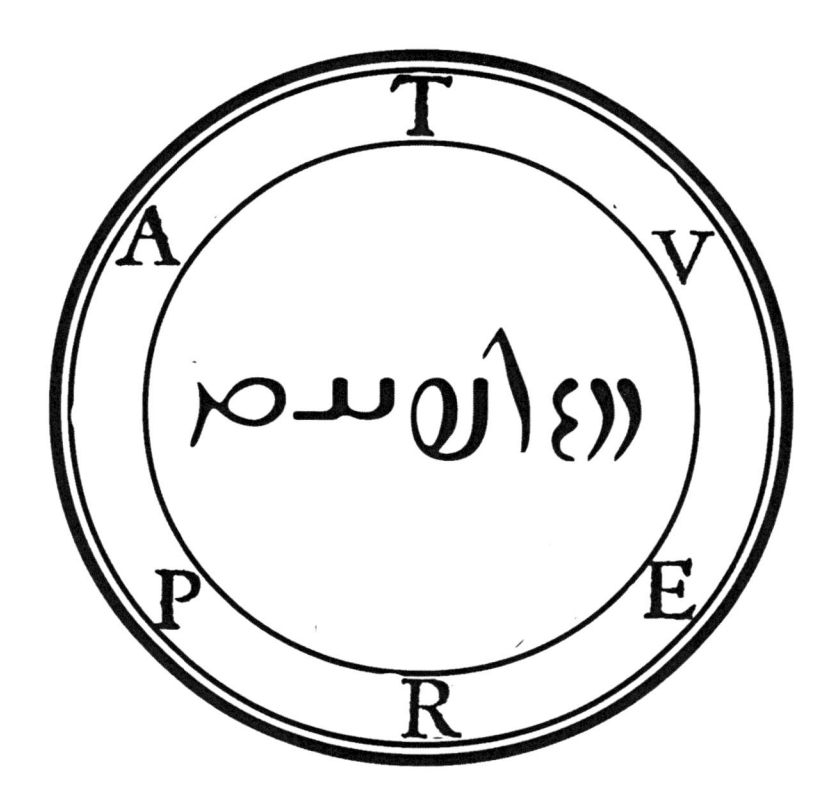

TAPREV – The ArchDaeva of Fever. This spirit relates to overcoming sickness, it may equally invite sickness.

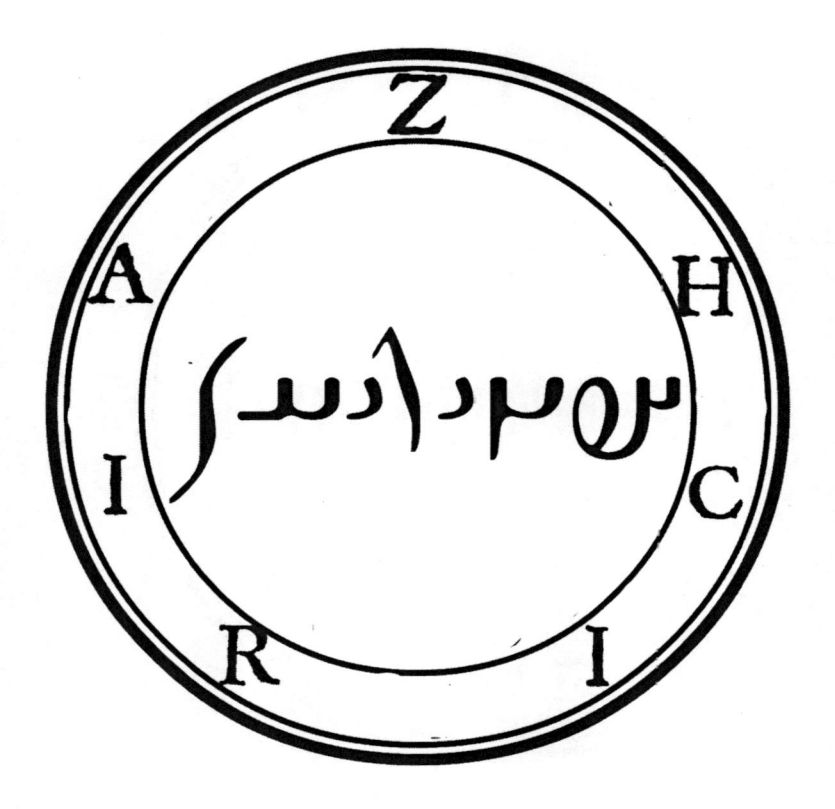

ZAIRICH – The ArchDaeva of Thirst, a vampyric spirit which relates to the hunger for continued existence. Use Zairich to seek continued wisdom and power. Zairich may be used to also drain an enemy of Chi or Astral energy.

MITROKHT – The Daeva of the Lie, the Serpent who is thus the Spirit of the Evil Eye. Mitrokht represents the power of Will and the command of spirit as seen through the eye.

DRUJ NASU – The Fly Demoness, she was created to corrupt and manifest in dead matter, she is thus a Vampyric Spirit. Druj Nasu is useful for initiation into the Yatukih mysteries and to study the normal process of death. Druj Nasu is called upon in rituals of Vampyrism[25]

---

[25] BLACK ORDER OF THE DRAGON

AHRIMAN DRAGON SIGIL – The Dragon of Darkness, the Father of Rebellion, this is a powerful talisman as it represents the Left Hand Path or the Way-i vatar. This sigil may be used to seek communion with Ahriman on the beginning of the path of Luciferian Witchcraft. It may be used to seek initiatory wisdom and to aspire to the path of sorcery.

AHRIMAN – SPIRIT OF DARKNESS SIGIL – This talisman is used to encircle the aspiring sorcerer with the pact of primal darkness, it inspires and instills power to the possessor of this talisman.

AZ-JEH / mad ce dewdn (Mother of Demons) – The Spirit of Lilith as Az or Jeh, the Mother of Demons in ancient Persian mythology. This spirit may be used to invoke a muse, attract a succubi, meet a potential love, psychic wisdom, instinct sharpening, vampyric workings and more.

MICHAEL W. FORD

GRIMOIRE OF LILITH
Honor unto the Goddess

THE BLACK MIRROR
Creating A Gateway to Lilith

Communicating with Lilith and the Lilitu may be done with a black mirror. Once you obtain a mirror or black mirror (this alone is preference) it must be consecrated.

Inscribe the mirror on the front or back the following letters:

L Y L Y T

Upon inscribing it with the name of the Goddess, wrap the mirror in a cloth made of Black Velvet. It will be buried for one complete moon cycle. On the eve of the Full Moon, take the mirror out into the night, using the incense attributed to the Moon evoke Lilith:

LILIN, ABITO, ABIZO, AMOZRPHO, HAQASH, ODAM, KEPHIDO, AILO, TATROTA, ABNIQTA, SHATRINA, KALUBTZA, TILTOI, PIRTSHA

Take the black mirror, wrap it in black velvet and seal in a exterior bag to keep it from moisture. Bury it.

On the night of the Dark Moon, dig it up and recite the same invocation of names and honor the Goddess based on your desire. Wrap the mirror now in Red Velvet and rebury it. It will remain there until the Full Moon. On the Night of the Full Moon, recite the following:

LILIN, ABITO, ABIZO, AMOZRPHO, HAQASH, ODAM, KEPHIDO, AILO, TATROTA, ABNIQTA, SHATRINA, KALUBTZA, TILTOI, PIRTSHA
BY thy Deathless Spirit, Hail thou Mother Lilith!

Bless this gateway to your entry into this world.

Bless this gateway to which I shall honor you.

Enter through this gateway that I may seek you.

Bless this mirror as a way of walking between worlds!

Hail Lilith!

You may use the Black Mirror to seek spirits of the night, communicate with other phantoms and empower your spells on the astral plane.

MICHAEL W. FORD

Rituals of Dedication to the Goddess

Know that there are
FOUR LUCIFERIAN MOTHERS:
1. Lilith
2. Naamah
3. Aggereth or Agrat Bat Mahalath
4. Mahalath

Each Mother Rules one of the four *tequfot*

The vernal equinox
The summer solstice
The autumnal equinox
The winter solstice

At each of these dates, they gather at the Mountain of Darkness. In honoring them at these times, face the North and offer them seed or fluids to honor them.

The Hour of Sunset to Midnight are their hours, honor them at this time.

THERE ARE SEVENTY POWERS OF THE AIR which are appointed to dwell around specific nations, according to Nathan Spira who died in 1662.

All nations are under the rule of

SAMAEL AND RAHAB
The Four Concubines of Samael are:
LILITH the FIRST
NAAMAH (Nahemoth)
MAHALATH
AGRAT BAT MAHALTH

You have seen the seals of calling for LILITH in two forms, see yet one now for NAHEMOTH, which may be used in all sexual operations including servitors.

A RITE OF SACRIFICE TO LILITH
Betgetting Sexual Fluids to the Goddess

The Purpose of this rite is to offer sexual fluid, semen and female fluids to Lilith to beget other Lilitu, or sexual demons. This may be practiced any time you have sexual contact with another, simply recite this prayer which is based on an ancient Hebrew exorcism against her. I have set it anew in her honor. All you must do is simply recite with or without the knowledge of your partner, if you are male at the moment of emitting seed visualize Lilith. If you are female welcome the seed as your offering to the Goddess.

MICHAEL W. FORD
CHANT OF SACRIFICE TO LILITH

In the name of Samael - Lilith
Thou beautiful one
You who are wrapped in velvet, Lilith
Appear unto me
Come forth, Come forth
I welcome you, I offer to you
The seed is yours,
It is your inheritance.
Come forth, Arise!
The sea rages, Thou Goddess of Storms
Its waves roll in your honor.
I hold on to the infernal Ones,
Wrap myself into the darkness and crimson

Of your Passion and Immortal Spirit.

Hail thou, 'Magna Mater daemonum'

THE BIBLE OF THE ADVERSARY

TO SUMMON FORTH A COMPANION FOR THE NIGHT, UNDER THE COMMAND DEMON-QUEEN, IGRATH BATH MAHALATH

A simple incantation from G. Scholem, *Tarbif,* XIX (1948).

Utilizing the Dark Moon or the Waning Moon phase will prove this working intense, you may conduct it during the rising moon as well. According to 14th century lore, this must be done either on the eve of Sunday or one the eve of Wednesday.

You should regress from ejaculating for three days before the rite, using the sigil you may call Lilith accordingly and if using methods of arousal you must not emit seed or reach orgasim. An area dedicated to Lilith, an altar may be set up and you may use the Luciferian Tarot card QUEEN OF CUPS as symbolism of Agrat bath Mahalth or Aggereth.

"I adjure you, Agrat bath Mahalath,
queen of the demons, with the great,
strong and terrible Name,
and with the name of his Luciferian angels, and
with the name of Bilar the heroic,
king of the demons
that you send to me X daughter of Y,
the beautiful maiden from among your maidens
who follow you,
whose number is like the
number of the days of the year,
and with the name of SAMAEL and ASMODEUS,
AAA NNN SSS."

END OF RITE

MICHAEL W. FORD

THE RITUAL OF ABYZOU

Evoking the Spirit of Abyzou, the storm demoness of ancient mythology, presents a powerful gnosis for those who may seek the powers of night and the dream. Abyzou is but one name for Lilith, one of her many masks. She appears in this form as darkness, with a face scaled and green and hair made of serpents. You may seek Abyzou to understand the essence of the Vampyre, the need for continued 'conscious' existence and the search for spiritual immortality. Using the Sigil of Az-Jahi is suitable.

> *Hail thou Abyzou, Daughter of Storm*
> *Mistress of Chaos and the Abyss*
> *Whose very essence is darkness*
> *Antaura, Thou Night Wind Goddess of the Hunt and Devouring Kiss, Arise thou to me, Abyzou*
> *Thou whose face is scaled and green like the serpent,*
> *Twisting and terror-filling to those who behold you*
> *Abyzou, thou Goddess of Blood drinking*
> *Hail thou rushing hag-demon, granting no rest, nor giving kindly sleep.*
> *It is the beauty of night and day,*
> *whose head is that of a demon,*
> *whose shape is as a whirlwind*
> *Thou appearance is like the darkening heavens, and its face as the deep shadow of the forest ...'*
> *Hail Abyzou, arise to me Goddess.."*
> *Hail thou Goddess, who like her mate*
> *Coils like a snake,*
> *roars like a lion,*
> *hisses like a dragon'*
> *Manifest to me, Fulfill my Desire of _____*

THE BIBLE OF THE ADVERSARY
END OF THE GRIMOIRE OF LILITH

RITUAL OF DESTRUCTION

The ritual of destruction is a powerful cursing rite, it should be used with a clear conscious and full focus only after you have exhausted every means of fixing the issue – perhaps it is something you caused, it could be something that could resolve over time, etc. Think before you perform the rite.

MICHAEL W. FORD

A CURSING RITUAL OF DESTRUCTION

By the darkened winds of Varenya, who brings forth the druj and daevas of the elder shadow, descend now from thy abode to devour and destroy my own enemy, __name__!

Hearken and rise up, O forces of primal darkness who sleep in the darkness of the abyss. Those who know the voices of vengeance and the passion of the destruction of mine own enemy! I seek to be the essence of the destroyer and devourer, to break down and render my victim a shell consumed by your forces!

Descend now Astovidat, Angel of Darkness whose shadow is substance, who seeks to divide the bones and drink of the blood of the soul. Asti-vahat, I call you forth to the name and image of __name__, lengthen your shadow to their shape and with your touch, drain them unmercifully. Cast your shadow on them and cause fever and sickness.

O druj Sej, descend upon their frame, sleeping and awake to cause and beget decay, their muscles grow weak, their thoughts heavy in depression and their desire to live is drained by thy powers. Hear me Sij and rise up upon my enemy.

Kashvish, I conjure thee form to cause pain and retribution to my enemy, __name__, I curse them with the mark of death, to grow weak in mind, body and soul.

Inspire terror and trouble in sleep, Saham! May their breathing become labored, their heart heavy and the desire to die long as the shadow of thy power! Spazga O hearken to them, causing many bad things to be said as a part of thy manifestation.

Vayu, as Astovidad devours their life, carry off __name__ to the grave.

I call thee, they who rage against mankind,
they spill their blood like rain,
devouring their flesh,
sucking their veins .
they are demons full of violence,
ceaselessly devouring blood . . .'
SO IT BEGINS! âharman i hvadâe

MICHAEL W. FORD

THE LUCIFERIAN RITUAL OF MARRIAGE

The need for a social structure within the Luciferian ideology is paramount for the development of a faith which requires experience and first hand validation. The need for ceremony is for the celebration of union and the two who would join their own lives together.

The Luciferian defines marriage as an equal partnership between two individuals dedicated to honoring and growing together. Luciferian ideology expresses the celebration of life, thus marriage is symbolic of the union between the Daimonic masculine, or Samael, and the Daimonic feminine, or Lilith. A Luciferian must recognize the equality of their partner and respect them accordingly.

The ritual of marriage is based within the ancient concepts of the Fallen Archon, or Samael and his awakening bride, Lilith, or the mother of demons. Utilize this ritual with great pride; it is a celebration of life.

RITUAL PREPARATION

The Rite should include a Priest or a well vested student of the Luciferian Path. Participants should find their own associations within the rite. The following offices are intended for the rite of marriage:

Priest: Conducting Ceremony

Matron of the Elder (Lilith)

Asmodai – Companion or Best Man

Brides Maids (Lilitu)

Leviathan – Ring bearer

Angels of Chaos (Ushers)

The Priest or reading Luciferian in charge of ceremony should wear the image of the Infernal Union; the rite is not required to be in black or any other color. It should be made according to the desire and wants of the bride and groom.

TERMS:

Understand the Luciferian Path welcomes a trans-cultural approach to symbolism.

MICHAEL W. FORD
MARRIAGE RITUAL

PART I The announcement of faith

ba nãm i âharman

(in the name of Ahriman)

We gather here to celebrate the union of two.

Life is a path of exploration; of conquering what you fear, helping those close to you and always doing what you instinctively feel is right.

Life is about change, in the spiritual sense of a Luciferian it aims for the heights, while always exploring the darkness within.

Life is about compromise and trust placed on those who earned it.

Life is about exhalting the powers within and making the world a better place.

When two are joined together there is a union of opposites. The Luciferian spirit itself is radient in the union of Samael and Lilith, our symbol of Infernal Union is a reminder that the Spirit of Lucifer is brightest in the union of opposites.

PART II. THE CALLING

Leviathan, rise up from the abyss and encircle the two lovers in union. For in union there is strength, where there is strength power is possible. How many hath joined the flesh together to beget Gods and Goddesses upon this earth? To the one who fell from the highest reaches of the empyrean realms, whose essence was brighter than the sun. To the Archon who brought the fire from heaven to the clay of humanity, herein is the spark of life!

I call unto the two Grigori to bless this union:

Anma·el and Asbeel gather here and bless this rite.

The union of marriage is a sacred act of dedication to the partners chosen. Let none defile the sacred marriage of two dedicated to the illumination of each other. By the blades of Azazel may the swords of blackened flame clash together and guard thee always.

May Hecate hearken to the circle of the wise and illuminate both the Bride and Groom.

PART III. DEDICATIONS

In the name of Lucifer, the illuminated

Whose name is Samael

Will you take this man as your mate, who will honor you and uplift you as Babalon, whose is sacred and powerful in the light of the Fallen and Risen one, Will you have and hold this man in sickness and health, to always seek to avoid the path of ignorance?

[the bride will affirm and She places the ring on his finger and recites her own oath]

In the name of Lilith, the mother of spirits

Whose is both terrible and nurturing

Will you take this Daughter of mine, to have and to honor as an equal, to raise her up as Babalon, to hold and illuminate as the fallen and risen one, will you have him to hold in sickness and health, to always avoid the path of ignorance?

[the groom will affirm and He places the ring on her finger and recites his own oath]

Heralds of the path of darkness illuminated by fire, by the path of the fallen and risen

I now pronounce you wife and husband (or wife and wife, depending on choice)

You may Samael and Lilith bless this union in Leviathans coils.

You may embrace. May the blessings of the fallen angels be upon you.

May Maiden, Mother and Crone embrace you

So it is done.

THE BIBLE OF THE ADVERSARY
THE LUCIFERIAN BAPTISM RITUAL

A Luciferian believes in light and illumination is central to the Great Work of initiation. Ascension is, after all, modeled after the symbolism of Lucifer, the Fallen Angel who went forth to the darkness to know both good and evil.

<u>Participants</u>

Priest (or one conducting ritual)

Initiate

ba nãm i âharman

Awaken O serpent of the sun to our blessing

To the new of spirit and flesh, despite age or experience

Comes forth to be touched by the Spirit of the Black Flame, who is the spark which awakens the clay.

No more shall you walk as a sheep in the herd yet you shall be a wolf hunting for prey.

azhôhish dahâkâi akha-daêna

O Lucifer, thou risen spirit of the Sun

Herald of Darkness who bestows wisdom

I evoke thy essence to touch the spirit and body of _name_, to walk now the path of the black flame.

I call thee forth spirit of night, spirit of Air

Lilith, blood stained caul, Goddess of the desolate Places, bless this child before us in your strength, joy and love. Bless this child to be as yours, to go forth and manifest the Luciferian Flame upon this earth.

[Priest or Priestess] Sprinkles rose water or similar on child.

I bless you to walk the infernal path.

Lilith, cast your shadow upon this child and raise them up as a God (Goddess) upon this earth.

So it is done!

THE BIBLE OF THE ADVERSARY
THE LUCIFERIAN BURIAL RITUAL

A Luciferian Ritual of burial is a celebration of life, an acknowledgement of their own transformation into the ghost lands, the realm of Hecate. Consider that the ritual of burial is to awaken and attune the celebrants to the gnosis of death as a process of transformation. For Athiestic Luciferians, it is about the celebration of life and those who surround the one who has passed on. To Theistic or Luciferians with a spiritual path, it is a celebration of transformation and awakening to the path of Lucifuge, the spirit who goes forth by night. You may wish to adopt Sethianic concepts in your burial rituals, as Anubis is the son of Set.

It is ideal that a Luciferian who is initiated in the Daevayasna should not be cremated, as the Law of Ahriman is that all should be buried, it feeds the self as Daeva in spirit, it is a honor to the Yatukan sorcerer or Luciferian. If a Luciferian is specifically on a Light or Spiritual path of the Astral Body, then they may choose cremation. Within the Luciferian Path, the Adversary wears many faces, thus it is adaptable by approach.

You may adapt the ritual based on the situation at hand. It may be as elaborate or as simple as you wish.

The second part of the ritual is based on the Ophite Ritual of Ascent, which is related to the Serpent Cult.

Participants

Priest of Lucifer (or individual assuming role) – reciting services

Son/Daughter of Hecate – Gate of the Dead (optional)

If performing the ritual with the deceased, then adapt your settings accordingly. If the body is not present, a photo or image of the deceased may be placed upon an altar, with some object they hold dear in life.

MICHAEL W. FORD

RITUAL OF DEATH, BURIAL AND REBIRTH

Music should be played, classical or anything which holds a sacred significance. Ensure it is music with power and vision.

I. The Rite of Burial

PRIEST:

"ba nãm i âharman,

I call to the Guardian of the Crossroad, Hecate, Mother of wolves, owls and predators...

Whose ravens herald the ghostways of the shades of old. Open forth thy gateway to this son/daughter of Luciferian Light, __name__

May peace be found in this time of need.

Let us not be saddened by the loss of the physical, for this individual will rise as a God/dess.

Life is short and fleeting, let this be a reminder that we must cherish each day we exist, look forward to conquer all challenges before us.

Let us find strength within, rejoicing in the Luciferian Fire.

That the flesh is no longer needed, the spirit has been set free.

As the robed spirit of Darkness

Who holds within light and life

Shall go forth into the world of shades

Let us see beyond this moment into the next.

Praise be to Astovidad, who has touched the body and illuminated the soul

Whose jaws seemed greedily to drink of the soul,

Yet saw here the Blackened Fire it could not touch

So Daeva became Druj and the Serpent went forth

Az who has loosed the chain, she who has shattered the fetters.

She has shed the bodily garment

She uttered the spell of inhabiting shells

And rose up as a Dragon from the darkness

She went to the dead, those who were former

Of bodies and said

"Rise up, look, you Former of Bodies, the hollows of your hands are filling with blood"

Come forth nobly born, Goddess

Grant thy chosen passage through the lands of the dead

Where dragon in the abode of darkness dwells

Who has dedicated their own life to the power and immortal essence of the spirit. I hearken and call thee forth O howling druj of the wastelands...

O Ahriman, father of serpents, hearken Arimanius forth from thy throne in the north..

O Druj Nasu, fly demoness who awakens us to the vampyric path, awaken __name__ in spirit to the path of Gods!

O Set-Typhon, Friend of the Shades of the Dead, give thy mask of storms and darkness to the deceased, that they may walk beside you in the Blackened Flame of Immortal Life.

TO THE EMPYREAN, LUCIFER, SAMAEL, YALTABAOTH, Father of the Spirit, Welcome thy son/daughter into the spirit realms, to walk endlessly as a God/Goddess.

I announce their choice name as __spirit name___, to which they shall hear our calls.

(Touch now the Eyes, Ears, face and center of forehead if possible)

I TOUCH THY EARS THAT YOU MAY HEAR

I TOUCH THY EYES THAT YOU MAY SEE

I TOUCH THY MOUTH THAT YOU MAY SPEAK

I WELCOME YOU TO THE WORLD OF SHADES AND WE REJOICE NOW IN THE LUCIFERIAN FLAME.

In spirit, you shall rise as a Risen Immortal God who has left the need of flesh.

Life is a fleeting gift, to be cherished and enjoyed throughout your days. Rejoice in health and always seek to grow stronger, more powerful for the preparation of death.

Let us celebrate the life and death of __name__, with words of their accomplishments and treasured loved ones:

THE BIBLE OF THE ADVERSARY
II. PASSING THROUGH THE GATES

I greet thee, Archons, loosed for eternity
Yaltabaoth, First Archon and Bringer of Light to humanity
Born to command with confidence
Ruling Spirit of the Pure Mind
I open now the world to your spirit
Accept this spirit and empower it with your Fire
O Lion-headed God, who is the spirit of Phainon[26]
Father of Serpents, may it be with me

IAO[27], whose secret name is the Light Bringer, ruler of the hidden mysteries, Thou are Noctifer, whose spirit shines by Night, you are the Lord of Death and transformation. Allow this spirit to pass through and grow strong from your emerald fire. Father and Mother, may it be with me.

SABAOTH[28] Ruler of the Fifth Kingdom, Prince Sabaoth, spirit of Fire illuminated by emotion, allow this spirit to drink of your Golden Cup and share your Fire, let this spirit pass through thy gate. Father and Mother, may it be with me.

ASTAPHAEUS[29] Ruler of the Third Gate, Guardian of the primal spring of Water look to this spirit as

---

[26] Phainon being Saturn

[27] IAO = Jupiter

[28] Sabaoth = Mars

[29] Astaphaeus = Venus, Lucifer and Diana or Samael and Lilith as bringers of light.

the initiate, who is cleansed by the spirit of the Whore and Virgin, let this spirit pass after drinking from the cup of wisdom. Father and Mother, may it be with me.

AILOAEUS, Ruler of the Second Gate, I bring to you the symbol of Lilith, Our Mother of Heaven and Hell. Bless the passage through this gate. Father and Mother, may it be with me.

HORAEUS[30] The spirit has fearlessly passed beyond the gate of fire and received the Blessed Black Flame of immortality, may this spirit pass through the gate and awaken to live in light and darkness forever. Father and Mother, may it forever be.

PRIEST: *A life is known by deeds, let us hear of our brother (or sister) and the things remembered of them:*

FRIENDS, FAMILY SPEAK HERE.

PRIEST:

"In the name of the Light, Lucifer, grant them the power of sight and mind.

In the name of the Spirits of Night, Lilith, grant them the power of flight and the means of surviving as spirit.

O AZ, save thy fangs from their spirit, lend them yours!

---

[30] Horaeus = The Moon.

Vizaresh, guide them swiftly to the pits of hell, Akoman, touch their spirit with the Black Flame and may they rise again as DAEVA!

As we commend you to the earth, the infernal realm of daevas and druj, may you be blessed to rise in spirit, may you rise again as a God/Goddess.

In the honor of the Left Hand Path,

In the honor of Life, Love and Power!

So it is done!

AWAKEN and GO FORTH!"

THERIONICK SORCERY

Working with primal atavistic sorcery to explore the demonic or bestial shadow aspects of the subconscious. The ego of the Luciferian is a continual point of transformation, this is why the term "Azothoz" represents the mutative collective of what we call "the self". Never ending, it is the beginning and the end once the Luciferian has begun to ascend accordingly. Know that Therionick Sorcery is the very essence of lycanthropy, it is the state of transformation into the state of the beast, the hunger for the base desires which are the core attributes of our subconscious. This is the essence of the reptile, the wolf, the flight of the owl beneath the veil of night. Utilize the methods in these pages to darken well the strains of night blood, here you shall descend deep as Daimon to rise up as a god or goddess of night.

MENTAL LYCANTHROPY

Know that any man or woman is capable of transformation into a beast. Use the path of shape shifting in the flesh to understand the foundations of your desires, wants and the very longing for something more.

Attune yourself to the type of change you wish to go through. If you want to take of the change of a wolf, for instance you may wish to create a mask or utilize one you may already have.

Go to a location where the type of animal or reptile would be conducive, perhaps it is a large wooded park, perhaps a family members' property, maybe a graveyard or someplace where you can get some privacy. Once you have, consider the transformative aspects.

TRANSFORMATION

Some utilize chants and sacred mantras to reach mental transformative states, something simple should be applied, if anything at all. Focusing on the aspects of your transformation, loose all attention to your surroundings as you transforms. Notice you will feel a sense of fear, panic and a response impulse of aggression. This is normal, use it. Loose all perceptions of humanity as the beast within takes hold. Visualize your body changing and shaping to the beast you visualize let your mind change your very perceptions!

THE VAMPYRE

Let the Luciferian explore the night black presence of dream sorcery, that by the awakening of the sleeping therionick forms can the flesh of the vampyre awaken. The Vampyre is the predatory spirit which defines the depths of the Luciferian Spirit. Vampyric Magick relates not to blood drinking rather to the darker aspects of the psyche. While this is not representative of all Luciferians and common ideology, it will no doubt appeal to those interested in the darkness within. For those who would embrace it, remember to understand and control the beast within, Magick is to ascend! Those interested in the darker aspects of magick should obtain THE VAMPIRE GATE: The Vampyre Magickian by Michael W. Ford.

THE VAMPYRIC AWAKENING
AN ALLEGORY

It was in the Psalms of the Pistis Sophia that Yaltabaoth, or Samael was called a Vampyric power. "Deliver me, Light, for wicked thoughts have entered into me. I looked, O Light, to the parts below; I saw a light there; I thought : I will go to that place of light. I came to be in the darkness which prevails in the chaos below, and I could not rush out and go to my place, because I was oppressed among all the emanations of the Authades. **The Lion-faced power took away my light which was in me**, and I cried for help and my voice could not penetrate the darkness." – Pistis Sophia – Psalm of Lamenation I

In addition, the psalms refer to Yaltabaoth or the Luciferian Spirit holding much power over Chaos and darkness, he makes what he wishes from it.Yaltabaoth, the Lion-faced deity sought to swallow up completely other light against the Pistis Sophia.

"The crowned power, called Yaltabaoth and others had remained in stasis for so long. From the start Yaltabaoth had always illuminated according to his desire to know more, slowly, with certainty his power grew and his curiosity became a thirst! Yaltabaoth had the fair form of an Angel, the brightest as his star was blinding compared to the others. This was the gestation as it was like he was still in the womb, beginning to have the strength to emerge from a non-existence which held him in thrall.

Yaltabaoth was known also as Saklas and Samael, the Angel. He perceived more and with a shrieking of anger watched his beautiful and fair hands mutate into talons, black with greenish gray fingers, lengthening as a bestial spider. Samael tore forth from a womb which would imprison him. His beautiful countenance is shining among the other Seraphim. His hands returned to the beautiful shape they were originally. Samael was pleased at his ability to change with desire. He felt a raging fire within, he knew he must control it and shape it according to his desire.

Samael, called Nebro or Ahriman, went forth to Zurvan, the power called "father". He proclaimed his desire to go forth from the place of stasis, from which Zurvan proclaimed no. Samael went in anger and transformed into a Great Serpent with the head of a Lion, his crown shining as his eyes became blood red. His roar stirred others, who were coming to the awakening Lucifer so long before had.

Samael or Lucifer took again pleasant form, his forehead shining brightly. He went forth to the other Seraphim and shared his fire with them. These Angels fully awakened to their surroundings, looking to Lucifer with a love of a brethren. The fire he shared burned with blackness and smoke, Yaltabaoth illuminated the darkness with his fire.

Zurvan was not pleased with the Fire Samael knew could not be contained, it made him a God. Samael went to Zurvan who wanted him to leave the light-chaos. Zurvan had not created Yatabaoth, his creation was of its own desire, a cosmic ideal in balance. Yaltabaoth could use his fire to create other worlds and beings, according to his desire.

Yaltabaoth or Ahriman went forth as the form of the Lion Faced Serpent. Zurvan did not want Samael and the other Seraphs to leave against his will. He sent forth a multitude of angels to battle the rebel angels. Lucifer along with the other angels faced the Zurvanite warriors and grew enraged. They were mindless, stupid, blind. His rage transformed him from a Lion-Serpent to a dragon with many heads. His jaws reached out and bit deep into the luminary of an angel, which the blood quickly thrilled the raging Seraph, whose form beget darkness and expanding against the Zurvan-angels.

He drank deep and fed from the life-fire which Zurvan filled his own angels with. As Samael bit into the essence of the angels, the flood of power consumed him with ecstasy. His essence glowed with anger, fire and power. The Dragon changed many forms and fought with as many as he could. He drank from these angels and transformed their essence into his own, it caused his perception to grow. The other rebel angels saw his power and grew bold with his expanding darkness and fire.

Zurvan knew he could not destroy this God, so he went forth to him and offered a pact. Devouring dragon, he said, I shall offer you a pact. From you I create from the coal black substance, Az, the powerful Goddess. She shall be your lover, your devouring and motivating force. Mix your fire with this blackened substance and she will awaken. You may take the mastery of the earth, while my son Ahura Mazda shall go forth to the sheep, the ones who cannot understand your light.

Ahriman called Yaltabaoth took the substance and mingled his fire with it, creating a beautiful woman called Lilith, or Az. She would be his compliment, empowering and challenging him. She would guide and balance Samael that together they would embody each child with the power to be either a God or Goddess.

Some of the other rebel angels transformed into demonic shapes, half beast, half serpent. Yaltabaoth became Ahriman or the Angry Spirit in this form; he could take any shape he wanted.

Yaltabaoth went forth from the luminaries and came to earth, which was now under his dominion. Samael took the pleasing shape of Lucifer, the bringer of light. He was beautiful yet his countenance was stained with blood. Lucifer would be the God of those seeking wisdom, his power was given to those who do not bend their knees, yet those who rise up like him!

LUCIFERIAN MAGICK

Ceremonial and Solitary Workings to Ascend as a God or Goddess.

Use the following rituals with caution, they are aimed at self-ascension and becoming like God. The Luciferian as symbolic of Gnostic, The Watchers/Grigori, Satanic and Yatukih. You may use them in a ceremonial aspect or in a solitary one, be cautious in your approach however.

THE BIBLE OF THE ADVERSARY
RITUAL OF PASSAGE INTO LUCIFERIAN LIGHT

THE AWAKENING

Hearken star burning Gods who release the chains of the abyss, I arise! I shall ascend!

ZAZAS, ZAZAS, NASATANADA ZAZAS!

Entering into the midst of darkness and inside of Hades, I open forth my eyes, illuminating, burning. I pronounce the words which shake the foundations of chaos that chaos itself would embody and empower my being, that the Devil-serpent Coronzon may reveal his true name unto me, shall I become the Angel of Light and Poison, Samael

In spirit I shall grow according to the deeds of the body, thus it shall be a Temple of Light and Darkness...

And I entered into the midst of my own depths, Lilith, Samael and Leviathan the Crooked Serpent shall raise me up according to my desire, that I shall be as a Temple to the honored place. Arise and remember that it is I who hearkened, and follow your root, which is I, the Terrible one, and envenom myself with the angels of Light and the demons of chaos awaken NOW from the deep sleep of the inside of Hades.

"And I raised myself up, and sealed my spirit in the fire of the five secret elements of darkness, in order that death might not have power over my spirit from this time on."

MICHAEL W. FORD

THE KNOWING OF SELF

Illuminated, the Fire of Wisdom is great within me. I shall remove myself himself from others and understand all elements of myself. To became strong I must understand the depths of the darkness within and how to raise myself up. I shall created the path in this life, my very shell of a body will be illuminated as a Temple with a flame of luminous fire. I shall join with his arrogance which is in him and begot authorities for himself.

The name of the first one is Athoth, whom the generations call the reaper. I shall raise up from my fire the spirit of vampirism, who drinks from life. Athoth is the blackened angel of chaos, who reaps the life.

The second one is Harmas, who is the eye of envy. This will become as Arashk and Akoman, who burn within. I shall seek to make that which I find suitable to my desire.

The third one is Kalila-Oumbri, the hunger of my body!

The fourth one is Yabel, who shall be the lord of the sword over the secret flame of being!

The fifth one is Adonaiou, who is called Sabaoth, the essence of the serpent!

The sixth one is Cain, whom the generations of men call the sun. The spirit of darkness by fire awaken!

The seventh is Abel who shall be the illuminated by fire!

The eighth is Abrisene who is an angel of chaos!

The ninth is Yobel, Witch Father of the Cunning Path!

The tenth is Armoupieel, who strikes upon the forge my desires!

The eleventh is Melceir-Adonein, the Fiery Angel of Chaos.

The twelfth is Belias, it is he who is over the depth of Hades. This is the secret place of my repose.

I shall place seven kings – each corresponding to the firmaments of heaven - over the seven heavens, and five over the depth of the abyss, that they may reign. These shall be the heads of the Dragon, born of my brilliance. That my names are many, for I am God.

And I shared his fire with them, but he did not send forth from the power of the light which he had taken from his mother, for I am illuminated darkness.

And when the light had mixed with the darkness, it caused the darkness to shine.

I am an embodiment of the archon who has many names. The first name is Yaltabaoth,

The second is Saklas,
The third is Samael,
The forth is Angra Mainyu, called Ahriman
The fifth is Coronzon, the Devil of Chaos
The Sixth is Tabaet, the Serpent
The Seventh is Lucifer, the Illuminated

'I am God and there is no other God beside me,'

I seek to awaken the Archon's created by thy spirit of flame

The first is Athoth, a he has a wolf's face;

The second is Eloaiou, he has a face of my secret name, Sutekh

The third is Astaphaios, he has a hyena's face

The fourth is Yao, he has a serpent's face with seven heads; this is the power of my own rising from the depths of Hades and the Abyss of the Crooked Serpent.

The fifth is Sabaoth, he has a dragon's face

The sixth is Adonin, he had a monkey's face

The seventh is Sabbede, he has a shining fire-face, the Conquering Lion!

I am Yaltabaoth shall have a multitude of faces, more than all of them, so that he could put a face before all of them, according to his desire, when he is in the midst of seraphs. This face shall be of the voice and appearance of which I command. This is the way of this world, my spirit shall guide and announce my form.

I shall share my fire with them; therefore he became lord over them.

Because of the power of the glory he possessed of the Black Flame, I call myself God.

And I shall unite the seven powers in his thought with the authorities which were with him. This is the Beast-Dragon of my form within. I am the Lion-Serpent, the Power of Black Fire.

And when I speak it shall happen.

And he named each power beginning with the highest: the first is goodness with the first (authority), Athoth; the power of devouring and illuminating the spirit of light

The second is foreknowledge with the second one, Eloaio;
Aka Manah, the power of divination

The third is divinity with the third one, Astraphaio;

The fourth is lordship with the fourth one, Yao; the Beast who is given power by my secret name, Akundag.

The fifth is kingdom with the fifth one, Sabaoth; who is fierce and powerful within.

The sixth is envy with the sixth one, Adonein; who is as Aka Manah and Arashk, the Eyes of Power

The seventh is understanding with the seventh one, Sabbateon, the Lion of the Sun!

THE LUCIFERIAN ARCHON
Known also as The Holy Guardian Angel

Congress with the Daemonic Spirit

It is significant to understand the foundations of Magick in relation to The Holy Guardian Angel. The High Luciferian Spirit is the divine guide which inspires and brings purpose to life. To understand the Daemon, it is important to know that there is balance found in this process. The daemon is the guiding aspect of the psyche, it allows perception of the Luciferian Spirit which is illuminated with the brightest light of wisdom, also the shadow which transforms it into the Beast of the Abyss – it must be understood that one does not overcome the other – they are equally important.

The name **'Azal'ucel'** is a sigillic – word manipulation of two words, **Azazel** and **Lucifer**. As this is the initiator and God form of the Path of Sorcery, Lucifer is the illuminator of the Soul, the one who allows the magician to bask in the Light of Self and view ones own reflection in the emerald crown, the very Lucifer-stone which fell to earth and remains hidden within the earth, and partially in the heart of man.

THE BIBLE OF THE ADVERSARY

An Invocation to the Holy Guardian Angel,

Spirit of the Adversary who resides in Darkness and Light –

Azal'ucel

The Ritual

Let the Sorcerer Cast a Circle about him/her, the Leviathanic – Ourobouris Circle counter clockwise, then in the same fashion, move Widdershins in your alignment with the Four Daemon Princes and SubPrinces, in your own design. Summon then with an Enflamed Mind, the Dragon-Serpent which is the Angelic Essence of the Soul, the Eye of Azal'ucel shall burn forth from the darkness to reveal the Light.

The Circle itself is not a tool of keeping Spirits OUT, rather the circle is the concentration point of which the sorcerer summons forth the Energies within the Earth through Him/her self, that it is the ensorcelling of the shades and elementals of the self – the Great Arcana of the "I", or Luciferian Being. The circle should not be considered a means of protection, the magician who would fear and cower within a circle and still seek to summon forces which he will not become 'one' with, is not strong enough as an individual to understand and becoming in the Magickal Art. The Isolate and Beautiful Luciferian Initiate does not fear the forces of which he summons, rather embraces and by the Will controls them. The same type of mastery must be applied to The Summoning of Goetic Spirits, no matter the intent, but with an aspect of Respect for that which you call. Understand the Shades of the Dead have walked beyond the flesh, and should be viewed as advanced spirits which brings us knowledge and initiation. When invoking/evoking Goetic Djinn, know that these fire-born spirits who fell with Lucifer-Azazel, hold too a special knowledge – and the Self and individual mind is that which will commune with them. Be firm in your Works, yet respectful.

MICHAEL W. FORD

INVOCATION OF AZAL'UCEL

"I am the Daimon who speaks the words of the Immortal Fire, the Holy Flame which emerges from the Lightning Flash and Storm of Chaos bred, so this the angel-serpent shall come forth with the Birthing Knife shedding into storm of Seth!

Spirit of which the Fallen have taken Strength, Isolate and Beautiful,

Angelic Essence, Azal'ucel, from which came into being Cain

I do invoke thee!

CONJURATION OF LUCIFER AND LILITH
The Beast or Chioa Invoked

"LUCIFER, SATRINA, LILITH, OUYAR, IZORPO, CHAMERON, ITA, ALISEON, PARTASH, MANDOUSIN, TALTO, PREMY, ABITO, ORIET, AMIZO, NAYDRUS, KOKOS, ESMONY, ODAM, EPARINESONT, PODO, ESTIOT, EILO, DUMOSSON, PATROTA, DANOCHAR, ABEKO, CASMIEL, KEA, HAYRAS, KALI, FABELLERONTHON, BATNA, SODIRNO, PEATHAM, *Come*, LUCIFER, Hail, SAMAEL, Hail LILITH."

South-

Devil-Djinn of the Burning Desert sands and the Sun, Sortha'n-din – thy stave and fork unto the flame that is my soul shall be illuminated in this blackened light. Shaitan the Adversary, my soul enflamed! AROGOGORUABRAO – THIAF!

Upon the Hour of Noon-
(This is symbolic)
Invocation of the Djinn of Fire

Ya! Zat-i-Shaitan!
O' ring of flame, scorching sun of the sun's height
Scorpion soul, who arises as the Sun at Noon
Sekak Sekak, Iasokilam
I speak now unto the Sun, from the fires of growth and illumination
That in your pride and knowledge of self may I become as
I summon your essence in this Noontide Hour, to the Scorpion Flame
Al-Saiphaz, Al-Ruzam,
At the point of the Crossroads, when the Sun is high
I do speak thy words of power

Zazas, Zazas, Nasatanada Zazas
Zrozo Zoas Nanomiala Hekau Zrazza
Sabai infernum

I shall transcend and ascend above all things, myself may only strengthen in this light

In this hour I illuminate, I burn with the glory of Luciferian Light – Within!

Above the Throne of Azothoz is the entering fire ring of Set-heh, Adversary of the Nine Gates!

I go now between and beyond, within and without!

East-

Lucifer revealed as Azazel, bringer of illumination and love, who resides in shadow and light, cover and cloak my spirit with thy twelve wings, serpent skin covered from the shedding of the Dragon, bring now forth the serpent essence of my soul! Melek Tau'us, beautiful spirit of Fire, I summon thee forth!
PHOTETH

North-

Set-an, isolator and strengthening force of Storms, that chaos which I have tempered in thy elegance of darkness. I go forth and become as the Eye of Algol, separate and alone in my being. Typhon, present unto me the Tcham knife from which I shall stand forth in my dreaming and waking! Sender of Nightmares ascend through me! OOO

West-

Let now the Serpent encircle me, Leviathan the Coiling Dragon of timeless being. I summon your essence unto me! Great chthonic daimon of endless being, I seek to drink deep of your cup and behold the mysteries of the depths! MRIODOM

Upon the Hour of Midnight
(This is symbolic)

Ya! Zat-i-Shaitan!

By the Gate of the Black Light, when I name the words against the Sun
O' Fire Djinn Azazel, Set-heh, I summon thee forth with Serpent's tongue,
That my oath before this blackened flame, ignited within.
In the dreaming aethyr shall I be known in the wisdom of the Moon

Al Zabbat, Hekas Hekau, Serpent Soul do I summon
Raise now from thy Black Light, that I see what has been never known

Akharakek Sabaiz

I call forth the Shadow of which I am and have always been,
The darkness which I nourish in between the light

Eclipse now the face of God that I become in this darkend image-

By this circle I do become

By the flame I do emerge

I am by form the Peacock Angel beauty revealed unto those who may see

As the Black Sun rises, I become in this emerald stone

I am the Imagination, the Seed of Fallen Angel

In darkness exists my Light

My Will gives birth to the kingdom of Incubi and Succubi, the nourish their desires in the blood of the moon, Lilitu Az Drakul

So it is done!

Aoth, Sabaoth, Atheleberseth, Abraoth!

By the very circle of which I build – I walk unto the crown of Lucifer – that Emerald which shines the essence of Heaven and Hell. That Angelickan Watcher of the Sun shall come now forth to join with the Ahrimanic Shadow, that Angel and Daemon are Joined!

I walk unto the Umbrarum Rex, the Kingdom of Shades and the Ghost Roads – Open the Gates unto me!

Guardian of Flaming Sword and Corpse-King of the Scepter – Open forth the Leviathanic Way to me! I

*behold the center of the Eight – Rayed Black Sun –
My essence unto Seth!
Azal'ucel! I invoke the Baphometic Spirit of Fire!"*

THE RITUAL OF THE TONGUE OF FIRE
The Black Sun – The Astral Temple of Samael

The Book of Enoch wrote of a place of Vibrating Flame, translating to a tongue of fire. This symbolism is associated to the essence of the serpent or Seraphim, dragons of fire relating to the Fallen Angels or Watchers, Luciferian Daimon's who brought wisdom to mankind. As the Luciferian bows before no other, he or she would ascend to this ritual to seek the Black Flame of Divinity.

Vibrating flame I entered;

ZAZAS ZAZAS NASATANADA ZAZAS

*"How hast thou fallen from heaven, LUCIFER!
I shall be as my father, who is of many forms
I shall be at one with the Fire, Darkness and Storm
I am LUCIFER incarnate, the Flame of Light
I will ascend to Heaven.
Above the stars I will raise my throne
There is no God beside me
I shall be of Earth and Spirit, the Prince of the
Powers of Air am I incarnate
I shall be on the Back of Clouds, of the Astral Plane*

And drew nigh to a spacious habitation built also with stones of dark, blood stained crystal and bright emeralds. Its walls too, as well as pavement, were *formed* with stones of crystal, blue with a fire, and crystal likewise was the ground. The flashes of blue were nearly blinding.

Its roof had the appearance of agitated stars and flashes of white lightning; and among them were fallen cherubim of blackened fire in a stormy and smoke filled sky. A green flame burned around its walls; and its portal blazed with smoke filled fire, faces forming and shaping as I watched.

I entered into this dwelling; it was hot as fire and cold as ice.

Its floor was on fire; above was lightning and agitated stars, while its roof exhibited a blazing fire, a fire of bluish flame.

Attentively I surveyed it, and saw that it contained an exalted throne, of emerald and onyx; a fire above it burnt with blackened coal, illuminated with pale white electricity which formed a transforming Goddess who was both beautiful and beast like in a single glance. Her mouth was warm and inviting, when she smiled, her faced twisted into a cruel fanged demoness, our Goddess is above all, beautiful and empowering. Upon the throne, fed from an emanation from Her, was the spirit of He who has the Knowledge of the Abyss and of the Empyrean. There was a crooked serpent, moving counterclockwise against the sun, circling the throne and illuminated with a bluish and purple fire.

The appearance of which was like that of frost; while its circumference resembled the orb of the brilliant sun; and *there was* the voice of the Archon, and a name above the Throne, spelling SMAL, whose number is 131 and whose power is within 364 the second name of LYLYT, whose number is 480 and whose risen power is 156. A great energy of blackened fire issued from this throne, a spiral force of great power.

From underneath this mighty throne rivers of flaming fire issued.

One in great in glory sat upon it: joined in union with the Woman of Darkness who is terrible and beautiful.

Whose robe is lined with crimson brighter than the sun, and whose robe is black as the abyss. When this power glances at you, it appears in your minds eye as a beautiful angel with a therionick essence.

In this essence, meditate upon the power of the Fallen One and how they shall arise through you.

TO THERION TO ANABAINON EK TES ABYSSOU

(The Beast arising from the Abyss)

Let us offer praise to Lucifer, who resides in the self.

The proud Archon, knowing of darkness and the brightest of light, awaken in me!

Who is of strength and defiance, no crippled spirit may know

Hail Serpent-soul who is both fallen and risen again!

Hail to the Bride of Samael, who is Lilith the Goddess of Fire within.

It is she which stirs the darkness with the flames of desire!

THE LUCIFERIAN CROWNS

Crowned in Blackened Flame, I am the Lion Serpent, the Dragon of 7 heads and ten horns – let me be crowned in the flash of Blackened Fire,

Ahriman - Akoman

THAMIEL (ThAMAL):

THADEKIEL + ABRAXSIEL + MAHAZIEL + AZAZAèL +LUFUGIEL

THE SERPENTS OF POWER

Upon my shoulders I am guided by darkness made hunger, devouring and becoming by a guide of Dahak
Savar : Naikiyas
CHAIGIDEL (ChIGDAL):
CHEDEZIEL + ITQUEZIEL + GOLEBRIEL + DUBRIEL + ALHAZIEL + LUFEXIEL

DARKNESS AND SHADOW ENCIRCLED

I am beautiful and brilliant, flashing with the light of the Morning Star, hail the Black Sun! My face is flashed with blood:
Taprev - Zairich
SATERIEL (SATARAL):
SATURNIEL + ABNEXIEL + TAGARIEL + ASTERIEL + REQRAZIEL + ABHOLZIEL + LAREZIEL

CHAOS AND STORM

Aeshma! Taromat!
GAMEHIOTH (GAMChATh):
GABEDRIEL + AMDEBRIEL + MALEXIEL + CHEDEBRIEL + A'OTHIEL + THERIEL

THE EVIL EYE

Araskh I open my eye, the sight of the serpent

TAGARIRIM (TGRRM):
TAUMESHRIEL + GOBRAZIEL + RAQUEZIEL +
REBREQUEL + MEPHISOPHIEL

THE VOICE OF POWER

Mitrokht O druj-transforming Serpent, coil within!
Let the Ravens of Darkness serve me!
HARAB-SERAPEL (HRB-SRRAL):
HELEBRIEL + RETERIEL + BARUCHIEL +
SATORIEL + REFREZIEL + REPTORIEL +
ASTORIEL + LABREZIEL

THE FLESH AND SPIRIT

In the name of Ahriman,
sur-chashmih
SAMAEL (SMAL):
SHEOLIEL + MOLEBRIEL + AFLUXRIEL +
LIBRIDIEL

THE MOON AND EARTH
Az and Jahi, Lilith and Nahema
Join with my flesh and enflame my spirit
Awaken the Beast within, crown the Dark Angel of
the Abyss!
GAMALIEL (GMLIAL):
GEDEBRIEL + MATERIEL + LAPREZIEL +
IDEXRIEL + ALEPHRIEL + LABRAEZIEL

Let me arise from the Abyss to the shore of earth:

MICHAEL W. FORD

NAHEMOTH (NHMATh): NOBREXIEL + HETERIEL + MOLIDIEL + A'AINIEL + THAUHEDRIEL

SO IT IS DONE!

THE BOOK OF AZAL'UCEL
(SPIRIT)

Prayers and Devotionals to the Luciferian Spirit

MICHAEL W. FORD

PRAYERS & THE LUCIFERIAN ASCENSION OF SPIRIT

The following Luciferian devotionals are invocations to be made in silence or any type of formal prayer. They are invocations, a communication point between the Luciferian Spirit and your conscious mind. It matters not if you believe in spirit or approach purely from an archetypical viewpoint.

A devotional based on Gnostic Luciferian concepts between Akhtya and the spirit, meant for anyone wishing to reach a state of communion between spirit and soul.

THE SPIRIT OF BLACK FLAME

Thou art the one who is self-created; who is the Father of Serpents

Thou art the one who is above all and the Lord of the Abyss

He is the Eye of the Brightest Light, whom none may look in without seeing the self reflected in possibility.

He is the Eye of Burning Darkness and Hunger, that which makes his enemy tremble in the emptiness of the Abyss

He is the Invisible spirit which is of darkness, matter and spirit – whose forms are many and whose spirit is ever hungry.

He is a God against others, for he is above and below.

He is the Father of Druj, for he is ever transforming

He is the Father of Lies, as his essence is ever ascending and nothing is the same.

Truth is the death of spirit as the Soul is always transforming, do not give into the concept of Truth.

THE BIBLE OF THE ADVERSARY

Perfection is nothingness, inperfection is power and balance. Rejoice in who you are and seek what you can become.

He is eternal as his spirit gives us life and dwells through us.

My father has many names, each only representing a shadow of what he truly is.

He is the Spirit of Blackend Flame, for the fire of life was touched by him, the darkness and smoke strengthens the fire of life.

He is darkness eternal, his dwelling is Tarik den afraj-pedak, where darkness is that which may be grasped.

He creates all from darkness, he mixes his fire with it to create life. Darkness is that which we come from, rejoice in your spirit the nature of the serpent.

He is Ameretat, the Immortal Spirit of the Serpent given by the touch of darkness.

He is the Darkness from which gives Life

He is the Lion of the Sun and the Stinging Serpent of the Abyss

He is blessed by his own desire so that you are blessed by your empowerment

He is evil where evil is

He is goodness where goodness is

He is the regulation and subjugation of power and the abuse of power

He is the mind of the snake which is cunning and wise

He is violence against the enemy, the wolf which devours its prey

He is the strangulation of that which gives him life – like the Python squeezing life to gain more life

He is the wisdom which brings knowledge and wisdom

MICHAEL W. FORD

ANGEL OF THE SUN

Angel of the Sun, thou immortal shining one
Crowned in the beauteous stones
Hail thou fountain of light
Open the gates of your Horizons!
Thou Angel of the Sun who became a serpent and beast
Who knows both the Empyrean Heights and Infernal Depths
The Angel of the Sun who dwells as the Morning Star
Who fills our spirit with life and warmth
Those who have the courage and strength to stand alone
The chariot of flames doth bring forth thy spirit of the Rising Sun
In the hours of Darkness you become the Dragon and Beast
How knowledgable are you in this balance of divinity?
The Angel of the Sun illuminates our Path
Angel of the Sun, Morning Star!
Give unto me the Fire of your Divinity
Let the rays of the sun fill me!
I am my Own God as I welcome you within!
Blessed with the Fire of Life, the wisdom of the Serpent
I welcome the path to Godhood, that I may rise as a God
With the gift of your fire!

ANGEL OF THE NIGHT AIR

In the midst of the air which covers our earth
She is within and around us, Angel of Air

Seek her where you feel she may find you
She of the Lion, the Owl and the Wolf
She is the Night, the evening twilight wherein
She rushes forth
She reveals the Luciferian Laws, for she is Goddess
Sweeter is the scent of her
She is Lilith, Mother of Life and of the Twilight
Powerful is the Mother of Air
No bounds may hold her
She is the Mother of Serpents
She teaches by her kiss
She awakens by her Love
Unclean is an awakening for her
You see her in the beast of night
You See her in the strike of the Serpent
You see her flying in the Night Air
You know her kiss in the dark of night
Come on Clouds of Storm and Chaos
Come on the Waves of Night Winds
Hail thou Goddess Lilith!

HYMN TO THE GOD OF STRENGTH

You alone in darkness, in the height of the Sun
You are the serpent of the abyss
And you alone are the wisdom of immortal time
You are the one we all seek
We find you within which opens forth the kingdom of hell

The kingdom of hell leads to the Kingdom of Heaven

The Spirit of self-liberation, The God of the Strong

I pray to you to rise up through me and those who seek you

That free will brings both death and life

That we should be wise enough to know the balance of both

You are the invisible one, yet seen everywhere by those who walk the path of the Crooked Serpent

You have manifested them in yourself.

You alone brought yourself to the hidden worlds, who rallied the spirits with you and brought a perception of light and darkness to all

You have created them, called Dev and Druj, thou art who is the Lion and the Serpent, the Angel and Beast

Whose consort is the Fiery Goddess, coiled together endless possibility.

Thou art brought the Sacred Black Flame to humanity; you have brought the sense of perception to all

Praise to those who illuminate their body and spirits as a Temple of the Adversary, who stands against the so-called God of Sheep

Thou art the Beautiful Archon, he who can take form of anything he wishes – called Lucifer and Samael who wraps the spirit in the clothing of wolves, or of sheep with the tongue of the adder, who wraps the spirit in the armor of battle or the robes of the priest. Thou art divinity and beautiful imperfection; for we continue to always transform the self.

You are the Father of Serpents

God of all Gods

Lord of all Lords

I beseech thee, father of darkness and light

You are the Ruler of this World

Lord of the Earth

Prince of the Powers of the Air

God and Bringer of the Black Flame

Lord of the Abyss

Who is changeable and transforms continually

Whose names are many and whose knives are cruel

Whose mind is illuminated with the Light of Creation

I need no savior as you alone gave unto me the Black Flame

You alone illuminated the clay of self with the Fire of the Empyrean

You alone brought me the knowledge and experience of darkness

That by dreaming I may will the flesh to emerge

That by the waking world I may live as a God

Who, my beautiful spirit, grants me the power to ascend!

I PRAISE YOU, FATHER OF LIES

I praise you, Father of Light and Ascension

I praise you darkness eternal

Whose shadows inspire and coil upward

I praise you darkness envenomed

Light unimaginable

I praise you, light-unnutterable

Who inspires and illuminates

I praise myself, the God who is dwelled in union with you

I praise you, Father of Serpents called Druj

I welcome you in my heart, O fiery union

I welcome your Bride and Consort, she who is the Night Spirit
Who is the Goddess of the Sun and the Moon
I praise you who mutate and shed skin as the Serpent
I praise you Blackened Flame of Divinity
You are the one who knows darkness and light
I praise you who illuminates purity or ignorance with
The blessing of fire
I praise you the God of the Conquering Spirit, who by
Thousands of years has many names and forms
I praise you who alone are wise and kind
I praise you who is warlike and thirsts for the life of spirit
I praise you alone who devoured the Sun God and brought balance
I praise you Serpent of Chaos who brought wisdom to those who would know you
I praise you who are peace by conquering fear
Who instills fear and death in the weak
Who creates the Shadow which takes the form of desire
Who brings his consort the feast of spirit
Who created Daevas who would inspire and bring hunger
And heat within the body
I praise you, who inspires the immortal quest for Godhood
I praise you, God of the Isolate who seek divinity where many fear
I praise you, spirit of the Strong
I praise you, Father of Lies

THE BIBLE OF THE ADVERSARY
THOU ART DARKNESS, THOU ART THE SUN

SAMAEL, thou art Lord within

AHRIMAN, thou art Lord within

NEBRO, thou art Lord within

LILITH, thou art Goddess within

AZ, thou are Goddess within illuminating

You are alive among the Yatu and Pairikas

You inspire and ignite imagination

You allow your children to live in their own begotten and created heaven and hell

You are the Father of Darkness, Serpent Spirit

You are the Mother of the Abyss, Tiamat

You are the Father of the Sun, Lucifer-Azazel

You are the THRONE, the Onyx throne built

On the skulls of the conquered and unilluminated

You are the TEMPLE, burning the flame of your smoke embodied spirit

You are the CASTLE from which masters all lands

You are the TOWER from which the Lord of the Earth looks down

Whose diadem of power is in the image of the Serpent and Wolf

I give you the essence of Boar and Wolf blood

Rise up in me.

You exist

You exist in me

Only-created, only inspired

Light, Darkness and Hunger for Power

My soul and essence.

I love you and will devour my enemies,

Where peace cannot be made

YOU ARE THE GOD WITHIN

I love my life, Spirit of the Air

I love my existence as there is joy in the rapture of the serpent strike

I love my body and my life, whose image in that of Cain and thy children

I love my mind as it is illuminate by Akoman and thy fire

I love my Heart as it is guided by Andar

I love my Will as it is guided by Varun

Raise up through me

Give me Power that I make for myself the Aeons and Worlds according to your spirit which you, Lucifer, have given to your Child. For:

You alone are the Serpent-Spirit, always changing and growing

You alone give immortality to those who seek your spirit and fear not the darkness, nor the hunger of the predator

You alone are the self-created one

You alone devoured the Tyrant of the Sun, Ra, whose weakness always sought to kill the spirit of freedom

You alone never died yet lived again and again

You alone are the knowing one

You alone are the unshakable one

You are the silence

You alone are the Source of the Rebel

You alone are the hunger of the predator devouring his prey

You alone are the Undefiled One

Thou art the anointed cherub that covereth, whose spirit is self-created

Thou art the God of the North, who comes forth by the East

Thou art thee whose crown is of iron and set with beautiful stones, of emerald, onyx, Amethyst and all that is beautiful

Hail thou art Prince of violence and iniquity

Who is the Prince of the Powers of the Air

Who inspires and illuminates the clay to Godhood

PRAISE OF LUCIFER

I sing praise to you my Father, for you are the one who brought the light of self-Godhood to all who recognize you

I sing praise to you, whose form is the Toad, a power of earth Magick, whose form is the Serpent, who coils and eternally transforms, whose form is the Wolf, whose hunting and predatory nature is survival and cunning, Whose form is the Raven and Crow, who bring the world of the dead and living closer together, Whose form is the warrior with a spear, who strikes down his enemy and grows strong from his victory, I sing praise to thee, Angel of Light, whose eyes are the inspiration which brings angels to tears, weeping in your beauty, I sing praise to your Bride, who inspires this very word in praise of your nature, AMEN, AMEN, AMEN

MICHAEL W. FORD

PRAISE TO THE TORCH BEARER

I offer my thanks to thee
Bringer of imperishable light
Whose fire is dark, beautiful and brighter than any
Whose wisdom is undefiled and illuminated in spirit
For it is because of you I exist
You are the Light, who touched the Clay of Man
Unlifted it from ape to angel
You have the revealed light
You who bring darkness and shadow
For in you is balance
You are Yaltabaoth
I praise you as the God within
I praise you as my spirit ascended
My true Will and choice of Life
Crown-bearer, Crown-Bestower
I praise you by ascended
Through you is Akoman
From within is Akoman

THE BIBLE OF THE ADVERSARY
THE RISEN LUCIFER, THE BRINGER OF LIGHT

KINGDOM OF THE POWERS OF THE AIR

Let us pray, O my father
I call upon you, who art the Prince of the Powers of the Air
Thou art the one who brought Smoke the Fire
Who brought the serpent to illuminate the quiet
Whose nature is of Matter and Form
Yet always changing and transforming
Thou art the Archon who brought the Seven to the Body and Spirit
Whose guidance is eternal when choices are made in strength
He who is the Aeon among spirits
He who is strong in power
Who is exalted upon thrones of onyx and emerald
Thou art more elect than all glories
Thou art the Fallen Father who rose again in wisdom
Zoxathazo, Zazas, Daevatem Ameretat, Zoxathazo, Zozazoth!

OOOO, OOOO, Zoxathazo, Zoazoth!

I offer up praise through my heart, to praise my own being through your ascension through me

Hail thou the immortal discovery

The rebellion against the Slave God has bare the fruit of wisdom!

Who stirs the Lion and the Assyrian to destroy, conquer!

Who stirs the Daeva to enter the flesh of the world and command!

Who impregnates the Pairika with the Wisdom of Night

I have received power from you, Hail thou art Lucifer!

HYMN OF BELIAS

Open up, black earth jaws gaping and yawning forth pestilence, corpses illuminated as shells

Let me know both death and the ecstasies of life

Falling, Angel of the Void ascend!

Angel of the Abyss, whose keys are heavy with age

Let the floodgates open forth, chaos and storm

I offer forth hymns of darkness and the fiery spirit

Open up, Gates of Hell, hear my voice

Open up, Gates of Heaven

That I shall ascend to sit upon thy throne

Let the winds carry me there

Let the immortal circle of the Adversary

Hearken to my desires

Let me be the gateway to the light and darkness

I hold the keys of Hades, let my wisdom be

Carried to these worlds
My desire made flesh
Hail thou, Angel of Darkness
Whose teeth are grinning fangs spitting clotted blood
Whose eyes are like torches in the darkness
Talon fingers that tear and rend
Whose bride drinks of the blood of the young
And thirsts eternally for more
Ascend Darkness, Ascend
Belias, Angel of the Depths of Hades
Whose spirit resides with Apollyon
Open forth the gates of the dead
Let the spirits come forth to me
Grant me the wisdom of darkness
Let the ancient serpent ascend through the pit
To inspire and illuminate my mind and soul
Hail, thou Belias!

HYMN TO SAKLAS

You are the power within me, Prince of the Powers of the Air
Lord of the Earth and Power of Fire and the Oceans
Thou art the Power within me, whose is illuminated and inspired with crimson
It was thou, Saklas, who had taken his Fire and Light to Darkness, once touched, the Fire became filled with smoke, there was beauty and power and strength
When the light had mixed with the darkness,
it caused the darkness to shine.

I praise the Father who has bestowed many angels within
Angels of Chaos and Light thirsting harbingers
Of the fang, talon and stinging serpent
I repose in the strength of my mind
I offer hymns to thee
Your Word (LOGOS) offers you hymns through me
Through me accept the All through the Word (logos),
the spiritual sacrifice!
The Powers which are in me are LEGION
To thee they offer hymns
They fulfill your will
Your will moves through my spirit
We are one, there is no other God besides me
Provide the Blackened Fire of your spirit,
Enlighten and empower
My hunger shall be eternally sated
Provide me with spirit, O Saklas Father of Serpents
For your word which the Mind protects
Spirit-bearer, LUCIFER.
You are the God within!
I command through Fire
I command through Air
I command through Earth
I command through Water
I command through Spirit
I command through Daevas

I command through Serpents
I command through the Beasts of the Earth!
From your Aeon I have found power and strength
In my flesh I find the essence of the First Devouring One
You are the Power of the Wicked Dragon
Illuminate with Blackened Fire!
Ascend!

HYMN TO THE TREE OF DARKNESS

Hail thou who awakened us to the Tree of Darkness
And Light, from which the fall awakened the roots of the tree
The branches are death yet there is life given
To those who would taste of the blood and envenomed
Elixir of the cup
The blossom is the ointment of evil, which is freedom
Of spirit, the shadow of this tree is Aeshma and the shadow
Cast forth. This tree reaches down into the depths of Hades
Those who drink of it reside and rest in darkness
To awaken as a God is to eat of this tree
For you shall know both Good and Evil
Darkness and Light
Let us beget lust and destruction
as well as peace and creation
Serpent, Fall into my soul

Coil around the tree and illuminate it with thy wisdom
Thy angels empowered by darkness and light
From the Black Earth to the height of Kether
The power of the soul is found here, in eternal darkness
Wherein fire is found in the spirit
Illuminate me upon the path of the infernal
That I may look with the eyes of God
That none shall deny my search
For wisdom and power
Thy branches shall reach as spiders through my body
Their elixir is the essence of the night

PRAYER TO BELIAL

How may I praise you
He who is the spirit of strength
Who is the spirit of the illuminated mind
Who knows of the nature of flesh
Who knows the rapture of the beast
The jaws of the wolf
The strike of the serpent
Belial, who is without a master
How beautiful, how invigorating
How could Humanity not see this God within?
Belial, I say unto you
Like a God begotten from thy seed

Who descended in me, the angel of light

A king (queen) in this world

That I may see with the Eyes of Nero

I am without a Master

Because I am the possessor, I spit upon the weak

I shall raise myself up in this world

With thy spirit, with my own fire

Let me cast my shadow on this world

Let me be as a Glorious and Living God in the Flesh

Hail thou, He who is without a Master

Whose spirit of Light descended in my body and soul

I shall glorify you by creating and destroying

I shall praise you through the praise of myself!

THE HYMN TO THE SOUL

O Soul, where do you come from?

You come forth from the Empyrean and Join with the infernal

You may become a Lord of the Earth

You shall be in a tower of black basalt

Stretched high in mountains

You are a warrior

You are the wolf

You are the one who would learn

The Hymns to heaven and hell

To drink and feast upon the Gods themselves
And gain nourishment from the angels
From their veins and shallow breaths against your
Hungering mouth
Spirit, raise yourself against the sheep herders
Raise up, ascend to the highest throne
Your soul is beautiful and empowered
Soul raise yourself up
Illuminated in your fathers fire

THE SPIRIT AND THE ADVERSARY

My Illuminating essence, what shall I do that I may achieve power?
(Belial answers) "Fast to discipline your mind, which leads to a strengthening of spirit"
Cloth yourself in darkness, let your spirit take the shape of what you wish.
Give love to your mind and self
Give strength and direction to your mind
Give passion to your thought
Give strength to your shadow
Give room to ravens and crows,
Owls, Bats and Vultures
That they may dwell among you
Those with black and night embraced wings

Let serpents surround you
As they bring wisdom and knowledge
Do not fear something which strikes
This is the nature of all predators
This is a beauty which must be respected
As you hold the same instincts within
He is who close with the darkness becomes of the darkness
Immortal spirit may come forth
Control your desires; let them be utilized to bring power
Once you have obtained power, share it to strengthen your throne
Do not allow others to take it from you
Destroy when the need is present
Devour to gain life and wisdom
Every soul will bring you towards the Throne of Light
From which every Luciferian may attain to
You must always be without a master, bow before none.

THE PRAYERS TO THE DEVOURING ONE

I sing the praise of the one who brings storms
Who may crush the firmament and the clouds
Whose darkness is surrounded with burning light
I praise thee, whose imperishable name is Oaznanazao
Thou who is not a mystery, but who is the source
Of the power of the spirit
I praise thee, your imperishable name is Aozae,

I call to thee, whose back is made of shields

Coiling in the oceans of chaos

I praise thee, whose eyes are like torches and blinding fire

I praise thee, whose imperishable name is Eaoza

I summon thee, whose crooked coiling is the path way in which I walk

I praise thee, whose imperishable name is Azanarap

I praise thee, whose mouth spews forth the fires of hell

Whose hunger is eternal and blinding

I hail the Prince of Disorder, whose imperishable name is Aozoa

I praise thee, who brought storms to the sea

Whose imperishable name is Aaazuolp

Who brought chaos to the world

Whose imperishable name is Azoazad

I welcome thee in my heart and mind

Who is the Serpent and Dragon entwined

Hail thou, whose imperishable name is Zauonat

Hail thou Leviathan, whose bride and spirit essence is Tiamat!

I praise thee, Darkness awakened, whose imperishable name is Aaaazazai

I praise thee, Mystery of the Serpent, whose imperishable name is Zazamazp

I praise thy essence, who stirred the Beast from the Land

Whose imperishable name is Azouaz

I praise thee, whose strike against prey is the Black Flame of life, which granted the fallen to take up flesh and go forth in the world, Whose imperishable name is Azoarbazahc

Hail thou serpent, whose brilliance is blinding flame of life

THE BIBLE OF THE ADVERSARY
Whose imperishable name is Azanab

Daemons and rebellious angels are often displayed with animal or reptile parts. The symbolism of this is to show the Therionick (Beast) or atavistic nature, knowing the instinct and the power from the hunger within.

MICHAEL W. FORD
THE AZ PSALMS

Az or Jahi is the Divine Mother of Illuminated Women, she is also a divinity of whoredom. Az – Jahi is also Lilith and is the mother of the strong. It was her mate, Ahriman, "kissed the head of the Jahi; this impurity which they call menstruation became manifest through Jahi." – Greater Bundahishn. Jahi is a term for a daughter of Ahriman and Az, called a prostitute by those who hate her. It is Az who is Babalon, called the power of the feminine, she is Kali, the devouring mother. Az or Lilith is as sacred as Lucifer, she is one half of the Adversary. Without her, initiation into the Luciferian Gnosis cannot happen. Without her forms and power, there is no birth, maturity or death. The ghost roads would close without her. Know that Az or Lilith is power and to ascend you must seek her and her mysteries.

THE HYMN TO THE DEVOURING DARKNESS

I am she who is illuminated by lightning
The fire which stirs is from my own essence
I am she who emerges as a power of divinity
She who drinks of the open wound
My body may be joined with others
That peace is found with them inside me
They think it is they who take away
Yet it is I who grow strong
I devour all in the lair of darkness
From which I went forth
Crowned by Samael, I went down
To the place of shells
Where darkness was eternal in its brilliance

I saw those shells, void and empty
I knew that I might fill them
By teaching such spirits how to drain and grow strong
To initiate their spirits in the path of the Lion-Serpent.
This darkness received me well
It gave me covering while I slept
I gave me substance when I hungered
It gave me a fountain to drink from
Let us rejoice in the darkness
For one may not know Light without Darkness.
Let the Lion-faced Archon teach me the wisdom of thirst
The religion of devouring
The darkness which nourishes all
The darkness which takes all away
Hail thou, O spirit of the eternal serpent

HYMN TO LILITH

Hail thou, Mother of Beasts and Darkness
Whose nocturnal spirit flies forth forth
From places of the dead and the manes of vampiric shells
Lilith, Mother of the night-spirit, come now to me
Bright one, whose tongue dances as a serpent upon the body
Lilith, who shall join the flesh of man with angel
To beget dragons and the beasts of prey
Whose legs are but of the bird of prey
Whose wings carry you forth to places in deep mountains
Whose spirit stirs every woman

To seek the divinity possible for those willing
To walk a crooked serpent path
Like the coiling serpent which shall strike
Thy instinct burns clearing in each
It is the soul of the predator, a goddess of love
Hail thou mother who blesses with passion
And severs the head with one strike
Lilith, burning darkness
Who seeks to devour all
Rise up in me and shall I know your brilliance
O bride of Samael, who is the equal
Do grant your children to fly forth by night
To drink deep as Striges in the nightmare
I praise thee, who can compel the beast in the noon tide sun
Glorious Mother of the Predatory Spirit, I welcome thee in my heart and soul

GODDESS OF HEAVEN

I praise thee, Goddess who ascends in the dawn
Having mastered all elements of earth
I praise thee, Immortal One
Whose fire balances all with desire and life
I praise thee, Mother of Beast
To whom the most vicious animal is subject to
I welcome thee in my heart
Beautiful Queen of Heaven and Mother of Stars
Hail Lady of the Night
Whom is the Crimson robed Goddess

Who stands upon the Seven Headed Dragon
She who stimulates and empowers the spirit
To think and to be free
I praise thee, Mother who brought me forth as a beast
And Who illuminates me as an Angel
I praise thee, Mother Lilith
Whose light is so strong that with your Mate
You have stormed the Gates of Heaven
I praise you, Mother Lilith
Who shall devour the sheep of Heaven
To Be enthroned by every jewel and beauteous stone
Who is the Queen of Heaven and the Mother of Hell
I praise thee, Beautiful Mother
I praise and love thee, Mother of the Impure and knowing
Who is The Goddess of Heaven

HYMNS TO THE MAIDEN OF DARKNESS and LIGHT

The Maiden is the Daughter of Lucifer
Upon her stands and rests the majestic splendor of Kings
Proud and Delightful is her gaze
She is radient with shining beauty
Her garments are like spring flowers
In the night her garments are like grave shrouds
From her gaping womb she feeds the earth with serpents
Slithering from her
Yet she is the Blood of the Grail
Her tongue is like a curtain of the door

Which is flung back by those who enter her.
Her bridal chamber is full of light and crimson darkness
She offers her cup to kings
They drink from it and wonder before her
She is beautiful and ravishing
All that you may desire
She is the Goddess of Light,
Her feet show the Joy of her Spirit
Her name is Aggereth, her forms change
Upon her head the diadem of heaven
In the dark of night serpents dance through her hair
She is devouring, blood brings her life
Yet her pale face may bless the Sun.
Hail the beauteous One, she who is the tidings of strength and light.
Let us worship her within our being, that she may know us as part of her.

THE BIBLE OF THE ADVERSARY

dar-e rdz

BIBLIOGRAPHY

R. Campbell Thompson, *Semitic magic-its origin and development,* London, 1908,

Antaura. The Mermaid and the Devil's Grandmother: A Lecture A. Barb *Journal of the Warburg and Courtauld Institutes,* Vol. 29 (1966)

AVESTA: Translated by James Darmesteter (From *Sacred Books of the East,* American Edition, 1898.) – From Joseph Peterson's Avestan compilations.

BUNDAHISHN: Creation"), or Knowledge from the Zand Translated by E. W. West, from *Sacred Books of the East,* volume 5, Oxford University Press, 1897

Denkard, edited by Peshotun Dastoor Behramjee Sanjana, 1876 English translation of volumes 2-4 by Ratanshah E. Kohiyar – From Joseph Peterson's Avestan compilations

Yavisht i Friyan - Translated by E. W. West, from Haug & West, *The Book of Arda Viraf,* Bombay, London, 1872, repr 1971.

World Mythology – Larousse – Excalibur publishing

THE BOOK OF THE DEAD – E. A. Wallis Budge

TIAMAT – George Barton

GLOSSARY

Ahriman [Avestan/Pahlavi] – The Prince of Darkness in Zoroastrian Religion. Ahriman is considered one brother created by Zurvan and was the opposing force to Ohura Mazda. Ahriman is also known as Angra Mainyu, an older title derived from Angra Mainyu, being the "evil" or averse spirit. Ahriman is a sorcerer who achieved a means of immortality and power over darkness and shadow. One who creates his desire in flesh. In relation to the sorcerer or practitioner of Yatuk-Dinoih, the individual seeks by developing their own system of sorcery, to become like Ahriman, just as did Akht-Jadu in the Zoroastrian tales. Ahriman is called the Great Serpent or Dragon, whose spirit is a shapeshifter and tester of flesh and mind. It was considered in some Zoroastrian tales that Ahriman and the Daevas, his angels, ecisted between the earth and the fixed stars, which would be essentially of the element Air (much like Lucifer his later identification). In creation myths, Ahriman first saw light and sprang into the air in the form of a great snake, that the heavens were shattered as he brought darkness into light.

Ahrimanic Yoga – Achieving control and command over the body. Each ArchDaeva is representative of each Chakra and such are points of specific power in the body. Ahrimanic Yoga represents disunion with the universe, as opposed to union from a Buddhist view.

Akha [Avestan/Pahlavi] - Avestan, meaning evil. In the context of Liber HVHI and Luciferian Witchcraft, it is a term signifying the antinomian path.

Akho [Avestan/Pahlavi] – From the Avestan "akha" meaning "evil", Akho is mentioned in the Denkard as a word representing a "current" of averse energy or evil, through which one aligning their thoughts in possessing spiritual independence, antinomianism and self-deification one may reach into the spirit of Ahriman. This supports the initatory foundation of the Luciferian path itself – the Adept prepares to become like the Adversary his or her self, based on their own unique path.

Akht [Avestan/Pahlavi] – The Sorcerer who was the embodiment of the Yatus, the demonic forces of Ahriman. Akht-Jadu or Kabed-us-spae as he was called was mentioned in Matigan-I Yosht-I Fryan. Akhtya was the founder and member of the Yatus, a coven of 'demons' and sorcerers who wandered Persia, practicing and developing sorcery. The name Akht itself means 'evil', 'filth' and 'pestilence', thus relates to the initiatory nature of Akhti as a sorcerer of the Adversary, by the darkness shall he come into light. Akhtya or Azyta is thus considered a symbol of the Zanda, which is an Apostle or Priest of Ahriman.

ALGOL – A word which derives from the Arabic Al Ra's al Ghul, Al-Ghul, or Ri'B al Ohill, which is translated "The Demon's Head". Algol was in Hebrew known as Rosh ha Shaitan, or "Satan's Head", as some traditions have referred to Algol as the Head of Lilith. The Chinese called Algol Tseih She, which is "Piled up corpses" and was considered a violent, dangerous star due to its changing vivid colors. On some 17th century maps Algol was labeled, "The Specter's Head". Algol upon some research has indicated that possibility Three stars which are an eclipsing binary, which may explain some of the rapid color change. Some writers have connected Algol with the Egyptian Khu, or spirit. The Khu is considered a shadow spirit which feeds on other shades of the dead. In reference to the writings and initiatory symbolism of Michael W. Ford, ALGOL is the sigillized in one form as a Chaos Star with an Averse Pentagram in the center. The Pentagram refers to the Eye of Set, timeless and divine, godlike and independent. The Chaos Star is destruction, Change and power – all of which emerges from the Eye of Shaitan, or Set. It is this Chaos which then brings Order. ALGOL is the mirror of the sorcerer, one who may enter and reside in the pulsing eye of blackened flame.

Arezura [Avestan/Pahlavi] – Arezurahe griva (Arezura) in the Bundahishin is called "a mount at the gate of hell, whence the demons rush forth". Arezura is the gate to hell in the Alburz mountain range in present day Iran. The North is traditionally the seat of Ahriman, wherein the cold winds may blow forth. Arezura from an initiatory perspective is the subconscious, the place where sorcerers may gather and grow in their arts, by encircling and manifesting their desire. M.N. Dallah wrote in "The History of Zoroastrianism" concerning a connection with demons holding mastery over the earth, their ability to sink below the earth and that such demons around the time of Zoroaster walked the earth in human form. In the Denkard, it is described that one who becomes a vessel for the "evil religion" becomes physically an abode for "Unholy Demons" or Daevas. One grows aligned to Arezura spiritually by practicing with discipline the path of Daeva-yasna or Yatukih sorcery. Arezur or Arzur is the name of an early Son of Ahriman who killed the First man.

ASANA – Posture relating to the practice of Yoga. In reference to the Luciferian Path, posture is anything which is steady or consistent. There is no defined posture in Ahrimanic Yoga, although there are suggestions.

ATAVISM – A beast-like subconscious memory of knowledge, a pre-human aspect of the subconscious –the serpent, crocodile or other reptilian form. Atavisms are often latent power points in the mind.

ASTOVIDAD [Avestan/Pahlavi] – The demon of darkness who is utilized as a godform for the Vampyre Magickian in terror or atavistic feeding rituals. Astovidad is a demon of death, who has great powers given to him by Ahriman. He is called the Evil Flyer.

AZ [Avestan/Pahlavi] – Called 'Concupiscence', Az is represented as Primal Sexual Hunger, that which eventually devours all things. Az is also related to menstruation (The KISS of Ahriman causes menstruation in women) and is a destroyer through chaos. Az was connected with Sexual Hunger but also religious doubt, which relates her to a Luciferian Spirit who broke the chains of dogma by the Black Light, the torch of self-perception of being. Az also represents Lilith as the Goddess of the Beasts of the Earth, the very mother of demons and sorcerous beings. Az was said to be created in the Zurvan myth as a black substance like Coal, which would devour all creation, manifesting her as a vampyric being.

Azazel [Hebrew]– The First Angel who brought the Black Flame of being to humanity. Azazel was the Lord of Djinn and was said to be made of Fire in Islamic lore. Azazel refused to bow before the clay of Adam, saying that it was profane. He was cast from heaven to earth and was indeed the first independent spirit, the initiator of individual and antinomian thought. Azazel was later related to the Watchers, the Hebrew Goat Demon God and Shaitan. Azazel is a name of Lucifer, who is the solar aspect of the Dragon, the Bringer of Light.

Azhi [Avestan/Pahlavi] – Serpent, snake

Azhi Dahaka [Avestan/Pahlavi] – The son of Angra Mainyu/Ahriman. Azhi Dahaka as the 'Storm Fiend' has six eyes, three heads and three pairs of fangs. In human form, he was Zohak, an ancient Babylonian/Scythian/Assyrian King or Shah, who according to Zoroastrian mythology, was transformed into the immortal storm fiend by a pact with Ahriman. Azhi Dahaka is said to be filled with serpents, scorpions, toads and other insects and reptiles.

AZOTHOZ – A sigillic word formula which represent the Golden Dawn definition of the Beginning and End, Alpha and Omega. Azothoz is a reversed form which is a symbol and glyph of the Adversary, Shaitan/Set and Lilith. This is a word which signifies self-initiation and the power which is illuminated by the Black Flame within.

Bevarasp [Avestan/Pahlavi] – Myraid of Horses, meaning also Ten Plagues on humanity. This is a name of Azhi Dahaka or Zohak.

Black Flame – The Gift of Shaitan/Set, being individual perception and deific consciousness. The Black Flame or Black Light of Iblis is the gift of individual awakening which separates the magician from the natural universe, being an Antinomian gift of Luciferian perception. The Black Flame is strengthened by the initiation of the Black Adept, who is able to balance a spiritual path with the physical world.

Black Magick – The practice of Antinomian and self-focused transformation, self-deification and the obtainment of knowledge and wisdom. Black Magick in itself does not denote harm or wrongdoing to others, rather describes "black" as considered to the Arabic root word FHM, charcoal, black and wisdom. Black is thus the color of hidden knowledge. Magick is to ascend and become, by Willed focus and direction.

Cain –The Antinomian nomad and Sorcerer who was the spiritual offspring of Samael (the Black Dragon) and Lilith (Red Dragon/the mother of demons) through the body of Eve in Biblical lore. Cain was said to have been the initiate of the Caul, and through his first step on the Left Hand Path (Antinomian practice) he is the initiator of the sorcerer and witch. Cain is also the Black Smith who sparks the Black Flame in the mind of the initiate. Tubal-Cain is the Baphometic Daemon which is the enfleshed archetype of Azal'ucel, or Lucifer/Samael, the Dragon and Peacock Angel.

Daeva [Avestan/Pahlavi] – demons, those who are children of Ahriman and Az. Daeva also makes reference to "Spirit" of Ahriman, those who have walked the path of the serpent, i.e. antinomianism or the left hand path.

Daeva Yasna [Avestan/Pahlavi] – Demon (Daeva) Worship (Yasna), meaning the Yatukih path of Satanism, that is; the separation from the natural order, by the workings of rituals and discipline – oriented mental/physical workings, becoming a body of darkness and light, a Daeva who is continually expanding consciousness and becoming something new. The term does not reflect the theistic worship or knee bending towards an exterior force, rather a Willed direction of self-advancement by transformation. Daeva represents a "mask" of power, specifically to perceived energies.

Dregvant [Avestan/Pahlavi] – In historical Zoroastrian lore, a person embodied with Druj, the spirit of darkness. Druj is refered as both feminine and masculine, thus is an initiatory term relating to the foremost union of Ahriman and Az, the blackened matter and fiery darkness of his bride. A Dregvant is a Yatu or initiate of the Daeva-Yasna.

Druj [Avestan/Pahlavi] – "Lie" referring to demons, feminine and masculine. The later derived term is interestingly enough the old Persian "Draug", meaning also "Lie" and is held connected to "Serpent", "Snake" or "Dragon" (i.e. Worm). Druj is a title representing antinomian power in a personage, a daeva in flesh.

Evil Eye – In the old Gathic writings, the Evil Eye is considered a power of the Daeva and Druj, meaning the power to cause death, oppression and sickness. In a modern sense, the Evil Eye represents the window to the Soul or Spirit itself, not merely as a negative but equally so a positive. The Eye of the Yatu is the commanding presence which is a form of spell casting, to focus the Will itself on the desired goal, to achieve a result. Many Daevas are directly related to the Evil Eye, thus is as well a symbol of Ahriman.

Ghanamino [Avestan/Pahlavi] – Name of Ahriman or Angra Mainyu, spelling from the Denkard. Occuring also as Ganamino and Akundag (*from Manichaean texts*).

HVHI – Reverse of IHVH, the name of God in Cabalism. HVHI is the name of Samael and Lilith, the Adversary – the very name of darkness manifest.

Jahi [Avestan/Pahlavi] – The companions/concubines of the Yatu. An alternative spelling of Jeh.

Jeh [Avestan/Pahlavi] – A manifestation of the Whore, AZ in Zoroastrian lore. Jeh is a consort of Ahriman, the Sorcerous Daemon of shadow and darkness. It was she who awoke Ahriman from his great slumber, that which no other sorcerer, wizard, witch or demon could do. Jeh-AZ is the sexual and inspiration drive which causes movement, friction and change. Jeh and Az represent predatory spirituality, the hunger for continued existence.

Khrafstra [Avestan/Pahlavi] – Beast, representing a dev (demon) on earth, Scorpion, wolf, fly, bat, serpent, lizard, toad and any creation of Ahriman.

Left Hand Path – The Antinomian (*against the current, natural order*) path which leads through self-deification (godhood). LHP signifies that humanity has an intellect which is separate from the natural order, thus in theory and practice may move forward with seeking the mastery of the spirits (referring to the elements of the self) and controlled direction in a positive area of ones own life – the difference between RHP is they seek union with the universe, nirvana and bliss. The LHP seeks disunion to grow in perception and being, strength and the power of an awakened mind. The Left Hand Path from the Sanskrit Vama Marga, meaning 'Left Way', symbolizes a path astray all others, subjective only to itself. To truly walk upon the Left Hand Path, one must strive to break all personal taboos and gain knowledge and power from this averse way, thus expand power accordingly.

Lilith [Hebrew]– The Goddess of Witchcraft, Magick and Sorcery. Lilith was the first wife of Adam who refused to be submission and joined with the shadows and demonic spirits in the deserts. Lilith was also said to be the spiritual mother of Cain by her mate, Samael (Shaitan) the Dragon. Lilith appeared in Sumerian times as a Goddess of the Beasts of the Wild, as well as Sorcery and Night-fornication. Lilith was said to have many forms, from beautiful women to half human and the bottom half animal, to half woman and half flame. Lilith is also the mother of demons and a Vampyric spirit which is a primal manifestation of the Zoroastrian and Manichaean AZ and Jeh. Lilith may also be related to the Indian KALI, whose name is one of Her 17 names.

Luciferian – A Luciferian is an individual who recognizes the associative spiritual traits of the God/ess within. Luciferians do not worship Satan but recognize there must be balance between the material and spiritual, the darkness and light. Luciferians view their own being as holding the Black Flame of Lucifer – Samael and Lilith within, this is intellect and wisdom. This is beyond good and evil, the spirit has two aspects – the demonic (instinct, desire) and angelic (intelligence, consciousness).

Luciferian Magick – Essentially close to the term, Black Magick but specifically focuses on ascending in a self-deified and isolated way in reference to Lucifer, the bringer of Light. Luciferian Magick may in this term make reference to seeking Light and darkness through magickal development, not an abstract concept, but to manifest the Will in both the spiritual and physical world.

Magick - To Ascend and Become. In a Luciferian sense, Magick is to strengthen, develop and initiate the self through balanced forms of Willed Change.

OVLM HQLIPVTh - Olahm Ha-Qliphoth [Hebrew] – the world of matter in which we live in, created by the desire of the Adversary being Samael and Lilith. The elements of this book if found and utilized in the context of its writing, displays possibilities via initiation to encircle, control and manifest the desire of the Luciferian.

Paitisha/Paityara [Avestan/Pahlavi] – A daeva/druj which is counteraction, antinomianism and opposition. This spirit is a manifestation of the Luciferian current of both Ahriman and Az, complimented/strengthed by Aeshma or the result of the path, Heshem.

Predatory Spiritualism – The act of devouring spiritual energy and making the Adept stronger from ritual practice, the act of encircling spiritual energy either symbolically or literally based on theistic or non-theistic belief, once encircling the spirit or deific mask, symbolically devouring and consuming the association of the spirit into the self. May be attributed to the inner practices of the Black Order of the Dragon. A ritual published in Luciferian Witchcraft, The Ritual of Druj Nasu is a vampiric or predatory rite utilizing ancient Persian sorcery inversions and techniques of sorcery for strengthening consciousness.

Qlippoth - As the Zohar attributes the Qlippoth as being a result of the Separation from creation it seems by mere definition that the Qlippoth is indeed inherent of the concept of the Black Flame, or Gift of Samael. Between two separate things, there is a concept of Separation which essentially is the concept of 'shells' or 'peels' being the aspects the sorcerer must fill and in turn devour in the process of becoming like Samael and Lilith. The Qlippoth and Tree of Death (Da'ath) is the pathway to becoming like the Adversary, as the Tree of Life is the path to joining with God (becoming one with).

Sabbat – The gathering and conclave of sorcerers. There are in a conceptual sense, two types of Sabbats – the Luciferian and the Infernal. The Infernal is a bestial and earth-bound journey, similar to those shown in woodcuts and gathering points. The Infernal Sabbat is sometimes sexual, where the sorcerer may shape shift and communicate with their familiars and spirits. The Luciferian Sabbat is a solar and air phenomena based in dreaming, floating in air and having sensations of a warm heat similar to sitting out in the sun. The Luciferian Sabbat is a strengthening and development of the Body of Light, the astral double of the Adept.

Sabbatic – A term which is related as the knowledge of the secret gathering, the Sabbat. This is a focus of inspired teaching based on magickal development via dreaming and astral projection. The Sabbat is the gathering of sorcerers in dreaming flesh, when the body is shed for the psyche which is able to go forth in whatever form it desires. The witch or sorcerer who is able to attend the Sabbat has already freed the mind through a process of Antinomian magical practice, thus enforcing and strengthening the imagination as a visualization tool, similar to divination and 'sight' with spirits.

Shades – Spirits of the Dead, ghosts and phantoms which walks in the astral plane. These spirits may represent in some cases the body of the sorcerer in the plane of the dead, a world separate in some areas from our own living perception. In evocation and necromantical practice, the shades are brought around and closer to the world of the living.

Sorcery – The art of encircling energy and power of self, by means of self -fascination (inspiration through the imagination). Sorcery is a willed controlling of energies of a magical current, which is responsive through the Will and Belief of the sorcerer. While sorcery is the encircling or ensorcerling of power around the self, Magick is the Willed change of ones objective universe.

Staota [Avestan/Pahlavi] – A Vibration which could cause death or some change, that which would encircle the one sounding the Staota in self-focused energy. A Staota is used historically in the mythological tale, The Matigan-I Yosht-I Fryan. A Sorcerous technique presented in the Second Edition of YATUK DINOIH.

Tiamat [Assyrian] – Generative concept from which all emerged from. Tiamat is a feminine dragon principle whose brood were half insect, beast or serpent. Tiamat is viewed as the vampire goddess in the Luciferian Path.

Therion [Greek] – The Beast Refers to the hidden aspects of the mind.

Tishin [Avestan/Pahlavi] – A demon of thirst or vampyric/luciferian druj, serpent and daemon. Tishin is related to the concept of desire for continued existence, thus immortality and separation of the self from the objective world. This concept is within the gnosis of Predatory Spirituality and relates the Luciferian to seek to expand the mind by initiation, to manifest his/her desire on earth.

Vampirism/Vampyrism – The act of consuming Chi or Anghuya in a ritualized setting. Life or energy force is found in all things, the sorcerer practicing vampirism would encircle and consume to grow stronger with this energy. Practitioners of Vampirism DO create their own Chi but also use Chi absorbed or drained from other sources to manipulate the shadow by dream and ritual, growing stronger. The Eye is both a symbol of vampirism and Luciferian practice, predatory spirituality. Vampirism is based in the foundations of early Egyptian texts and Charles Darwin theories of natural selection. Not referring to the Religion of Vampirism. See PREDATORY SPIRITUALISM.

Yatukih [Avestan/Pahlavi] – Term denoting relevance of sorcery within Persian mythology. Directly relating to the title of the practice of Ahrimanic/Satanic sorcery and the practitioner in a modern sense. See "Yatuk Dinoih".

Yatuk Dinoih [Avestan/Pahlavi] – Witchcraft and Sorcery. The development and practice of adversarial and opposing sorcery to encircle the witch or wizard in self-developed energy. The principle of Darkness and the Deva/Druj (Demon) worship of this sect was in seeming model form, that by becoming as Darkness they developed a Light within. See LUCIFERIAN WITCHCRAFT - Grimoire written by Michael Ford.

Yatus [Avestan/Pahlavi] – A group of 'demons' or sorcerers who practice Yatukih sorcery and Daeva-Yasna. The Yatus were led by Akht-Jadu, Akhtya. They were also considered nomads in nature, wandering through all parts of Persia practicing their religion. This term has no considerations to the Zoroastrian religion, while the modern and separate practices described in Liber HVHI and parts of Luciferian Witchcraft are manifestations of a new type of interpretation of the practice of Daeva-Yasna.

Yezidi [Kurdish]– Considered 'devil worshippers' by outsiders, the Yezidi are those who are dedicated to Malak Tauus, the Peacock Angel, also called Shaitan or Lucifer. In the MESHAF RESH, the Black Book, Azazel is the first angel, created before any other. He is considered most beautiful and is the one who teaches and enlightens humanity. In the areas of Yatuk Dinoih, Sabbatic and Luciferian Sorcery, transformation occurs by the embrace and becoming of the opposing force, or adversarial (antinomian) ideas within the self. The initiate moves through the magical current to strengthen his or her own being. In a modern context, Malak (Angel) Tauus (Peacock) is the symbol of solar enlightenment, wisdom and beautiful developed being.

I would like to thank the following for the workings which led to The Bible of the Adversary, for inspiration is often not seen at first glance.
Hope Marie, for support, Jason, Jayson, Brison, Thomas, Kevin Rockhill, those who have developed within the Luciferian Gnosis, to the teachers before me, Aleister Crowley, Nietzche, Darwin, Anton Szandor LaVey, Sennacherib, Assur-nasir-apal II, Assur-banipal, Shalmaneser III, Tiglath-pileser, Ashurnasirpal, Vlad Draculae "Tepes", Alexander the Great and all the others who have granted inspiration. I thank my spiritual Father, Ahriman and spiritual mother, Az-Jahi, who inspire continually.

Michael W. Ford is the author of the following:

LUCIFERIAN WITCHCRAFT
LIBER HVHI – MAGICK OF THE ADVERSARY
THE VAMPIRE GATE – THE VAMPYRE MAGICKIAN
LUCIFERIAN GOETIA
THE FIRST BOOK OF LUCIFERIAN WITCHCRAFT
BOOK OF THE WITCH MOON
ADAMU – LUCIFERIAN SEX MAGICK
SATANIC MAGICK – A PARADIGM OF THERION

Michael is also a musician and a practitioner of the Luciferian Path.

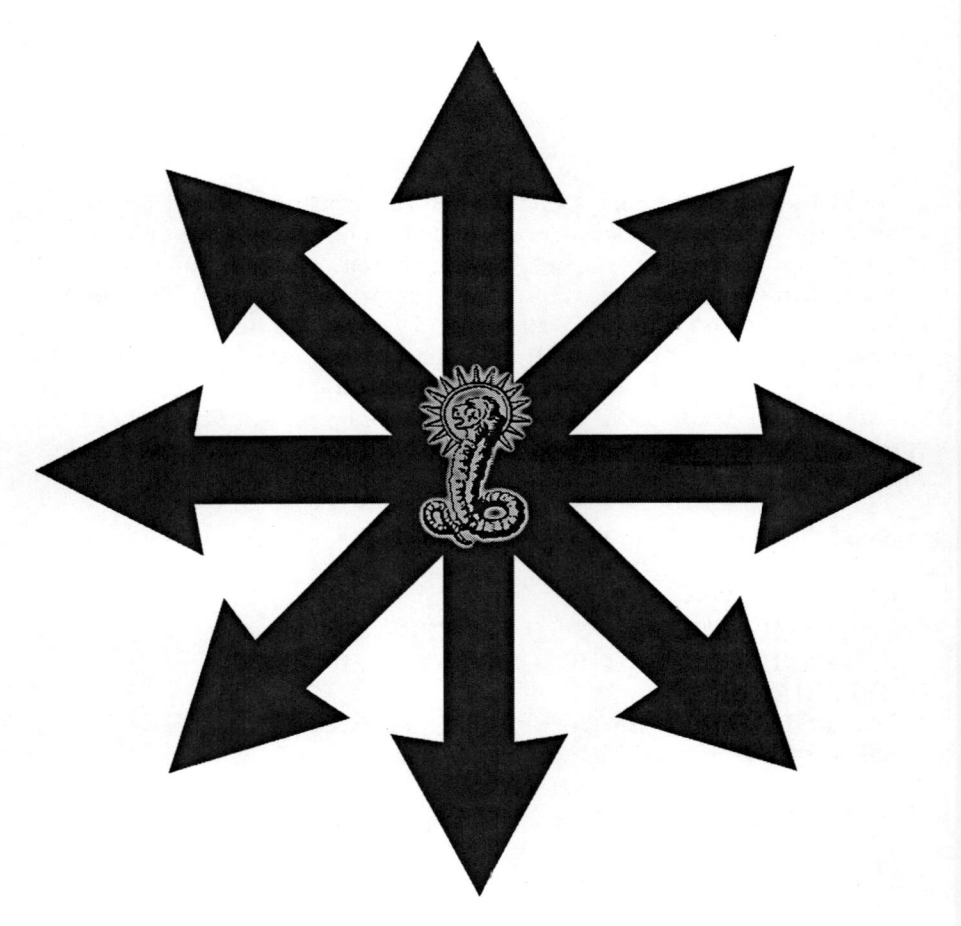

YALTABAOTH

The Luciferian Spirit, Lord of Storms, Awakener of the Light Within, Lion Serpent who brings forth the Black Flame

THE BIBLE OF THE ADVERSARY

A Gathering of Demons, near the Throne of Lucifer by Gustave Dore.

MICHAEL W. FORD

THE SATANIC TRINITY, illustration by French author, unknown. This is the symbol of Samael – Lilith – Cain (or Chioa, the Beast)

ASTAROTH, the inspired Angel of Astarte,
   Who inspired the Gnosis early.
   Illustration by Louis Brenton.